Covid Stories from East Africa and Beyond:

Lived Experiences and Forward-Looking Reflections

Mary Njeri Kinyanjui
Roopal Thaker
Kathryn Toure
(editors)

Langaa Research & Publishing CIG
Mankon, Bamenda

Publisher:

Langaa RPCIG
Langaa Research and Publishing Common Initiative Group
PO Box 902 Mankon
Bamenda
North West Region
Cameroon
info@langaa-rpcig.net
www.langaa-rpcig.net

orders@africanbookscollective.com
www.africanbookscollective.com

ISBN-10: 9956-551-54-6
ISBN-13: 978-9956-551-54-5

© 2020 Mary Njeri Kinyanjui, Roopal Thaker, and Kathryn Toure,
copyright for each of the chapters is with the chapter author(s)

To reference this book:

Kinyanjui, M. N., Thaker, R., and Toure, K. (Eds.) (2020). *Covid stories from East Africa and beyond: Lived experiences and forward-looking reflections*. Bamenda: Langaa.

Cover design includes a photo of a mixed media painting by Anna Rarity;
see the end of the book for more information and her bio.

Praise for the Book

It is inspiring to read the many voices of African women and men telling their stories, rich in the value systems of our cultures. The stories bring out the class issue as well. They endorse justice as a central issue of our continent. We are proud that Africa *is* telling its stories. Timely too!

— Fatma Alloo, Founder,
Tanzania Media Women's Association (TAMWA)

* * *

We are in a season of tremendous change, and it is important that we hear from Africa. As we move forward during the 21st century, while dealing with the consequences of covid19, we are challenged to examine our priorities and pivot to focus on what matters most. The writers of *Covid Stories from East Africa and Beyond* generously share what they're encountering during the season of covid, but more importantly, they share their strategies of coping and resilience. Africa can help us understand ways to live our lives more fully.

— Joanna Grace Farmer, Building Community Capacity…
Remembering our Legacy of Love

* * *

This book, privileging the voices of ordinary people, will open your eyes to covid19's impact on the African continent, the ways the virus has disrupted daily life, and how people are coping and adapting to the pandemic.

— Michèle Foster, Professor and Henry Heuser Jr. Endowed Chair for
Urban Education Partnerships, University of Louisville

* * *

These covid19 stories are a revelation of our 360 degrees of human struggle and triumph – matters ultimately of heart, mind, body, and soul. These are all expressed in the chapters in personal and structural ways, addressing policy and practice, the macro and the micro. A new normal must-read...

– Karindi Odindo, Psychologist and
Conflict Transformation Counsellor

* * *

We are delighted by the publication of *Covid Stories from East Africa and Beyond* and by its success in revealing how African people have responded to covid19 with resilience and creativity.

– James Giblin, Professor of African History, and
Blandina Kaduma Giblin, Lecturer in Kiswahili, University of Iowa

* * *

Brilliant and timely. This book shares the stories of real people during the coronavirus pandemic on the African continent. It shows people dealing in so many ways with this shocking moment in history when, like in some improbable science fiction movie, a deadly virus comes from nowhere with little or no warning and shuts down our lives. The question on everybody's lips is "How will I cope?" The book provides valuable insights of how Africans were coping eight months into the pandemic. It begins with stories of everyday life and then gets into structural issues.

– Sitawa Namwalie, Kenyan, Poet, Playwright and Performer

* * *

The African continent is so diverse, yet these covid stories from East Africa and beyond resonate with experiences here in West Africa. Happy to see mention of Ghana, The Gambia, Senegal, Sierra Leone, and Nigeria as well.
— Adwoa Agyeman, Social change strategist and co-founder of EPIC-Africa, enhancing philanthropic impact

* * *

This is an important and extraordinary collection. With books and articles being written and published about life during this pandemic, this book is not just another one. It is gripping, depressing, inspiring, and very thoughtful about both the present and the future. Its authors are primarily women from African countries, but its reach ought to be far wider.

Immediate reactions to the pandemic may be largely shared by people in many other regions of the world, but I love how this collection also asks about a post-covid19 world, how some things ought to change, how some things may well be transformed, what we might want in a post-pandemic world, and how that future world can learn from what this pandemic has made palpably visible.
— Virginia R. Dominquez, Gutgsell Professor of Anthropology, University of Illinois at Urbana-Champaign

To all those who supported each other during covid19 and those who lost someone during the pandemic.

Acknowledgements

Every book is a collective effort. This is no exception. Many people contributed in different ways to the realization of *Covid Stories from East Africa and Beyond: Lived Experiences and Forward-Looking Reflections.* Through small acts like circulating the call for chapters, encouraging and supporting one or more of the authors or editors, or reviewing and commenting a chapter to two, people from diverse horizons have raised the quality of the overall oeuvre. We do not take your efforts or contributions for granted and cannot thank you enough. Please feel acknowledged and appreciated.

Thanks to all those who in their daily endeavours invite interrogation of history and culture and power relations and promote understandings of African contexts in an interconnected continent and globalized world. Thanks, as well, to all those who support Langaa Research and Publishing to promote the circulation of stories and analysis about Africa and Africans and exposure to African worldviews and ways of thinking.

table of contents

Responding rapidly

chapter 1

The Covid Outlaw

Didi Wamukoya

chapter 2

**What I Learned
Surviving the Apocalypse**

Awuor Onguru

chapter 3

**Emotional Highs and
Lows of Quarantine**

Susan Karungi

chapter 4

**Making Covid19 Manageable
with Gospel Music**

Catherine Mongella-Kalokola

chapter 5

School Closure and Panic Mode

Meseret Kassahun Desta

Introduction to
Covid Stories from East Africa and Beyond[1]

Mary Njeri Kinyanjui
Roopal Thaker
Kathryn Toure

Coronavirus happened and is still with us. Its impact has been far reaching, and many lives have been deeply disrupted, even lost. Africans have sought to cope with it in various ways, including giving it names of derision, names of defiance, and names that point to a determination to overcome it. In one of Kenya's languages, it is referred to as *kinguki giki*. Kinguki means uproot, upheaval, disruption, destabilization, something that goes against the grain of established order. True to the word, coronavirus has shaken to the root the fundamentals of the neoliberal economy and our current lifestyles.

This book opens a window to how Africans in different contexts respond rapidly to covid, adapt to new realities, work with the most vulnerable, engage systems, and begin to transform towards a better world. It comprises 29 chapters about lived experiences of coronavirus in East Africa and beyond. The collective of 40 authors from over 20 countries narrates experiences through various socioeconomic, political, and cultural lenses. Regardless of their circumstances, coronavirus had an impact on every one of them and on their families. The stories in this collection highlight challenges, new opportunities, and ultimately the deep resilience of communities across the continent.

Covid19 has left a trail of problems. It has affected livelihoods and jobs, small businesses, and large industries. It has deeply affected education and schooling, exacerbated physical and mental health issues, affected agricultural production and markets, increased social problems such as

---

[1] Kinyanjui, M. N., Thaker, R., and Toure, K. (2020). Introduction to covid stories from East Africa and beyond. In M. N. Kinyanjui, R. Thaker, and K. Toure (Eds.), *Covid stories from East Africa and beyond: Lived experiences and forward-looking reflections* (pp. xix-xxviii). Bamenda: Langaa.

domestic abuse and police brutality, compromised personal and public safety, and much more.

Yet, *katika hali zote* ("across the board" in Swahili), each story in this collection reveals innovation, nimbleness, shifts in paradigms, and a variety of strategies for human agency and mutual support to prevail.

Coronavirus happened rapidly and caught many unawares. **Part 1** of this volume, on "**Responding rapidly**," highlights initial disbelief and early shifts in understanding and behaviour.

Wamukoya's protagonist quickly takes her children to a rural area, a safe haven, to improve their chances of survival during the pandemic. Her characters are daring and self-reliant, do with what they have, and do what they have to do. They are outlawed and their speaking the truth does not matter, but through solidarity they work together to face the emergency.

For Onguru, news of the pandemic and imminent lockdowns meant unexpected panic buying where shoppers grabbed all they could from supermarket shelves. "I eventually decided that leaving my cart at the till and dashing back and forth was my best bet," while her mother was "rapid-firing lists of items to me by text, and I could barely keep up."

Karungi in Uganda considers herself a "typical African mother," conditioned to "suck it up" in the face of challenge. During quarantine, she learns important lessons on mental health from her daughters and their "self-awareness that is the norm for today's child."

For Mongella-Kalokola, like for so many others, daily routines were "overhauled when covid19 came into the picture." What helps her to get through it? Taking a deep breath and "playing music from a playlist on my phone." Readers may find themselves dancing alongside her to Relax by Christina Shusho or Wewe ni Mungu (You are God) by Daddy Owen, strategies to detach momentarily from the chaos of the pandemic and find solace and peace of mind.

Desta goes into panic mode when schools close. "Day by day, it became clearer that unknowns would be the norm during the covid19 pandemic. I was quite stressed." How to manage her full-time consultancy researching and writing on the Horn of Africa and at the same time ensure her extroverted daughter – an only child who misses her classmates and playmates and insists that "virtual learning is boring" – has the attention and support she needs? Tensions escalate.

While juggling her responsibilities as a mother, Din shows leadership by ensuring people-centred disease surveillance and care at a major hospital in Nairobi. This was not a moment to boss people around but rather one of innovation, collaboration, and joint action to save lives and jobs at the hospital. "'Don't let your guard down' were the closing remarks of every taskforce meeting."

LoWilla tries to calm her own worries about family spread across eastern Africa by looking to the innovative ways in which youth in her home country of South Sudan share information, including through the #WagifCorona or Stop Corona campaign.

In this first part of the book, authors describe their experiencing of responding rapidly to needs during a pandemic, from grappling with surprise detention at a quarantine site, stocking supplies, learning about mental health issues, and developing coping mechanisms to reorganizing work and school at home and working together to keep staff at a major hospital safe, sane, and motivated. This part of the book wraps up with a reminder from Din and her team to "spread calm not chaos" and an appeal from LoWilla to manage our state of mind and Keep things Hopeful.

In **Part 2** are stories of "**Adapting to new realities**." A sense of deeper understanding and change develops. Coronavirus happened and became a moment for self-discovery, a moment to rethink lifestyles that had been overtaken by the neoliberal modernity of going to work every day and not having enough family time. Coronavirus compelled people to stop their everyday routines and creatively adjust to new normals.

Kinyanjui describes the abrupt act of women retracing their steps back to the home in 2020. Is home the anticipated safe haven? And a site of fulfilment and self-realization for women? How can it be the healing space it is meant to be?

Creatively rethinking dating is the subject of Muraguri's chapter, and the process if full of self-discovery. In a well told story, she introduces her challenge as "I'm not good at normal dating by any standards. I figured I couldn't be that much worse at covid dating." On Quarantine Day 14, Muraguri "stumbles" into her "first covid date."

The protagonist in "The Girl Who Met Her Shadow" by Ball-Burgess realizes that the physical mask she has to wear now, to protect herself and others, is similar to many other masks she has worn to hide and shield her herself – from herself and those who might cause her harm. Others struggle with the invisible monster outside. This girl struggles with the monster inside.

Eikelschulte opted to stay in Rwanda as the pandemic unfolded rather than return to the Netherlands. She takes time to learn some Kinyarwanda, which comes in handy in explanations to police officers on her first trip out of the house after the lockdown. She also learns the intricacies of MoMo or mobile money, especially for responding to requests for solidarity "in these bad days." Eikelschulte and her husband in turn experience the "caring people of Rwanda."

Kariuki shares an illustrated story titled "No Hugs in Weeks." Just after people make their New Year's resolutions, news of covid filters through, and before we know it, it can't be muted or avoided. What to do? Comfort each other, laugh, and keep moving. The drawings by Kariuki let us take a step back to look in on the situation and smile before figuring out how to stitch life back together.

Bitrus-Ojiambo shows another aspect to the pandemic, highlighting how humour is used to communicate and stay connected. She explores the "carnivalesque" and satire in 15 videoclips, memes, and images that circulated on social media, from "Laundry room prayer" to "Heading home past curfew." A very insightful read!

Hamelink and Nassor describe an unexpectedly enriching Ramadan experience with family and scripture, including an unanticipated deepening of faith during a time of isolation. Nassor also discovers the useful role the Niqab plays in social distancing.

Hamelink and Rubaba describe how Rubaba, a fourth-year medical student, leaves Dar es Salam when schools and universities are closed. She learns to balance chores at home and online learning, while enjoying the unexpected time with family and missing friends.

In this first of three "collective voice" chapters, titled "Working and Showing Solidarity from a Distance," Fabiano shares thoughts from professional women in Malawi who echo the advantages and challenges of working from home, which she considers a "sneak peek into the future of work." Njie describes the difficulties in the beginning for people in The Gambia to respect social distancing, when "social interaction constitutes one of the fundamental values of Africa." Abdullahi describes how Muslims find creative ways to show generosity to kin and provide alms to the needy, even when congregating is not possible.

The stories in this second part of the book speak to working from home, dating in new ways, and understanding more about the masks we wear. Ordinary life takes on an extraordinary character, as evidenced by the couple discovering new layers in their relations with Rwandans. Humour is important in adapting to new realities and provides insight. Religious practices and university learning change, and people surprise themselves in their adaptability, disciplining themselves to stay physically apart when possible, even when they yearn for sociality.

Part 3 of this collection addresses the extraordinary impact of coronavirus on humanity and comprises stories related to "**Working with the most vulnerable**."

The pandemic created problems for many domestic workers. Their employers asked them to stay away from work for a while or completely released them from their services. Amuyunzu-Nyamongo, Kinagu, and Mumma share the stories of some of these people who opted to sit "silently wearing masks" along a roadside in Nairobi, "watching cars and passersby," and waiting for work.

Domestic violence has intensified, as families shelter together during curfew hours. Sikuku and Amuyunzu-Nyamongo explore this reality in their chapter titled "When Home is Not Safe." They discuss societal norms and efforts to shift them and call for more strategic responses.

In a second "collective voice" chapter, "Wanting to Feel Safe and Secure," Wahito stays with the theme of the previous chapter, describing what it is like to be a schoolchild at home and *not* feel safe. Machina takes the reader to northeast Nigeria where people displaced from their homes because of insurgency have to deal with covid in addition. He relates examples of creative community mobilisation and calls on "leaders in formal positions of authority to recognize the resilience of the communities" and "work with them to respond to their needs and aspirations."

In many communities, "maintaining good respiratory hygiene by wearing a mask was not affordable to many people." Bultcha, Léautier, and Nyamwiza entrepreneurially decide to do something about it. They describe Muundo Barakoa as a creative shift during this moment of crisis, whereby women seamstresses link to markets to be of service and assure their livelihood.

This part of the collection does not cover all dire situations provoked by the covid19 pandemic. It rather shines a spotlight on four issues. First, the plight of **domestic workers** and how some former domestic workers – all women – take the situation into their hands as best they can, for the wellbeing of their families. Second, the longstanding problem of **domestic violence**, aggravated during the pandemic, and how human rights and women's rights organizations are responding and advocating. Third, how the pandemic inordinately affects **people displaced from their homes** and who may be living in camps, the actions of such communities to respond to covid, and the expectations of leaders in formal positions of authority. Fourth, how **women in the informal economy** benefit from the mobilisation and organization of local industrial capacity and thus are able to contribute meaningfully to public health efforts while assuring a livelihood for their families. This section speaks to the power of agency and solidarity but also the need to address patriarchal norms, other root causes of discrimination and physical and symbolic violence, and systems that perpetuate inequalities.

The chapters in **Part 4** focus on "**Engaging systems**," knowing that systems structuring our everyday socioeconomic and political lives need to be questioned and evolved. In some cases, they need to be fundamentally changed in a post-covid world of global interconnectedness.

Coronavirus is challenging the fundamentals of the neoliberal economy but also the home and the family, including production and exchange, as described by Tankou. Small-scale African famers produce the majority of food consumed on the continent, yet transport restrictions have limited their access to input and output markets and to farm labour. Farmers' products are healthy and loaded with nutrition but highly perishable. What does all this mean when it comes to rural and urban development and linkages and rethinking agricultural and food systems? Tankou demonstrates how farmers can farm for self- and community-reliance.

The story by Fonchingong shows how unprepared Cameroon was when covid19 arrived. She describes the fear, rumour-mongering, and stigmatization to which the pandemic gave rise. As in any public health campaign, communication, public education, and community involvement are crucial. "To ensure community engagement and see changes in behaviour, we need to involve the persons being protected." She calls for true commitment going forward to the Abuja Declaration, in which African Union countries pledged to invest 15% of their national budget in health.

Mwangi describes what the stance of the Somali government should be in the face of the presence of terrorist organizations in the country in the midst of a pandemic. To serve all the Somali people, she stresses the need for leadership, unity, and the respect of human rights, especially for women and girls. She calls on neighbouring countries, regional organizations, and the international community to play their parts in fighting violent extremism. Because of the interconnectedness of people and economies, peace, security, and development in the greater Horn of Africa region depend in part on the same in Somalia.

The reflection by Londadjim is an exploration of the human heart and what connects and humanizes people. Her chapter shows how people thought covid was for Asia and Europe in the beginning – a disease for the rich that could not survive in Africa. But coronavirus happened everywhere, and everything stopped. "We also stopped" to "see clearly" and take better care of each other. "People who were invisible before the crisis have become visible." Londadjim marvels at how, in a short time, "collective intelligence flowed and functioned, and the pooling of energies worked miracles for the good of people."

Londadjim posits that we are "coming out of a long sleep" and searching for coherence in our human relations. The awakening and newfound consciousness, if applied to engaging systems, can contribute to a more equitable and harmonious world. But the "barriers that separate" rich and poor "are not only external to us, they are also within us." We need to work on ourselves, even as we work to transform societal constructs.

This reality about our common humanity needs to infuse our engagement with agricultural and health systems, and other systems such as education systems, and also efforts to counter violent extremism.

Coronavirus happened. It is time for Africa to reimagine its postcolonial and decolonial futures. **Part 5** of *Covid Stories from East Africa and Beyond* points towards the beginnings of "**Transforming towards a better world**."

Has the crisis "awakened an awareness that was already there" and that will help in transforming towards The Africa We Want? Londadjim suggests this, in her second chapter, also translated from French. She is encouraged by the resourcefulness, creativity, and solidarity evident in social networks "developed by youth associations in the neighborhoods and suburbs of Ndjamena, Chad's capital city." She suggests it is time to question imposed development models, partnerships, and solidarities, denounce exploitation and oppression, and move away from debts that cannot be repaid. She reflects on the Black Lives Matter movement, which is calling out "fractured society, where whole groups of people have been excluded and others privileged." She writes: "Humxn[2] beings are not the enemy of humxn beings."

In the third and final "collective voice" chapter, titled "Ubuntu, Social Justice, Gardens and Market Mammas," Mtasa asks if ubuntu will become extinct in the age of covid19. Fragilities in society have been made worse and blatantly exposed. "Life has been dismantled for many people across the continent," including through xenophobia, for example towards some Zimbabweans living in South Africa. "Where has ubuntu gone?" When we are "collectively responsible for each other's wellbeing"?

LoWilla in the same chapter describes how South Sudanese women around the world fight for social justice in the face of violence from patriarchal systems. Lukamba inspires us by sharing about market women in Kinshasa who not only increase their sales of therapeutic plants that boost the immune system, and "have been part of the culture for centuries," but also take "time to educate their clients on their use."

In "A Tale of a Mother and a Son," Bayeh describes rediscovering the importance of time with her son. She humbly reminds us, in charming style and celebratory fashion, to focus on what is important as we continue to make shifts in our lives. She commits to setting her priorities and organizing her life in line with realizations that surfaced during the time of confinement and before Ethiopian New Year.

We have all been afraid and humbled by the humbling coronavirus, according to Nyamnjoh. He suggests that migrants' rights are at risk and that "neoliberalism in its various guises and disguises runs the risk of losing

---

[2] "Why humxn is not misspelled," by Bunny Young, 15 May 2020, https://abetterplaceconsulting.com/why-humxn-is-not-misspelled

out to the virus [...] if current rates of transmission are not contained with imagination, creativity, and innovation." He calls for "appropriate action, creativity, and innovative modes of solidarity" going forward and embracing the composite nature of being African.

The solution to the postcolonial and decolonial futures of Africa lies in "Rediscovering Neptune" by Morena-Ruiz who shows how the ethics of care challenge neoliberalism. Neoliberalism thrives on patriarchal extraction and exploitative hierarchies. It is time to rethink prosperity, consumption, and happiness in our everyday lives. Coronavirus has taught us that what is important is life, love, livelihoods, and our relations with the planet. As human beings we can build community capital in an utu-ubuntu way to serve as insurance to support life, livelihoods, and fulfilment, beginning with those around us.

Morena-Ruiz calls for "a radical transformation" in the narratives that support the ways we organize our relations and economies, with profound implications for care. We hope that the 29 covid stories shared in this volume are an inspirational contribution in that regard.

The human experiences, brought and bound together here, constitute stories of individuals, families, and communities. They tell a collective and multi-layered story about the impact of the coronavirus on humanity in East Africa and beyond. Some of the experiences surpass our limited human imagination which has been shaped by science, economic status, culture, policy, policing, and everyday politics. The stories are of courage, solidarity, reciprocity, love, and resilience of the human spirit to survive and thrive in the adversity caused by coronavirus. Together, the stories bear witness to an important moment in history and will take on new dimensions when read in future years beyond the now already infamous year of 2020. Ultimately, love will help us dare to do the impossible and to prevail.

Mary Njeri Kinyanjui has published on women's movements, the informal economy in Africa, ubuntu business models, and how women experience anthropain in their everyday lives. She taught at the University of Nairobi's Institute for Development Studies and earned her PhD in Geography from the University of Cambridge in the United Kingdom and her master's from Kenyatta University in Kenya. She is author of Coffee Time, *based on the experience of her family.*

Roopal Thaker *is a highly experienced program manager in the non-profit sector. She is passionate about working with community-based organizations to shape public policy from the ground up. Born and raised in Nairobi, she has studied at Harvard University, McGill University, and the University of Ottawa and is now working on adolescent health and life skills education programs in Kenya.*

Kathryn Toure, *PhD in education, is a researcher and writer. She promotes the circulation of African worldviews and facilitates community inquiry to deepen understandings of her/history and culture. She worked at Africa Online and in international and comparative studies at the University of Iowa and studied at the University of Montreal (education), University of Abidjan (history), University of Grenoble (literature), and University of Kansas (political science).*

Responding
rapidly

chapter 1

The Covid Outlaw[1]

Didi Wamukoya

Kavai returned to her room and cried like she had never cried before. Should she reach out to Lennox? Maybe he would agree to take her children in for the time that she remained in mandatory government quarantine. She dialled his number.

"Hello, Lennox," Kavai said. "I am in a truly desperate fix. My landlord is threatening to throw my children out. He says I infected them with coronavirus. The neighbours are threatening to burn them alive so that they don't infect the whole village. Can you take them in for the next few days until I leave quarantine?"

"What?" Lennox exclaimed in shock. "These are truly unfortunate times. I have travelled to Kinangop to pick up vegetables. Unfortunately, my lorry has broken down and can't be fixed today. Once the lorry is fixed, I'll be able to travel back, because the police are allowing food deliveries into and out of Nairobi."

"I didn't know you're in Kinangop!" said Kavai. "Please call me as soon as you get back."

Her last hope was lost. What if Lennox's lorry did not get repaired? Who else could she turn to with Mama Mukami still admitted in hospital?

Maybe she should threaten suicide. That would get the authorities listening. She opened her window and looked outside to see how far the drop to the ground was. Disappointing! It was not that far down. She could easily jump and land safely on her feet.

But looking out the window made her realize something. She could literally touch the perimeter wall of the Medical Institute. Here was her

[1] Copyright © 2020 Didi Wamukoya

This is a work of fiction. All names, characters, places and incidents are either products of the author's imagination or are used fictitiously. Any resemblance to actual events, locales or persons, living or dead, is entirely coincidental.

Wamukoya, D. (2020). The Covid Outlaw. In M. N. Kinyanjui, R. Thaker, and K. Toure (Eds.), *Covid stories from East Africa and beyond: Lived experiences and forward-looking reflections* (pp. 3-14). Bamenda: Langaa.

opportunity to leave this place. She put her head out the window and looked to the left and to the right. There was an armed police officer manning each end of the block. She would have to wait for darkness to exit unnoticed.

She went and knocked on Omega's door.

"What is it?" Omega asked.

"I have a plan," Kavai said.

Kavai led Omega back to her room and showed him how close her window was to the perimeter wall, explaining her plan of escape.

"That is a good plan," said Omega, excited. "But the curfew would have started, and we will get arrested again and be brought right back."

"There are those makeshift kiosks across the road," Kavai said, pointing them out. "We can sit out the curfew there and then go home in the morning."

Omega began to picture his freedom. It was a good plan. A solid plan.

As the sun set, heavy clouds gathered in the sky. They heard the rumbling of thunder, and then the first fat drops of rain fell to the ground. The skies opened up and let down the first long rains of the season. God was on their side.

The police officers manning their building went in search of cover from the rain. The time was ripe for Kavai and Omega to leave their forced captivity. They quickly stepped out of her room window and onto the perimeter wall and then jumped down to their freedom. They crossed the road unnoticed and made it to the makeshift kiosks.

The next morning, they melted into the crowds of early morning workers and walked all the way to Kangemi. It took them a little over two hours to get there. They were hungry and exhausted, but they dared not go home because the neighbours would see them and raise an alarm. They went and hid in the bushy surroundings of Kangemi Dam. Kavai started making plans to get her children. After a while, she received a phone call from Lennox.

"I have very good news, Kavai," Lennox said. "My lorry is fixed and is up and running. I will be in Nairobi before five o'clock this evening!"

"Thank God!" Kavai said, not daring to tell him that she had escaped quarantine. "When you arrive, please go straight to Kangemi Dam. There is someone there I want you to meet."

"Who?" Lennox asked.

"Just go there. You'll see," Kavai said.

Curious, Lennox went straight to Kangemi Dam upon his arrival in Nairobi and was shocked to see Kavai and a strange man hiding out there. Kavai quickly explained their escape and begged Lennox to help them get out of Nairobi.

"I can transport you at the back of my lorry, hidden behind my empty vegetable crates," Lennox said. "But I can only take you up to Naivasha. In the meantime, get rid of your mobile phones. I hear that the police can use them to track you down!"

Kavai and Omega threw their mobile phones into the dam.

"I will take you to Hydra Bar and then go and collect your children," Lennox said.

Reuniting with her children was the happiest feeling Kavai had ever had in her life. She embraced them one after another and then all together. They hugged and cried and hugged some more as she introduced them to Omega.

Early the next morning, they were secreted behind the empty crates in the lorry and ready to go. It was a most uncomfortable ride, but Kavai did not mind. It was a ride to freedom.

God was still on their side. Heavy rains pounding the city had forced the police to abandon their roadblock at Uplands along the Nairobi-Nakuru highway. They arrived in Naivasha at seven o'clock in the morning, and Omega went around looking for lorries headed to western Kenya. He found a driver headed to Kisumu who was happy to give Kavai, her children, and Omega a lift for a minimal fee.

They arrived in Kisumu at four o'clock in the evening and boarded a Kakamega-bound matatu. Kavai and her children alighted at Chavakali bus stop and said goodbye to Omega, who had to continue his journey to Kakamega. The goodbye was difficult and more emotional than Kavai had expected.

"Make sure you look for me any time you come to Kakamega," Omega said.

"You know the fate of our phones," said Kavai laughing.

"Here's my brother's phone number," Omega said, writing something on a piece of paper and handing it over to Kavai. "You will be able to reach me on his line."

"Thank you," said Kavai taking the piece of paper and tucking it into her purse. "I am very grateful to you for everything, especially for taking Mama Mukami to the hospital."

"I don't regret it," Omega said. "At least, I made a friend in you."

Kavai turned away quickly to hide the tears in her eyes. She too was glad she had made a friend in Omega, despite the unfortunate circumstances that had brought them together. She ushered her children into a matatu heading to her home in Vohovole village, vowing to keep her promise and stay in touch with Omega.

Kavai sighed with relief as they approached the familiar landscapes of Vohovole. She confirmed from the clock on the dashboard of the matatu that it was five o'clock in the evening on the 9th of April. As if on cue, the matatu driver cranked up the volume on the radio, and the presenter's voice rose over the static: "In the latest news, the police have assured Kenyans that they will trace the two persons who escaped from mandatory government quarantine last night. The two had tested positive for the coronavirus disease, and it is feared they will spread the infection wherever they go."

Kavai smiled to herself. She and Omega had never been tested for the disease. That was the government trying to alarm the public into reporting any escapees. As the matatu hurtled into the beautiful sunset of Vohovole, she thought of her future. How would she exist for the rest of her life as a fugitive? A covid outlaw? How had she found herself in this situation?

* * *

Here is how it all began…

It was half past six on the evening of the 26th of March. A cloud of dust rose over the semi-permanent corrugated iron sheet-roofed houses of Waruku village in Kangemi, an informal settlement on the outskirts of Nairobi. A few wispy clouds had gathered overhead, a sign of the coming long rains.

A group of men and women seated outside Mama Mukami's Millennium Kiosk huddled closer together, in direct contravention of the social distancing directives. Kavai Amunavi was among them. She, like the rest of the group, wanted to catch every word that the Cabinet Secretary for Health was saying with regards to covid19. The Coronavirus Disease.

Just two weeks before, the Cabinet Secretary had confirmed the first case of covid19 in Kenya, and their lives had been turned upside down. They had been told things they had never heard before. Do not shake hands. Maintain social distancing. Wash your hands regularly. When that is not possible, sanitize your hands with an alcohol-based sanitizer.

Kavai recollected, like it was yesterday, the day they had heard that announcement on the radio. On that evening too, they had huddled around the radio outside Millennium Kiosk.

"This is a rich man's disease," Ligare had declared. "It catches people who fly around in aeroplanes."

"That is true," Kisala had confirmed. "I don't know why it should affect us who have never entered any aeroplanes."

That was on the 13th of March to be exact. About ten days after that, they had again huddled around the radio to hear even worse news. The government gave directives for bars, nightclubs and other entertainment spots to close. Just like that, Kavai had lost her job as a waitress at Hydra Bar in Flyover Village. The job had paid her bills and kept her and her three children comfortable, despite being a daily wage job. Her boss, Lennox, had called a team meeting and announced the bad news.

"Hydra Bar is a very popular joint," he had said. "I am certain it will recover when this lockdown ends. However, during the time it is closed, I will not be able to pay your wages."

That had been a big blow to everybody. The employees cried and then, ignoring the Cabinet Secretary's directives on social distancing, held hands and prayed for a quick end to the covid19 pandemic. But Lennox would be okay. He ran several businesses besides the bar. She knew that he owned a lorry and transported fresh fruits and vegetables every day. He would survive, and Kavai was almost certain that his bar would reopen after this crisis. She would get her job back. That is what gave her hope.

But today, there was more bad news. The Cabinet Secretary had just announced a dusk to dawn curfew. What was that he was saying? Nobody was to be found outside their home from seven o'clock in the evening until five o'clock in the morning.

"This virus must be nocturnal," Mama Mukami said, much to everybody's amusement. "I had better close up the shop and get home before this curfew starts."

"That is true," said Kavai. "We had better go to our homes before the police come here."

Kavai headed home worried about her immediate future. She did not know how long her last pay would stretch. Her rent of five hundred shillings was due at the end of every week. She had to put food on the table for herself and her three children. She had to buy water for their daily use. How would she survive?

Her phone rang, startling her out of her worries. It was Lennox.

"Hello Lennox," Kavai said, wondering why he would call her at this time.

"Hello Kavai," Lennox said. "How is the going?"

"Tough," admitted Kavai. "I am contemplating going home to the village. At least there, my children and I will be able to survive."

"Don't go just yet," said Lennox. "There is a lady in Loresho who buys vegetables from me for her business, Solar Greens. She dries fruits and vegetables for sale, and this virus has increased the demand for dried foods. She needs more hands to help process the vegetables. I recommended you to work for her."

"Oh my God!" Kavai exclaimed in joy. "Thank you so much! May God bless you abundantly! When do I start?"

"Calm down," said Lennox laughing at her. "The lady wants you to start first thing tomorrow morning. Are you able to do that?"

"Yes, of course," said Kavai excitedly.

"Be there at seven o'clock tomorrow morning," Lennox said.

"I will be there," Kavai assured him. "Thank you again."

What would she do without Lennox? He had come through for her yet again! Kavai, a single mother struggling to make ends meet, had only two real friends in the city: Lennox and Mama Mukami.

* * *

At seven o'clock on the morning of Friday, the 27th of March, Kavai reported to work at Solar Greens, a cottage industry that had begun as a hobby. Now, with the outbreak of covid19 and people wanting to stockpile food for bad times ahead, dried fruits and vegetables were a good idea, and Solar Greens orders had gone through the roof.

Kavai joined five other colleagues. Their jobs involved sorting and destemming the freshly delivered vegetables and then washing them and putting them into a solar-powered dehydrator. They then packed the dehydrated vegetables, ready for delivery. It was difficult back-breaking work for Kavai, but it paid even better than the job at Hydra Bar.

The first week of her new job went very well, and on Friday, the 3rd of April, she was paid her first wages. In addition to wages, the employer, Mrs. Moseo, gave them packets of dried vegetables to tide them over the hard times.

Orders for dried vegetables at Solar Greens kept increasing, and Kavai had to go to work on Saturdays. One Saturday, they worked until six o'clock in the evening. Kavai was not so worried about the curfew, because it usually took her 40 to 45 minutes to walk home from work. However, on that Saturday, as Kavai was leaving work, she received a distress call from Mama Mukami.

"I need help." Mama Mukami sounded like she was in pain. "I was taking a bodaboda home from the market. On reaching Flyover, a matatu hit us, and we fell off. The bodaboda rider and matatu crew ran away to avoid being blamed for the accident by the police. I have been left here alone and in pain."

"I am not far from there," Kavai said breaking into a run. "Where are you exactly?"

"I am at the Flyover stage," Mama Mukami said. "I think my leg is broken. I am in so much pain."

"I'm almost there," Kavai said. "Sit tight."

Kavai ran all the way to Flyover stage and on arrival found Mama Mukami lying on the benches inside one of the bus stop shades. Her face was dusty and bloody, and her clothes dishevelled and torn in some places. She tried to lift herself up when she saw Kavai arriving but lay back down in pain.

"Can't you get up at all?" Kavai asked.

"No," Mama Mukami winced. "My head is aching terribly, and my right leg is in so much pain."

"We can go to Jamii Health Centre," Kavai suggested, flagging down a mkokoteni handcart driver.

"Hello," she said to the driver. "My friend here has been involved in an accident. I need help to take her to Jamii Health Centre."

"Sorry, Mama," the mkokoteni driver said. "But can't you see that it is almost curfew time. I have to run home to avoid being arrested."

"But this is an emergency," Kavai argued. "Surely, the police will understand."

"Okay," the mkokoteni driver said after a little contemplation. "Help me to carry her onto the mkokoteni."

"How much will you charge?" Kavai asked.

"I won't charge," the mkokoteni driver said. "Jamii Health Centre is on my way home."

Kavai and the mkokoteni driver struggled to lift the weighty Mama Mukami onto the cart. They arrived at the Health Centre at ten minutes to the hour. The gateman, on seeing the state Mama Mukami was in, ran inside and returned with a stretcher and two nurses. They lifted Mama Mukami onto the stretcher and wheeled her inside. Kavai observed that the nurses were not wearing the protective masks or gloves that she saw doctors and nurses on television wearing when being interviewed about the coronavirus.

The mkokoteni driver remained outside, and Kavai sat in the waiting area. After what seemed like a long wait, one of the nurses came out and said to Kavai, "Your friend will be okay. However, we believe that her right leg is either dislocated or broken at the ankle. We will have to keep her here overnight and take her for x-ray in the morning. The Radiology Centre is closed for the day."

"Thank you," said Kavai. "Can I see her?"

"You can see her, but I don't think she will be able to talk," the nurse said. "She has been sedated and has likely fallen asleep."

Kavai went into the ward to see Mama Mukami, who, true to the nurse's words, was half asleep. Kavai said goodbye to her sleepy friend and left.

* * *

It was quite dark outside when Kavai left the Health Centre. The whole street was deserted because of the curfew. Kavai felt afraid. She walked a short distance and found the mkokoteni driver standing there, waiting for her. They walked together for a few hundred metres before they encountered a police roadblock.

One officer walked up to them and asked, "Why are you violating the curfew? And where are your face masks?"

Kavai was visibly trembling.

"What is your name?" the first police officer asked the mkokoteni driver.

"Omega," the mkokoteni driver responded.

"Are you a dog?" the officer asked angrily. "Only God and dogs have one name. And you are not God. What are your government names?"

"Omega Shitiyavai Shitsing'ung'u," the mkokoteni driver responded.

"Lord Jesus!" the police officer said in mock consternation. "Is that a name or a tongue twister?"

Omega did not respond.

"And you, Mama. What is your name?"

"Kavai Amunavi," Kavai responded.

"Is this your husband?" the officer asked.

"No," Kavai said. "This man helped me…"

The police officer cut her off saying, "Does your husband know you are out here fraternising with mkokoteni drivers?"

He did not give Kavai a chance to respond. The officers arrested Kavai and Omega and took them to Kabete Police Station where they spent a long cold night in the police cells.

The next day, their names were not among those who were called to go to court and take plea. They remained in the cells until about nine o'clock in the morning when a police officer came to collect them.

"The ambulance has come," the police officer said. "It is time to go into mandatory quarantine."

"Quarantine?" asked Kavai distressed. "But we are not sick."

"The Cabinet Secretary said that anybody caught flouting the curfew rules or not wearing a mask is guilty of spreading coronavirus," the police officer said. "You therefore have to go to quarantine."

"But my children," Kavai pleaded. "They have nobody else to take care of them."

"We were taking a sick person to hospital," Omega tried to explain.

"Not my business," the police officer said. "Enter the ambulance and go to the quarantine centre."

Kavai and Omega were bundled into the ambulance and driven to the Medical Institute where they were to be quarantined for fourteen days at their own cost.

* * *

After being assigned a room, Kavai took out her phone and made a few phone calls. The first was to her son Oguvasu. She was glad she had had the foresight to buy an old mobile phone and leave it in the house to ease communication with her children whenever she was away. The second call was to Mama Mukami. Mama Mukami confirmed that her leg was broken and that she would spend a few more days at the hospital. The third call she made was to Lennox, informing him of what had happened. The fourth call was to her new boss, Mrs. Moseo.

Kavai spent the first two days in quarantine feeling dejected and worried about her children. The only person she felt she could really talk to was Omega, with whom she had been arrested. She never saw any healthcare worker visit them. Nobody came to take samples from them to confirm whether or not they were infected with the coronavirus disease.

On the 6th of April 2020, her second day in quarantine, Kavai received a distress call from her son Oguvasu. The landlord had given them notice to vacate their house in the next three days. His tenants were threatening to move out, because they were afraid that Kavai had been found positive with the coronavirus disease and may have infected her children, who would in turn infect them. The landlord did not want to lose his business during these hard times. The children had to go. Mama Mukami was still admitted at the Health Centre, and Kavai felt helpless. Who would she turn to?

She called her sister Imburani who was back home at Vohovole village and informed her of her plight. The only reprieve for her children would be going to stay in the village. Imburani was ready to travel to Nairobi to pick up the children first thing in the morning.

At four o'clock that same evening, Kavai received a call from her sister who sounded agitated.

"What is it?" Kavai asked, worried.

"You have not heard the news?" Imburani asked.

"We have no TV or radio here," Kavai said. "We rely on news from the rumour mill."

"The President has just made an announcement banning travel to and from Nairobi starting at seven o'clock this evening," Imburani said.

Kavai lost all strength. Her phone slipped out of her hand as she sank onto her bed in shock. What would she do now? Where would her children go? Would Lennox agree to help?

She decided to approach the Custodian the next morning and try rationalizing with her. Hopefully, the Custodian would understand her situation and let her go. She requested Omega to back her up in her plea for freedom.

The next morning, they went to the Custodian's office and found her door open. On seeing them approach, the Custodian removed her spectacles and, raising an eyebrow, said, "Yes?"

"I need to go home," Kavai pleaded. "I… Omega and I are not supposed to be here."

"Yes," Omega put in. "We had taken someone who had been involved in an accident to the hospital. That is how we got caught up in the curfew."

"And how is that my problem?" the Custodian asked.

"I have nobody at home to look after my three children," Kavai cried. "Being here and out of work means there will be no money for rent and food. Please, I am here by mistake. Just let me go home and take care of my children."

"Speaking of money," the Custodian said, clearing her throat and referring to her computer. "You two have been here for three days now and not paid the mandatory deposit of 10,000 shillings. If you can't pay the deposit, then at least pay the 6,000 shillings to cover your three days' stay. If you fail to pay this amount by the end of day today, your meals will be withdrawn. You will have to tell your family members to bring you food."

"But why are we being punished like this?" Omega protested. "Have we committed a crime?"

"Please, madam," Kavai attempted one last plea. "If it is a crime we committed, then let them take us to court. At least there, we have a right to bail and can be with our families while we await trial. But this is like detention without trial."

"I am not a lawyer and don't know about legal rights," the Custodian said. "Go and await your test results. If you are negative, we shall revisit your case."

"But we have not been tested," Omega said.

The Custodian looked at him and then put her glasses back on, indicating that she was done listening to them.

Kavai looked at the Custodian and felt nothing but pure hatred for her. What kind of human being was this that was so heartless? She left the Custodian's office vowing to do anything she could, anything at all, to get her children to safety!

Didi Wamukoya *is an Advocate of the High Court of Kenya having been admitted to the bar in Kenya in 2007. She holds a bachelor's in Law and a master's in Environmental Law, both from the University of Nairobi. Didi is a trained wildlife crime investigator having undergone training at Kenya Wildlife Service Law Enforcement Academy and the International Law Enforcement Academy. She pioneered the creation of a Prosecution Unit at Kenya Wildlife Service and was the Head of Prosecution at Kenya Wildlife Service for seven years. Didi is now the Senior Manager, Wildlife Law Enforcement, at African Wildlife Foundation (AWF) where she is primarily responsible for implementing AWF's Wildlife Trafficking Law Enforcement Action Plan and serving as the technical lead on AWF activities to stop illegal trafficking of wildlife products from Africa. Her work involves training and capacity building of investigators, prosecutors, judicial officers and wildlife rangers. Didi is co-author of* Natural Resources and Environmental Justice in Kenya *by Muigua, K., Wamukoya, D., and Kariuki F. (2015, Glenwood Publishers) and a novel titled* Wamukoya Netia. *She is author of two blogs: Wildlife Law Africa (www.wildlifelawafrica.com) and Wooden Glass (www.nairobiborn.com).*

chapter 2

What I Learned Surviving the Apocalypse[1]

Awuor Onguru

By the time I had reached Carrefour at Sarit Centre, the floor manager was turning people away just ahead of closing time. Several shoppers stood in front of the sanitisation barrier, in different states of begging, negotiating, and shouting their way into the store. My dad and I had left the house quite late for a pandemic shopping trip – stores these days close at 4 pm to let everybody make it home before the 7 pm curfew. We had hit the road at 3:30, hoping to squeeze past the security barriers to get a few items before returning home. As I approached the said barrier, this seemed more and more unlikely.

Despite the disappointing appearance at the storefront, I decided to give it a go. The store manager was a big Middle Eastern guy, with a look on his face like he had been dealing with irritating customers for the past few minutes. As I made my way to the front of the crowd, his face soured, and he made a quick attempt to pick up his phone, so that when I asked if I could enter the store he gestured widely in the negative and walked away.

I turned away and walked back to the escalator, defeated. What was I going to do about all the stuff we didn't have at home? There was no way we drove all the way there to go back emptyhanded. At the peak of my anger (and at the top of the escalator) I turned around and rode it all the way back down.

The floor manager was *not* surprised to see me back.

"Look sir, my dad's got diabetes and his blood sugar is low. I've got to get into the store to get him candy otherwise he's going to go into shock."

The phone is put down. Success!

"Shock?"

"Yes, shock. He's sitting in the car, and if I can't get him something sweet his blood pressure is going to drop, and he could have a heart attack."

[1] Copyright © 2020 Awuor Onguru
Onguru, A. (2020). What I learned surviving the apocalypse. In M. N. Kinyanjui, R. Thaker, and K. Toure (Eds.), *Covid stories from East Africa and beyond: Lived experiences and forward-looking reflections* (pp. 15-20). Bamenda: Langaa.

This wasn't altogether a lie. My father *was* diagnosed with type II diabetes a while back. At that point, I would have said anything to get into the store.

I stood there and watched the store manager's facial expressions change – disbelief, distrust, worry. I thought about what happened to all the other people who had been turned away. What were their stories? My made-up one would (probably) grant me entry, but what about everyone else who was cast away from the store?

The store manager looked at me a while, and then nodded towards the sanitisation barrier. Three minutes of rubbing hand sanitizer on my hands and arms, and I was in.

Walking into the store was less nerve-wracking than I had anticipated. Most activity was happening near the till, where people were anxious to check out and get home before curfew. So I shopped calmly, and lightly.

That is, until the news of the lockdown came.

As I sit to write this, I realise that the news of the lockdown shouldn't have been as startling as it was – we needed to collectively control the transmission of the coronavirus after all. As we unpacked the shopping that evening, we learned that it was not a full lockdown, and that only the city borders as well as restaurants and other places were to be shut down. Businesses were to encourage their employees to work from home where possible, and schools would not be resuming for another month.

But in the middle of that supermarket, receiving my mother's warning phone call felt like the beginning of the apocalypse.

Almost immediately the atmosphere at the supermarket changed. People ran from the tills back to the store aisles, shoving anything and everything into their carts: frozen food, beans, ice cream, tissues, wooden brooms, salmon, feta cheese – everything was fair game. Anxious fathers who did not know their way around the store began to yell into their cell phones, seeking guidance, while mothers in the store began to push each other over to get to the essentials.

Me? I entered a sheer survival mode. Cruising down the aisles, I began to throw items into the cart as I thought of them. What would a four-person family need for a month-long lockdown? I had to quickly fill my cart and at the same time avoid the store manager, who was now skulking between aisles (I was just supposed to be getting candy, right?). The pressure of this game sent me into pure shock. I wasn't *thinking* about anything, just shoving item after item into my cart as I saw something and deemed it lockdown-worthy.

I eventually decided that leaving my cart at the till and dashing back and forth was my best bet, to not be discovered by Mr. Store Manager. My mother was rapid-firing lists of items to me by text, and I could barely keep up.

During one of my trips back to the till, I met two twenty-something men. "Can you please look after this for me? I need a couple more things. I'll be right back." I scurried away before I could get a response.

Those poor boys! Not only were they thoroughly confused about what was going on, but now they had to look after some random girl's cart as well. Their "watching the cart" turned into scavenging for items for themselves. It became rather amusing: every 15 seconds or so I would dash by with something else for the cart, and it was always something that surprised them.

"What do you need cotton wool for?"

"Injuries, ear plugs – it even works as gauze in a pinch."

"Gosh, you know everything, don't you? Where do you get those smarts?"

There we were – three millennials/Gen Z's – suddenly tasked with the challenge of sustaining our families for the next month. Though I was immensely grateful to have been granted entrance to the store, I couldn't stop thinking about those that had been turned away and those who could not afford to shop at Carrefour.

I voiced this to my shopping colleagues.

One of them responded, "Yeah, who's to say that everybody can prepare for a next-day lockdown the evening before? It's extremely irresponsible for the government to just put that on people and expect them to be able to cope."

It's a word that commonly floats around these days: responsibility.

The forcing of our lives into our (relatively) tiny homes has us spending a lot of time thinking, about who is or isn't to blame for our misfortunes. Whose fault is it that we have the virus in the first place? And then whose fault is it for spreading it? And whose fault is it that we can't stop it? That we can't shop, and socialise, and exist normally? Whose fault is it that I had to lie my way into that store near closing time? The more you think about it, the more and more you fall into a circle of non-accountability – the only end to which is to simply put on your mask and get on with life the way it is.

I spoke to my ayah a few days ago about how she was dealing with covid19. Aunty Judy, as we affectionately call her, lives in Kibera – one of the largest informal settlements in Nairobi[2]. Every day she dons the mask and hand sanitizer that we gave her to keep safe and journeys to our home to cook and clean, and generally be of assistance to my mother. The curfew has meant that we have had to shorten her working hours, so she can make it home before dark. The night I came back from the grocery store, I asked my mother why we weren't letting her go.

"She needs this work, Awuor," my mother replied, with a look on her face like she couldn't believe I had just asked that question. "What is she going to do in Kibera with no income, no protection, and no ways to access healthcare and food?"

Realising my horrible mistake, I sheepishly slinked back to my room – to read statistics on how covid19 was affecting those who face multiple structural barriers and systemic discrimination. The World Bank estimates

---

[2] According to *Nairobi's Informal Settlements: An Inventory March 1993*, the area covered by informal settlements is 6 per cent "of the land area of Nairobi that is used for residential purposes" (and 1.51% of the total area of Nairobi), but these informal settlements "house 55 per cent of the city's population" (p. 6). While the first percentage (rounded up to 6%) regarding land area does not seem to have changed, the latter figure, because of population growth and rural-urban migration, has evolved, and it is now estimated that Nairobi's 150 to over 200 informal settlements (commonly referred to as "slums") are home to "between 60 and 70 percent of Nairobi residents," according to a 2014 study by the African Population and Health Research Center (*Population and Health Dynamics in Nairobi's Informal Settlements*, p. xvii). See also *Mukuru, Nairobi, Kenya 2017 Statistical Analysis* by the University of Nairobi and others.

Keep in mind target 11.1 for Sustainable Development Goal 11 on sustainable cities and communities: "By 2030, ensure access for all to adequate, safe and affordable housing and basic services and upgrade slums." Numerous slumdwellers, politicians, government authorities, and organizations worked toward this goal, in part via the Kenya Informal Settlement Improvement Project (phase 1, phase 2, funded in part by the World Bank from 2011 through July 2025) of the Ministry of Transport and Infrastructure.

that the spread of the virus "could push 71 million people into extreme poverty in 2020" which would represent "the first increase in global extreme poverty since 1998."[3]

The partial lockdown means that it is harder for the financially poor in Kenya's capital city of Nairobi to access the help they need, help that comes from their employment. Forcing a lockdown on these people puts them in danger. It forces many of them to give up their income and the sense of security that comes from knowing it will help them provide for the family.

As I raced through the aisles of Carrefour, I thought about that. I could get groceries. Could everybody else? How would we all access healthcare and feel the comfort of friends and family?

The covid19 pandemic has put us in a health crisis and created one of the biggest social crises I have ever seen. Suddenly, we find ourselves struggling to maintain our physical health and our mental health, our sanity, in a world that changes literally by the minute. Those of us that can afford to keep safe face the horror of our own selves, clambering to get outside. We all face the fear of running out of whatever supplies we have left. We're fighting against ourselves to save ourselves — from the pandemic and from imminent social and economic ruin.

That evening, at the store, I bought Aunty Judy 5 kilograms of rice, 3 litres of cooking oil, 1 kg of tea leaves, 2 kg of ugali flour, and 1 kg of salt. When I unpacked her items, her face lit up the entire room. She had enough food to feed her family for the days to come. That deed was a small one, but it cleared both our minds. I found safety and security in the fact that I had fought to take care of those important to me, and Aunty Judy and her family found comfort in the fact that someone was looking out for them.

As I write this, covid19 is far from over. Everybody all over the world is desperately grasping at anything and everything they hope will end our suffering – vaccines, testing, contact tracing, isolation, physical distancing. We are watching the world fall apart from our homes and offices. We are listening to and watching the end from our radios and TVs and commenting it on social media.

---

[3] "Projected poverty impacts of COVID-19 (coronavirus)," 8 June 2020, www.worldbank.org/en/topic/poverty/brief/projected-poverty-impacts-of-COVID-19

Even though everyday seems never ending, I can tell you that our loved ones are what matters. From someone who survived a supermarket stampede at the onset of a lockdown of Nairobi, here is the one thing I would like to share with you: In the midst of the apocalypse, we've only got each other.

Awuor Onguru was born in Nairobi in 2002 and has been writing since she was 12 years old. She is a graduate of the International School of Kenya and hopes to begin her undergraduate education in 2020 at Yale University. Her work has appeared in Menacing Hedge *and* Polyphony Lit, *among other publications, and has been recognised by Hollins University and the Alliance for Young Artists and Writers. Awuor is proud, through her chapter in this book, to be part of a group of African women, and a few men, sharing their writing, their art, their experiences, their insights, and their reflections. She thanks her mother for encouraging her to share her writing with others, in Africa and beyond.*

chapter 3

Emotional Highs and Lows of Quarantine[1]

Susan Karungi

I am a mother of two daughters, aged twenty-one and fourteen. I live with my daughters, and occasionally my nieces, aged twenty-two and nineteen, join us. As head of the household, I attend to physical, emotional, spiritual, and financial needs and provide day-to-day guidance and care. I have had the pleasure of seeing all four girls grow under my tutelage. I have experienced the joy of witnessing every milestone – the energy, excitement (and sometimes defiance) of the teenage years, and for the older girls the morphing into young adults.

My girls think I am a typical African mother, pointing out my sarcastic answers to what I consider "silly" questions, the most common being: "Mummy, where should I put the jerrycan?" And my response "on my head." Or the "try that and die" stare if they are about to get into any sort of mischief. The side of my African parenting style that my eldest child perhaps feels strongly about is that as an African parent, I am limited in my understanding of mental health issues. I am conflicted on this one. Growing up, I was not exposed to the kind of information on mental health, the rights agenda or the self-awareness that is the norm for today's child. There is social media, there are peers and the information out there is endless. Maybe I was conditioned to "suck it up." Back to this later.

Our home is in a relatively quiet urban pioneer neighborhood in a Municipality in Wakiso District in Central Uganda, about twenty kilometers from the capital city of Kampala. It is a modest three-bedroom house that we moved into while incomplete. The process of completing the house has been slow and geared towards managing whatever emerges as an inconvenience to the family. For instance, when darkness became an inconvenience, we fixed power connections. When dust caused incessant coughing and sneezing, we installed tiles, and so on. The house has three

---

[1] Copyright © 2020 Susan Karungi
Karungi, S. (2020). Emotional highs and lows of quarantine. In M. N. Kinyanjui, R. Thaker, and K. Toure (Eds.), *Covid stories from East Africa and beyond: Lived experiences and forward-looking reflections* (pp. 21-27). Bamenda: Langaa.

bathrooms and three toilets, but only one is functional. The others are not yet fitted with accessories. This presented a tricky situation in adhering to the self-quarantine guidelines of covid19.

The covid19 pandemic brought back a phrase I learned during my European history lessons: "When France sneezes, the rest of Europe catches a cold." In essence, the actions of France at the time affected the rest of Europe in diverse and sometimes adverse ways politically, socially, and economically. The phrase often appeared in examinations and is one of those questions I found exhilarating to answer. They say history repeats itself, and the events that happened in Wuhan, China have caused devasting effects across the world. When China sneezed, the rest of the world caught a cold (or something like the flu) – literally.

It is easy to be aloof when a neighbor's house is on fire, but when the fire extends to your fence, you have to do something about it. When covid19 first broke out in China, I treated it as a Chinese problem. It did not occur to me then that China had become an international trade hub for many Ugandan businesses, a tourist destination, and an attraction for many Ugandan students. When Ugandan students sought government support to be repatriated, reality hit home. This was not a "neighbor's problem" anymore. It concerned all of us. Before the first case was registered, the Government of Uganda took radical measures to institute a phased lockdown with the closure of all schools and the close monitoring of national borders. Meanwhile next door in Kenya, the disease had crept into their backyard.

My eldest daughter studies at a university in Kenya. With the Government of Kenya instituting partial lockdown, educational institutions had to follow suit. Initially my daughter's school announced a two-week closure, and we thought she could stay put in Nairobi. However, shortly thereafter, the school announced that it would close until mid-May, so we arranged for her to travel home. At the time, the Government of Uganda had started implementing quarantine measures for all people coming through Entebbe International Airport. Institutional quarantine was mandatory for all travelers coming from high-risk countries such as Italy, China, and Germany. People returning from other countries including Kenya were to place themselves under self-quarantine.

The term "quarantine" is etched in my childhood memory because it was, and still is, applied to curtailing foot and mouth disease in cattle. So in a household, how does it apply to a young girl, just back from Kenya, who is carefree, fun, and full of laughter – and incessantly crisscrossing into and out of others' personal spaces? Do these spaces exist? I was very thankful and relieved that she was not placed in institutional quarantine, because of the costs but also because of the anguish of having your loved one near, yet so far.

When my daughter eventually arrived home, we could only do the elbow greeting instead of the long warm hugs that are our custom. I knew then that it was going to be an uneasy fourteen days. We carried her luggage to her room, and the self-quarantine protocols and standards began. I wondered if we could share meals with her at the table. The question itself sounded ridiculous. How would I stand for "thrusting" food in her room? How could she enjoy her meal alone, when the rest of us sat at the family table and enjoyed the banter that accompanies our mealtimes? Would she feel abandoned? Unloved? We decided right there that we would make her a part of our mealtimes, and that she would be part of our family prayer time. We succeeded with the latter but not so much with the former.

The self-quarantine prevention measures stipulated that the "quarantinee" should stay in a well-ventilated room, preferably with separate hygiene and separate facilities. My daughter stayed in an airy and spacious room, but with only one functional toilet and bathroom, we had to adhere to minimum safety standards. We regularly disinfected the sink and toilet and other surfaces including doorknobs, power switches and walls. We were strict with this process, alongside handwashing, sanitizing and coughing into our elbows.

This whole situation, however, tugged at my heartstrings. I could not help but feel pity towards my girl. Was she feeling stigmatized? Was she feeling lonely? Was she understanding of all the things that were going on and had to be done? How were her sister and cousins feeling? It was tense. Though it was not explicit, I could feel that there was "us" and "her." Was she taking it all in stride? Time would tell.

Fourteen days can quickly swing by if you are relaxed, vacationing or doing something great. In quarantine, the days seemed like a lifetime. We ticked off each day as it passed and trudged through all the days as they came. My daughter still had classes going on, I had started teleworking, my younger daughter had work sent through her school's e-learning platform, and one of my nieces – a final year university student – was immersed in preparing for her final exams that had been slated for May.

Dealing with my daughter's fear and anxiety, and my own for that matter, was one of the difficulties I faced. Just back from Kenya, my daughter kept abreast of the covid19 news there – the infection rates, the measures instituted by the government. Every time new cases were announced in Kenya, she panicked. "Mummy, what if I sat with those people in a *matatu*? What if one is the Uber driver who took me to the airport? What if one is a classmate of mine?"

Deep inside, I believed she had not been exposed at all. When these questions came up, I faltered but kept a brave face and reassured her that she could not have had enough exposure to worry about. Around day six, she developed some mild flu symptoms and a cough, and as the numbers kept growing in Kenya, she got diarrhea. We checked with a doctor who assured us that it was probably nothing to worry about. But what if?

I needed to be in the right frame of mind to provide the emotional support and reassurance my daughter needed. I needed to be available for her and the other girls. I needed accurate information and a reliable source of information, so I took several measures. I subscribed to the World Health Organization WhatsApp group to get real-time and accurate information on covid19. I ignored all the conspiracy theories, fake news, and unhelpful information on WhatsApp groups. I stayed on a work-related platform that had strict protocols. It included official updates from time to time and messages from our occupational therapist. The information was well researched before it was posted. I desisted from having useless and draining debates on other social media platforms. The social media age has brought across many "experts" on various matters. There are baseless arguments, analyses, counter analyses, conspiracy theories, and falsehoods. Covid19 was not spared. Finally, I engaged in prayer to help us connect with our creator. I, and the girls too I think, gained a sense of security, feeling how He's got our back.

I had put my mind at ease, by shutting out the bombardment of misinformation and sensational coverage, which only fueled my fear and anxiety. How do you give what you do not have? If I were consumed by fear and anxiety, how would I give reassurance to my daughter that she was going to be okay? For the girls, I encouraged them to do the same, and we created space where we could talk about what was going on with the filtered information we obtained from credible sources.

My older daughter is the family "comedian." Most of the time, she has her happy hat on. During the self-quarantine period, her happiness dissipated. Her routine changed. She came out of her room long after the rest of us had finished breakfast. She had her breakfast mid-morning or early afternoon. Was she trying to protect us? By the time we were having lunch, she would still be too full to join us. For the first seven days of the quarantine, this was her pattern. She was alone most of the time. My other daughter and nieces would be together. There was no "together" time for the four of them. No connection. This was a new normal – a disruption to the lively, playful, and amusing aura that usually animates our home.

My children insist that I am a typical African parent, the kind who speaks using some sort of sign language – a stern look, a pinch (when they were younger) – and sarcasm. What I did not know until this time is that this description extends to how I understand or respond to the emotional needs of my children. Everyone has their way of dealing with the challenges that life throws their way.

In my case, I talk about with my sisters. I pray. Sometimes, away from preying eyes, I cry on my pillow. Or I find something to distract me. Whatever I do, I maintain a calm demeanor, which may be mistaken for aloofness. Talking with my sisters is the most soothing of all my coping strategies. We laugh, and somehow the issues mellow.

Around the tenth day of the self-quarantine, my daughter had a meltdown. Things fell apart completely. She told me amidst heavy sobs that I did not care about and did not understand what she was going through. For me, she said, it was all something to joke and laugh about. I was taken aback.

The previous day, I had told one of my sisters that whenever my daughter heard about the surge in Kenya's covid19 cases, she got a running stomach. We laughed about it, and that was it. Little did I know that this ignorant and innocent action hurt my daughter to the core. I realize that in this time of the rona, sensitivities run high, all around, and we best be sensitive to that.

Yes, I am an African mother. Am I devoid of empathy? I do not think so. Am I aloof? Not entirely. Do I suck it up? Yes. Do I understand mental health challenges that these young girls face? I am a work in progress. I knew that if France sneezes, the rest of Europe catches a cold. But I did not know that because of a virus from the other side of the world, we suffer and are stretched not only physically and economically but also mentally and emotionally.

My daughter's conversation with me was a turning point for us. I did not how to react. I felt anger, regret, and a sense of failure. How could my love be interpreted as aloofness and indifference? I realized she needed even more of that love.

We had another conversation. Apart from the stress of being in self-quarantine, I understood my daughter was also dealing with deeper emotional issues arising from my separation from her father. Surprisingly, he and I, after eight years, are now in a good place, but sadly she still carries anguish from the separation.

On the third day of April 2020, the fourteen days of self-quarantine came to an end. The end coincided with the celebration of my younger daughter's fourteenth birthday. What a coincidence! In biblical numerology, fourteen refers to the perfection of the soul, to its purity and light, a double of God's power and coincidence. And so, the light shines on our journey.

I am glad that my daughter did not fall sick to this dreadful disease. I am glad that during the fourteen-day quarantine period, we were able to connect in new ways. I am grateful that she is again happy and joyful. We devoured the delicious pastries she made for the third of April. And we all had our share of long warm hugs!

I am thankful that we all seemed to grow emotionally. We still have emotional issues to deal with going forward. Our quarantine period was a time of revelation of character and disposition. We made it through difficult days. We will not be quite the same tomorrow as we were yesterday. Every cloud has a silver lining. My experience may not compare to that of the millions of people who have lost loved ones or been hospitalized. But it is my story. And I am thankful for the platform to share it.

Susan Karungi is a 46-year-old mother of two daughters. She also lives occasionally with her two nieces. She works with SNV Netherlands Development Organisation in Kampala, Uganda. Currently she is working on a project titled Water, Hygiene and Sanitation Project (WASH) that promotes household access to improved latrines and, more broadly, supports the strengthening of decentralized government units to sustainably assure household sanitation. She lives in the Wakiso District of Uganda. She has written a small biography titled Samson Bityo Kahima: The Birth of a Legacy *to commemorate her father's 80th birthday. Proceeds from the sale of the book go towards supporting the Kahima Trust, a foundation established to support bright but indigent children in her community to attain education.*

chapter 4

Making Covid19 Manageable with Gospel Music[1]

Catherine Mongella-Kalokola

Wake up, say a prayer, brush my teeth, put on my playlist, clean the house, prepare kids for school, and serve everyone breakfast. Go to work and come back home. Prepare dinner. Repeat the next day. This has been my basic daily routine for the past five or so years, a routine engraved in my memory. My normal.

This routine was overhauled when covid19 came into the picture.

Let me start by recalling the day I had a breakdown at home, trying to supervise my son doing phonics homework while I worked on a donor proposal. My son was just not doing his work. He wanted to watch cartoons instead. I looked at him and said, "If you are not serious, you will be repeating grade one."

My seven-year-old looked at me and his eyes welled up. Not my best mother moment, I know. My brain could not process why he did not understand that I had a lot on my plate and him doing his phonics homework would allow me to finish my donor proposal. But children do not think like that. I closed my laptop and locked myself in my kitchen store, the only place of solitude where my kids cannot open the door.

I took a deep breath and texted Naomi, my good friend and mother to my godson. Naomi had temporarily relocated to Ireland due to covid19. In my mini meltdown, the person I could call for help was miles away. I could not text an emergency "we need some wine and girl time." I had to figure things out – quickly – and get back to being a teacher. I texted her: "today I told my son he will repeat the first grade if he is not serious." My friend, though miles away, was able to do a WhatsApp call, where we did what we do best. We laughed at ourselves. She laughed at me and with me. I laughed

---

[1] Copyright © 2020 Catherine Mongella-Kalokola
Mongella-Kalokola, C. (2020). Making covid19 manageable with gospel music. In M. N. Kinyanjui, R. Thaker, and K. Toure (Eds.), *Covid stories from East Africa and beyond: Lived experiences and forward-looking reflections* (pp. 29-34). Bamenda: Langaa.

at myself, and after that good laughter I knew everything was going to be alright.

Pre covid19, this 36-year-old had the first half of 2020 planned down to a T, starting with a Charity Ball which would be the first in Mwanza in four years. All expatriates in Mwanza were looking forward to it, and I was over the moon at being part of the organizing committee. We had arranged a Gatsby theme, a venue at the most exclusive hotel in Mwanza near the Lake, a four-course menu, and a band to fly in from Arusha. This event was bound to bring donations to the organization I work for and awareness to our work of helping street children in Mwanza. Second, I planned to have my daughter celebrate her first birthday in school – a milestone. Mentally I had already picked out the cake which would have her favorite cartoon on it, and it would be the day we would get her ears pierced because she always takes my earrings. hinting she is ready. Third, a short trip to Greece to visit historical sites, enjoy fine dining, and of course break a few plates. Finally, I thought to end the mid-year on a high with a tour of the work we do in London with our amazing partner Amos Trust. Two weeks promoting our work and then two weeks on a mini vacation looking after no one but thyself. These ambitious plans and aspirations were suddenly put on an indefinite pause.

February 2020. News of covid19 starts to hit the airwaves. I am yet to understand the massive impact it will have on the work I do. Plans for my trip to Greece had been finalized. I received a text from my sister asking about the number of covid19 cases in Greece. I googled it and found there were only four cases and zero deaths. I stayed positive. I traveled to Greece, only to find that most of the places on my itinerary had been closed due to the outbreak, so I decided to cut the trip short and return home until the pandemic was more controlled.

On my return to Tanzania, my temperature was taken and the details of my travel noted. Mentally, I appreciated my country's preparedness. I made it back to Mwanza in one piece, not fully satisfied from my experience in Greece but happy to have gotten some time to relax. A few days later, Greece closed its borders due to the epidemic which was later declared a pandemic. I thanked God for being able to get back home when I did. Little did I know that this would be the beginning of me feeling the pinch of covid19.

March 2020. Tanzania announces her first case of covid19. All schools close for an indefinite period. I first thought of my two children. Them being in school allows me time to work while they are in a safe environment. Them being at home, I think of my nanny, an older woman who comes at 8 am and leaves at 4 pm Monday thru Friday. Without a doubt, the kids would be able to manipulate her to put cartoons on and let them play instead of reading and working on their homework. How could she supervise their schoolwork when they do it in English, and she speaks Swahili? I instantly knew I would have to adjust how I work.

I also thought about my staff of 50 persons: 27 women and 23 men. About 75% of them have children in school. If schools are closed and it affects me, chances are they will be affected as well. Again, I knew right then and there that I would need to strategize to keep my team functioning during this pandemic.

I thought of my husband who is a medical doctor at the only referral hospital in the Lake Zone. Per day, he sees a minimum of 30 outpatients at the government hospital, which currently is the only place which takes samples for covid19 in Mwanza. He also sees inpatients and outpatients at a private clinic. All these interactions imply a higher risk of contracting covid19.

Back at work, my email inbox is flooded with messages from donors and partners asking how I, as the head of the organization, was going to manage the situation for my team and our beneficiaries including 35 children at our residential center and 20 children at our drop-in center. I had to strategize how best to respond to everyone's concerns, while reassuring employees who were worried about their employment, their health, and their families.

I took a deep breath and started playing music from a playlist on my phone. Music is the one thing that calms me down and puts my mind at ease. I knew this was not the time for my preferred soft rock and R&B. What I was about to go through needed a good dose of uplifting gospel music. I put on one of my favorites, Relax by Christina Shusho. I closed my eyes and removed myself from the chaos of the pandemic. I replayed the song three good times. After the third time, I opened my eyes and made a mental speech to myself – reminding myself that I am strong and can take care of any situation ahead of me. I made it my personal mission to manage covid19 to the best of my knowledge and ability.

First things first – my kids. I registered them for online learning at their school, bought enough notebooks, pencils and crayons, picked out the shows they could watch if I wasn't home, and planned their lunches and snacks. I also talked with their nanny about the changes in the children's schooling and the basic preventive steps for covid19, including showering once she comes in and always wearing a mask if she steps out of the house. I took her through the proper way of spraying down her shoes and phone with spirit when she arrived for work.

Ms. Catherine must have this all figured out.

Wrong. I quickly came to learn that online learning for kids in preschool and grade one is easier read and said than done. Even with online school and restrictions on TV time, my kids still found something to play with and ruin in the process. Did this derail me in my mission to power through covid19? No, I kept moving forward and reminded myself to keep moving.

Second in line was my husband, who was working at the frontline. I took the liberty to research the best ways to support him during this time. I changed my routine to ensure he could shower after work and have a steaming hot cup of ginger and lemon tea waiting for him. I made a mental note to buy a box of masks, spirits, and hand sanitizer for him to take to work. I ensured his shoes were taken off and sprayed with spirit and his laundry done every day after work. Again, I hoped I could control the situation by helping my husband, not taking into consideration at first my husband's and children's emotional states. At the outbreak of the pandemic, I had to sneak my husband into our room so the kids would not see him and hug him. Children at such tender ages did not understand at first that Daddy could not hug them until after he showered and sanitized. They wondered why their father started wearing a mask and always kept it on his face. One may think all this derailed me in my mission to power through in the midst of covid19. It didn't – I continued moving forward and reminded myself to keep moving.

Next in line was work – 50 full time employees, 5 volunteers, and roughly 50 children. They were all looking to me for a sign that everything would be okay, a sign that things would get back to normal. With some funding put on hold due to the pandemic, seven members of my team – myself included – faced a salary cut in the blink of a week. I had to put that on the back burner, however, and strategize on how to continue to operate our Day Center while reassuring donor partners that covid19 would not keep us from doing our work. I needed to make them understand that funding during covid19 was essential for ongoing support to children living and working on the streets. Where could they self-isolate? They depended on our centers and on my team.

I took a deep breath and gave myself a double dose of inspirational music. This time I went for a more upbeat song, Wewe ni Mungu (You are God) by Daddy Owen featuring Rigan Sarkozi. I reminded myself that one is only given battles one is strong enough to fight. I moved forward.

I reassured staff that salaries would stay intact and that our Day Center would continue to operate. I then sat with my manager to set a roster of staff that could be in the field during this time. We then looked for funds and provided all staff with reusable masks, sanitizers, and spirits, along with training from a medical practitioner. After two weeks of rolling out these changes and communicating with partners and donors, our team was managing, and our work was continuing. If only it were that simple though. I received the sad news that my uncle passed from covid19. All gatherings and social events had been cancelled by the government, so we could not even organize a funeral.

I have rolled my eyes so many times during this covid experience. I have locked myself in my kitchen store and zoned out. I have done so much google research and watched so many news updates. I had to pause. I had to remind myself that my faith teaches that there is a purpose in everything. I had made my plans, for example to tour London, but God had other plans. This whole experience has taught me that sometimes we need to go with the flow rather than stick to a routine all the time.

Routine is what had worked for me. Planning and lists helped me maintain my sanity. With covid19, a lot has changed. My kids' school sends me their homework every day. I have to print it out and teach lessons and supervise and submit their work on a daily basis. My husband comes home every day from the frontline. My staff seek assurance about their jobs. This all came out of the blue. I never imagined such puzzle pieces.

Two months since the pandemic emerged in Tanzania, I am still a wife of one and a mother of two children under the age of seven. I have unapologetically had to add an item to my memorized routine: self-affirmation. Just as my staff tell our young mothers that they are doing the best they can, I self-affirm every morning that I am doing the best I can. I self-affirm that I – as an Individual, a Wife, a Mother, a Director, a Teacher, a Nurse – have got this. I can do it and I am doing it. I am solving the puzzle.

I still listen to music every day as I clean the house in the morning. The difference is that my playlist now has more inspirational songs on repeat. Also, I do more exercise – which means running after my children. I have come to learn that they give me a full workout.

Wake up, say a prayer, brush my teeth, self-affirm (I have got this), put on my playlist, clean the house, serve everyone breakfast, bathe the kids, prepare their homework, leave proper instructions with the nanny, make sure the nanny showers and changes when she comes in, prep myself for work, and do not forget mask and sanitizer. Go to work, wash hands, sanitize desk. Come back home, take shoes off at the door, do not hug the kids, wash hands, soak clothes, shower, hug kids, remind them how much I love them, prepare dinner while listening to the stories of who hit whom, check homework, prerecord shows the kids can watch the next day. Repeat the next day. This is my new normal. Hectic, yes. Loud and messy – very much so – but I have learned to see this as a chance to cherish every moment with my family. A chance to learn my weaknesses and strengths as an individual, what I can do and when I need to pour myself a glass of wine. I thank covid19 for showing me what really matters in life – my health, my sanity, and my family.

In concluding, I urge any mother or wife out there (whether working in, from, and/or outside the home), any woman out there, to keep strong and not lose their sanity. We are all doing the best we can. And for those who need some music, Head over Water by Avril Lavigne is the latest song I have on repeat.

Catherine Mongella-Kalokola is a resident of Mwanza and mother of two. At the time she wrote this chapter, she ran an organization that provided psychosocial support to children and youth living and working on the streets. Currently she is a consultant with HC&A Solutions.

chapter 5

School Closure and Panic Mode[1]

Meseret Kassahun Desta

The covid19 pandemic brought multifaceted restrictions to the social and economic affairs of every family, society, and country in the world. The Government of Kenya took various measures to prevent the spread of covid19 in the community, following World Health Organization protocols. Social distancing and school closures were among the first measures introduced, followed by stay-at-home orders. Home as a space for family life became a place of work for many people – in addition to being a "teaching and learning space" for families with school-aged children. These changes introduced multiple and varied challenges for households. Socioeconomic conditions, marital status, the number as well as the age of children (only or with siblings) in the household, and other factors contribute to differences in experience. I relate here, based on my lived experience, some of the challenges of suddenly converting home to a working, teaching, and learning space.

Panic mode

The announcement of school closures came in March, just at the end of the first term of the second semester of the 2019-2020 academic year. I panicked. Then I realized the break between terms would be a useful transition week, to prepare mentally and psychologically. I got organized and went into action. With my daughter, we designated spaces for her learning activities and otherwise prepared.

Another source of panic was the lack of clarity about how the market system would operate for the supply of goods during the pandemic. The rumor that Kenya might impose a complete lockdown exacerbated the confusion. I decided to stock up on supplies like crayons, paper, paint, yarn, colored paper, and canvases.

---

[1] Copyright © 2020 Meseret Kassahun Desta

Desta, M. K. (2020). School closure and panic mode. In M. N. Kinyanjui, R. Thaker, and K. Toure (Eds.), *Covid stories from East Africa and beyond: Lived experiences and forward-looking reflections* (pp. 35-40). Bamenda: Langaa.

We also upgraded our internet package. I worried about the hours and hours our daughter would be in front of a screen. During the transition week, we talked about it and negotiated new screen-time rules.

Day by day, it became clearer that unknowns would be the norm during the covid19 pandemic. I was quite stressed. Our eight-year old daughter is very sociable and outgoing and would stay outside the whole day if possible. Being sheltered at home meant we would not be able to follow our regular routines – out and about in Nairobi.

Weekends were when we went for a swim, a walk in Karura Forest, or horse riding and dined out on Saturday or lunched out on Sunday. The curfew brought so many restrictions. No more gatherings for birthday parties. No more playdates with school friends for our daughter. Like any child, she loves playing with children rather than hanging out with her parents all the time, especially because she is an only child.

She missed her circle of friends and regularly implored, "May I organize a play date today?" We felt bad when we had to say, "Not while the covid19 prevention measures are in place."

Usually, on Sundays after church service, we would visit friends and enjoy a meal together with several families. It was the best moment. We adults would sit and chat. Our children would play together. We missed those encounters while sheltering at home.

Parents as assistant teachers

My husband and I both have hectic work schedules. For my husband, it was a very busy time of the year. As for me, I needed to focus on several research projects in Ethiopia and more broadly in the Horn of Africa. I had to finalize data collection by phone, which was already a major challenge, and at the same time help our daughter settle into virtual learning.

Because of the travel bans, all meetings I needed to lead, or attend, went virtual. Sometimes the meeting schedules changed when colleagues in various locations faced power or internet outages. This disrupted my plans, requiring me to be flexible. Because of my career as a researcher and consultant, I was accustomed to working from home. Because my husband had needed to negotiate Nairobi's traffic jams during his long commutes to his office, I had been the one to drop our daughter off at school. He was thus free from school-related responsibilities.

Because of this preexisting division of labor in our household, after schools closed, I became the de facto person responsible for assisting our daughter with her schooling. I faced a multitude of additional responsibilities: responding to emails from our daughter's homeroom teacher, reminding our daughter about her zoom meetings, supporting her in the completion of daily learning activities. I took on these necessary – and time-consuming – tasks without an open discussion with my husband about sharing responsibilities.

The first day of virtual learning was fun. Our daughter made a to-do list on her iPad. She was excited to do her own planning. The second and third days were a bit rough, because she did not want to sit alone and do her class activities by herself.

She started saying, "I miss recess and time to play with my friends."

On the fourth day, she announced, "Virtual learning is boring."

We listened to her concerns and encouraged her to use her creativity to make her learning experience more fun and enjoyable. She decided to make a fort using the dining chairs and red and blue striped shuka[2]. Her colorful fort gave her a sense of accomplishment. She declared, "Whoever wants to enter my fort needs my permission." We promised to respect her demand and desire.

Escalation of tensions

The second and third weeks of school were more intense – with more and more activities introduced. I helped our daughter take pictures of her completed assignments and upload them to a Google Drive. On many occasions, however, my husband and I both had a zoom meeting when she needed help to meet her teachers' deadlines.

Our daughter eventually lost interest in attending her music, language, and art classes. I noticed that the 30-minute sessions were too brief for teachers to recognize who was present and who was missing and ensure every child participated.

"They don't even notice I'm there," she explained. "Why should I be there?" Although I did not pressure her to attend those classes, I also did not approve of her decision.

---

[2] Shuka is a large piece of fluffy cloth. Known as an "African blanket," it is often red with black stripes but also comes in other bright colors. It is worn by the Maasai people of East Africa.

The intensity of my work increased. Deadlines approached. Tension escalated.

As I reflect back, I realize I had totally underestimated the level of engagement parents were expected to have with school-related activities. Hence, my husband and I had not discussed how to share the responsibilities. This created a communication vacuum, which led to a heated argument.

I had to tell my husband that assisting our daughter with her schoolwork and trying to complete my projects had become too much for me to handle.

The initial tension subsided, and we were able to strategize about what to do. We decided to take turns in supporting our daughter. Eventually, though, my husband took full responsibility for assisting her for the rest of the semester because my work required my undivided attention to complete a national report.

Coping with lockdown: A plethora of activities

Our daughter became interested in do-it-yourself (DIY) topics on YouTube. She watched videos by kids and imagined herself as a YouTube star. She started trying the DIYs at home. She became obsessed with recipes and baking, to indulge her love of cake and chocolate. Baking took her attention away from the screen, so we were happy to provide the ingredients she needed. She baked cookies, brownies, cakes, pies, and croissants. Her favorite? Chocolate chip cookies and real-butter croissants! She started baking every Thursday. Her lockdown coping strategy brings the family something yummy to share and savor once a week.

Despite the fact that I did not want our daughter to spend excess time on screens, I subscribed to an online piano lesson. The "Simply Piano" app served us the best. The more she learned how to play chords, the more interested she became. In a few weeks, she was playing mostly classical music. She has an ear for music and plays with zest. Her sense of achievement when she passes from one stage to another is palpable.

Our daughter had a bike, but she was not interested in learning to ride it by herself. I decided to accompany and coach her. She started balancing and controlling her bike when she wanted to stop. Day by day, her fears dissipated. Biking quickly became second nature.

She also tried painting. She has a great sense of combining colors. Because she messed up our place with lots of paint stains on the floor and tables, a designated area for her artwork was prepared.

She also enjoys making slime. During this lockdown experience, we tried so many edible and non-edible slime recipes. I am not sure if I like slime. It is slimy! Whenever she wanted me to touch it, I showed her a disgusted face. Then she made sure I touched it. The whole process resulted in lots of laughter.

We know our daughter appreciates when we listen to her piano playing, taste her baked delicacies, and touch the slime she makes. It's a reminder about the importance of affirmation. I now plan my time more carefully, so I may avail myself and fully observe or work with her. The more she includes these non-school activities in her day, the better she does in school.

No more fear of going out

As the months went by, and we knew we had to learn to live with covid19, my friend and I decided to arrange some play dates, for our daughter and her son. We took our kids out for bike rides together. It was interesting to observe the kids talk when they first met, after two and a half months. They shared what they were doing while staying at home, how good they were getting at playing the piano, or what they had watched on Netflix. Although we kept reminding them about physical distancing and to keep their face masks on, they did not adhere strictly to the protocols. But we were reassured in knowing that neither of our families had much contact with others. We also decided to go for a walk in Karura Forest. The more our daughter and I interact outside, the more our stresses disappear.

End of school year: Hooray!

School was scheduled to end the first week of June. Hooray! My husband and I would be able to focus more on our work. A school break also meant freedom for our daughter. She constantly told us she did not like virtual learning.

On the last day of the school year, she baked a rice crispy chocolate brownie. She also wanted her hair to be fancy because "we are supposed to a have a party." The last day of class seemed fun. Students brought their snacks to the virtual party. Our daughter showed off her rice crispy brownie. She enjoyed the day. I could hear the laughter of the other children too. What a moment.

The conversion of our home into a work and learning space exposed the family to some level of tension. At the same time, it offered us an opportunity to engage in various activities that increased our family time and helped our child develop new skills and experiment creatively in exploring her aspirations.

Meseret Kassahun Desta is an Ethiopian woman working for inclusive development and social justice. She has a PhD in Social Work from the Jane Addams College of Social Work at the University of Illinois at Chicago and more than 10 years of experience as a practitioner, teacher, and researcher. Her research interests include gender issues, child protection, urban governance, migration, and peace and security issues. She has taught at the School of Social Work at Addis Ababa University. The major courses she has taught include Social Development and Social Change as well as Social Policy Development and Analysis. She is the founder and a researcher at EMAH Social Development Consulting. As a consultant, she has carried out formative studies and evaluations of social programs in Ethiopia and the Horn of Africa for different UN agencies and international NGOs.

chapter 6

What Is It Like Working in a Hospital During the Covid Pandemic?[1]

Toseef Din

In the covid19 era, "spread calm not chaos." That is the theme at our hospital, M. P. Shah Hospital, in Nairobi, Kenya. We are a level 5 healthcare facility[2] and play a critical role within the county and national health systems in providing essential medical care, treatment, and services to the community. During this crisis, our role became even more important. I am the Chief Executive Officer (CEO) of M. P. Shah, one of the oldest and busiest hospitals in the country and which has a legacy of over 90 years of care. We have 210 beds and cater both for adult and paediatric patients.

We discuss Africa in one breath, and the implication is that it's almost as though we are the poor cousin of the rest of the world. As an African, born, bred, and nourished in Kenya, I do not ascribe to this line of thought. Within Africa we have a whole range of people, education systems, economies, facilities, and infrastructures. And we have some of the best healthcare professionals and healthcare services. Our hospital, for example, marries basic and state-of-the-art services in various medical and surgical fields with local context and local needs. We maintain competitive pricing, in line with Universal Health Coverage, according to which healthcare is a right for all.[3]

---

[1] Copyright © 2020 Toseef Din
Din, T. (2020). What is it like working in a hospital during the covid pandemic? In M. N. Kinyanjui, R. Thaker, and K. Toure (Eds.), *Covid stories from East Africa and beyond: Lived experiences and forward-looking reflections* (pp. 41-55). Bamenda: Langaa.
[2] There are six different levels of healthcare facilities in Kenya; **level 5 healthcare facilities** "are the county referral hospitals formerly the provincial hospitals. They are run by Chief Executive Officers who are medic by profession and have over 100 beds capacity for their in-patient. They are also do research about health."
Source: https://actionfortransparency.org/kenyas-health-structure-and-the-six-levels-of-hospitals-roggkenya
[3] For information on the **importance of healthcare pricing** and how it should reflect the cost of the provision of care, provide the right incentives, and take into account the broader health system goals, see *Price setting and price regulation in health care: Lessons for*

At the same time, we are cognizant of the shortcomings and challenges that come with fragile healthcare systems in emerging economies and the scarcity and disparity in distribution of healthcare workers and health services in our part of the world.

I experience these challenges every day as a leader at the helm of a busy hospital in Africa and now even more so with the onset of covid19. The pandemic posed a significant threat to the ability of our healthcare organization to maintain optimal operational capabilities and continue providing service through a sustainable model[4].

I am incredibly grateful to all our healthcare workers for their unwavering support during this very difficult call of duty and applaud them for being psychologically resilient and remaining committed and diligent during this time. I dedicate this chapter to them; they are the hope of many Kenyans.

How it all began

It was my day off: the 13th of March 2020. After several weeks of working without a break, I had decided to take a breather and give myself some selfcare therapy.

Everything started off well. I woke up late, had a leisurely breakfast, and went for a relaxing spa treatment. Just before heading back home, I logged onto my phone and got the news of the first covid19 positive case reported in Kenya. My heart skipped a beat, and suddenly there was a feeling of panic all around me. My phone rang non-stop, and messages came in one after another. Of course, we were aware of the outbreak in China and what had been happening globally since December 2019, however, we hoped it somehow wouldn't come to Kenya, or at least not quite yet.

Several weeks prior to March 13th, the hospital had formed a taskforce that would handle the logistics and clinical aspects of our response. We had been deliberating on ways to handle this pandemic and had launched

---

advancing Universal Health Coverage. www.oecd.org/health/health-systems/OECD-WHO-Price-Setting-Summary-Report.pdf

[4] For more information, see the Introduction in this paper, "Promoting **healthcare sustainability**…," published in the *International Journal of Environmental Research and Public Health* in 2019, volume 16, issue 3, pages 508-531. www.ncbi.nlm.nih.gov/pmc/articles/PMC6388157/#B2-ijerph-16-00508 or https://dx.doi.org/10.3390%2Fijerph16030508

extensive training and education programs. The effort to overprepare was obvious to staff.

I drove to work. I activated the preparedness plan that we had discussed so many times, and we engaged all our teams. Communication was key, even to the extent of seeming to overcommunicate.

Over the next couple months, the Kenyan social landscape changed. We witnessed closed places of worship, empty malls and streets, and the continuing spread of the disease. Certain medications advertised to be the cure for covid19 gradually went out of stock, and so did several types of personal protective equipment (PPE). It was quite a depressing state of affairs, however, we developed resilience and built more care and compassion into our service delivery.

Our priority remained the safety and protection of our 1,000 employees, 70% of whom are clinical. Healthy, safe, and decent working conditions for *all* healthcare workers amidst the covid19 pandemic was our objective every single day.

I value the wellbeing of all my staff just the way I value my family's safety. As a person who plans, prepares checklists, and executes, I was initially rather lost. The situation changed daily. I quickly realized that we needed to collectively shape our approach and adapt continuously. I consoled myself with the teachings of the Persian Sufi poets: "This too shall pass."

We were aware that no matter how much we prepared, a prolonged, continuous spread of the virus could lead to rapidly increasing service demands and potentially overwhelm our capacity.

Nonetheless, our taskforce put our plans into action, built stakeholder relations, engaged in partnerships with other organizations, and activated operational changes to ensure the continuity of essential services.

Trepidation or alarm could potentially jeopardize established working routines, and so we introduced campaigns of "spread calm not chaos" via continuous education and training. We handled the situation with truth and science, not fear and panic.

Even for a hospital that is well prepared, coping with the health consequences of the coronavirus disease is a complex challenge. In the face of the difficult demands and foreseen obstacles, the proactive and systematic implementation of key actions facilitated effective hospital-based management during the rapidly evolving situation. Among the very important preventative measures, in keeping with Government directives, are physical distancing, avoiding crowds, and improving patient flow. Despite the newness and foreignness of "physical distancing" for us in Kenya, we quickly adopted the practice and accepted it as our new normal.

Below, I will detail specific actions and various experiences.

Learning from the past

The 2003 global SARS outbreak informed many populations, employers, and workforces in affected countries. There was panic, however, and there were many unknowns. Scientists weren't certain if they would be able to eliminate SARS completely, or if it would become a seasonal illness like the flu. Luckily, doctors and scientists were able to completely eliminate SARS by isolating and quarantining people until the virus passed out of their system and they could no longer transmit it to others. We in Kenya were largely spared exposure to that outbreak, and perhaps that is one reason why the covid19 reality was all the more distressing.

Now, there is so much information available, and almost everyone has an opinion that they share on social media. This is helpful in many instances but misleading in others. It behoves us each to choose what information we assimilate and what information we discard or ignore. The sharing of scientific information on clinical breakthroughs and advancements in technologies have fast-tracked humanity's understanding of the disease. Yet, we still need to use nineteenth-century practices to contain it.[5]

---

[5] The book, *SARS: How a global epidemic was stopped*, reminds us how "SARS shook the world." "The book is richly filled with facts and exclusive inside accounts of what really occurred in those fateful months" in 2003. It "offers insights into the lessons learned from this major public health crisis and provides key information that should be useful for dealing with emerging infectious diseases in the future." Three of the 13 lessons shared in the final chapter are as follows: (1) "transparency is the best policy," (2) "twenty-first century science played a relatively small role in controlling SARS; nineteenth-century techniques continued to prove their value," and (3) "animal husbandry and marketing practices seriously affect human health." The last chapter concludes "with the remark that 'it would be tragic if we did not learn from the experience of 2003 and make the most of it.' Indeed, SARS has shown us that **if we work together and better prepare ourselves, we can confront and conquer new emerging and re-emerging infectious disease threats with calm and confidence**" [emphasis added]. Source: Review of the book by Suok Kai Chew in *Bulletin of the World Health Organization*, April 2007, Volume 85, Issue 4, page 324, www.ncbi.nlm.nih.gov/pmc/articles/PMC2636331 and

Are we safe within the hospital? Our initial response

Since the 13th of March 2020, every morning our employees walk into the hospital feeling apprehensive, not knowing what the day will hold. We kickstart every day with a taskforce meeting to address concerns as diverse as admissions, discharges, brought-in-dead, infection control, patient confidentiality, and operational and administrative issues. These meetings are chaired by me and attended by staff from clinical and non-clinical departments. Members of the taskforce are at the heart of our hospital's response. The medical director, the head of nursing, and all doctors and nurses provide invaluable support. It is physically and mentally exhausting for all.

In the beginning, each day ended with tuning into the Government's press briefing, which included mention of the number of positive coronavirus cases being confirmed across the country, and every day we would tell ourselves: "Don't let your guard down." Encouragement, determination, and motivation were supporting pillars. However, gloomy faces always filled the room, and we didn't know where we were all going with this unpredictable situation. Initially, we organized dry-runs on how it would be if we started receiving positive patients, and this helped us to streamline our protocols and allay procedural anxiety.

One nurse asked me "What happens if I get infected?" and "What happens to our families? How do we safeguard them?" These important questions required straight, non-political answers.

I had a huge role to play to ensure that the safety of our staff was guarded at all times and necessary medical expenses were covered. Reassurances were key. I could imagine what might be going through our nurses' and other medical workers' minds, who risk themselves in responding to the call of duty. The hospital, of course, was going to take every measure to ensure their safety, and we implemented appropriate measures. The hospital formulated a covid19 policy, which was cascaded to all staff. It's often said that the true test of leadership is how well you function in a crisis, and this, no doubt, was my test.

---

http://dx.doi.org/10.2471/BLT.07.032763 or
www.who.int/bulletin/volumes/85/4/07-032763.pdf

It was one of the most challenging times of my career. We had to make decisions quickly. We had to make the best decision at that time, without knowing if it was the *right* decision. It was time to display courage and decisiveness and project a calm demeanour, but that is easier said than done.

We turned our attention to the flow of human traffic in the hospital. We receive close to 3,000 people a day, including patients and relatives and people from ancillary services. Guided by international and local guidelines, we deferred all elective operative cases and reduced scheduled clinics. We established a hotline number and started tele-triage. A visitors restriction policy was implemented. We restricted entry points into the main hospital. We started training and education of the general public through the use of stand-up posters.

The hospital corridors, usually as busy as a crowded mall, slowly turned almost empty. There was an eerie feeling with masked employees at every turn. Communication remained key – through a daily staff memo to all departments so all staff remained informed of what was being done for safety and wellbeing. We enforced physical distancing in all hospital areas and marked chairs and queues. Staff with direct contract with patients that had tested positive for covid feared exposure. We designed protocols and processes to enable effective triage for early recognition and isolation of people suspected to have contracted covid19.

We also simplified decision-making processes on appropriate modes of treatment (inpatient vs outpatient) and safe de-escalation and discharge of patients. To ensure timely detection and isolation of suspected cases and thus reduce the chances of infection transmission, we set up an Acute Respiratory Infection Tent outside the Accident and Emergency departments. Because they posed a risk for transmission, aerosol generating procedures were halted in the main hospital as was nebulization in ambulances.

Our local maintenance teams tested the efficacy of using one ventilator on multiple patients and the installation of portable sinks around the hospital. We also made our own face-shields using homegrown solutions and 3D printing. Because the N95 mask, one of the most precious PPE items, soon became out of stock, we decided to use UV technology to sterilize our masks inhouse. It was overwhelming to see our teams working so closely together to look for quick solutions.

A chain is as strong as its weakest link, and it was important that we were all reading from the same book. One failure could lead to the failure of the entire protocol.

I often say that the first step in looking for a solution is to acknowledge the problem. Once we identify the problem, we can look for solutions. There was always something new to do. We ran blood donation drives because blood banks across the city started running low. Every day was a new learning experience, and every day we devised and implemented new protocols.

About two weeks after receiving the new guidelines from the Ministry of Health, we had effectively shut down all non-essential services of the hospital. This was quite a demotivating scenario for a vibrant and dynamic hospital. Things went quiet, and we could almost hear ourselves breathe. I repeatedly told my team, "God does not burden a soul beyond what it can bear." Let's be positive always…

How we ensured continuity

In April 2020, our occupancy was down by 50% and our revenues and outpatient numbers dropped significantly. We had the quietest Easter. No bunnies, no eggs displayed around the hospital. The timely guidelines from regulatory authorities on deferring elective procedures had helped us secure resources for the predicted surge in covid19 patients and defer high-risk procedures like in ophthalmology, ENT (Ear Nose and Throat), and dentistry. Our staff felt confident about this decision and were ready to offer all primary services, without compromising on patient quality.

We prepared a business continuity plan and rolled it out in phases. It was assumed that private hospitals in Kenya would be bustling with patients, and we would have 100% occupancy. However, this was not the case for us, and we continued with a financially disastrous fall in numbers. It was not business as usual, but we were ensuring continuity of essential services with clear communication plans. Our ethos was that, after all, we were a hospital, not a "covid19 hospital," and health is everyone's right. We were determined to continue cultivating and inculcating an atmosphere of care based on compassion, sound clinical practice, and patient benefit.

The seamless running of routine and emergency investigations for the timely and safe treatment of all patients had been ensured, and proposals for increasing our capacity for testing of other respiratory infections together with covid19 were reviewed. Investigations not supported at our hospital had to be referred, and an efficient referral mechanism was instituted.

Safe processes for obtaining, packaging, and processing samples for covid19 were established. We adapted to increased demands for testing through a well-coordinated implementation plan of priority actions.

We then embarked into the austerity measures exercise that was feared by all. This involved a host of measures including curtailing capital expenditure and deferring new projects. What was on every employee's mind was the pay cut. Would it come? When? How much? This was probably the most painful matter that the management had to consider. After numerous meetings, analysis, and debates, it was decided that pay cuts would be instituted, only if and when we had exhausted all other options.

We had challenging times ahead, and we needed to buckle ourselves in and set our sails high to catch the wind.

What it really felt like

As the days turned into weeks, more quietness crept into the hospital, and on 8 April 2020, the hospital received its first batch of covid19 patients. With full protective gear donned to receive patients, no one was recognizable. We had to call out names of our colleagues to know if we were talking to the right person. We had a positive attitude but were also nervous. Our staff had been given the right training and education but drills and reality are understandably different. And the stakes were high. It seemed as if we had rehearsed for a movie, and now it was time to film. The separate ward we had dedicated for isolation became a covid19 positive ward and had its dedicated team of nurses and doctors.

The usual traffic into the hospital further reduced, and the place became even more silent. It's difficult to know what goes on in someone's mind in such a situation, until one personally experiences it. Most workers feared pathogen exposure. Some dreaded long working hours and fatigue that would drain them. Mental health was being tested and what topped the list of concerns were psychological distress, occupational burnout, and stigma.

Because international flights had by then been suspended, we feared the spread of coronavirus through community transmission. We were well aware of the clinical risks. Another concern that consumed people was the risk of personal and family financial difficulties. We were in a situation we could not control and felt anxious. We had to live with this pandemic, a constant worry for us all, and we were also aware of news from around the world about people losing their jobs and economies failing. Hence, we worried about our own finances and what would happen if we were hard hit.

Used to a close-knit network of relatives, I hadn't seen my mum, friends, or extended family in weeks. Feelings of loneliness crept in and couldn't quite be abated by occasional video calls and other virtual links with people. I yearned to have tea and cakes with friends. The fact that I had lost the possibility for simple physical contact like that was depressing. To make things even worse, there were limited options to vent, like going to the gym, because places of congregation were closed.

A new regime formed for me. Every evening, instead of hugging my children as soon as I got home from work, I would dash into the washroom and change all my clothes. My children joined virtual classes. Cricket and football were replaced by indoor table tennis and carom. More comfort and time were demanded of me by my children. I had to balance this diplomatically because the demands were those expected of a superwoman.

Among hospital staff, we encouraged open dialogue. Stigma and feelings of strain were experienced and discussed. When staff returned home, some family members feared they might be bringing covid19 into the home. This brought about anxiety and fear of isolation and rejection. Some staff feared they might have contracted the virus unknowingly. Emotions were labile and affected a multitude of relationships: nurse-doctor-patient, employee-employee, employee-employer, relationships with friends and family. And one's own health affects the way we eat, sleep, talk, behave, and relate with ourselves and others. After a taxing day at work, there was little energy left for activities such as playing, taking walks, exercising, or cooking.

Staff who had chronic illnesses like depression, hypertension, and diabetes could be getting worse because of difficulties in adhering to treatment regimens. We experienced poor concentration on assigned work and had to immediately take measures to arrest the situation, so it would not lead to errors or safety concerns. Some staff became defensive. Numbness and mixed emotions were evident, and some staff "played ignorant" as a way of coping. Stress from the experience of monitoring yourself and being monitored by others for signs and symptoms of coronavirus led to sadness, anger, and frustration. Many of us felt guilty about not being able to perform habitual parenting and family responsibilities and resented that we had very few moments to unwind. At work, we heard complaints about under/oversleeping, sleeping disorders. and under/overeating.

To support staff, we emphasized eating healthily, talking walks outdoors, attending counselling sessions, watching comedy shows, and looking for activities that brought happiness back into our lives. We offered clinics on how to maintain good mental and physical health and shared tips and suggestions. The whole process was overwhelming, but it was important to enhance our sense of control and resilience. We talked, in the clinics and in the hallways, about accepting circumstances we cannot change and taking steps to take care of ourselves. We kept up the regular staff interfaith prayer meetings at the hospital. And we prayed the Serenity Prayer:

> *God, grant me the serenity to accept the things I cannot change,*
> *courage to change the things I can,*
> *and wisdom to know the difference.*

The art of healthcare in a pandemic

This pandemic requires all hospital staff to stay prepared and alert at all times. "Don't let your guard down" were the closing remarks of every taskforce meeting. We had immense support from our entire board, especially our chairman who would come in almost daily to check on us and support us. We received tremendous support from our well-wishers and donors. There was uncertainty among staff about the overall preparedness of the national healthcare system, which can affect the daily lives of healthcare workers and their psychosocial wellbeing. We suggested staff develop routines they enjoyed and keep away from excessive social media.

The words of Florence Nightingale came to mind. "*Nursing is an art: and if it is to be made an art, it requires as exclusive a devotion, as hard a preparation, as any painter's or sculptor's work...*" It is humbling to know that the cornerstone of infection control today, which is handwashing and basic hygiene, was emphasized and implemented by her!

These words helped our nurses go ahead like heroes and treat patients with pride, compassion, and respect. We had to remind ourselves that the oaths that we took are bigger than our egos and fears.

Safe work practices were encouraged not only for staff but also for patients and visitors. Prevention of cross-contamination between patients was prioritized. Because of the dusk to dawn curfew, we had to rearrange the shifts of frontline staff and ensure no stoppage in service. We adjusted our outpatient operation times and temporarily suspended one of our outpatient centres to use the resources at the main hospital. We identified essential staff positions and considered the cross-training of employees. Staff at higher risk, for example pregnant women and those with chronic conditions, were redeployed to lower risk areas.

As the reel kept turning, we knew all this could lead to reduced morale and possible sick leave and other absenteeism. In the case of a full-scale outbreak, there could be a further depletion of the workforce due to the need for isolation of symptomatic and even asymptomatic staff, and we would have to supplement the workforce with mostly locum staff. We organized standby groups to be ready to assist in addressing such deficits. For new healthcare workers, we expected an expedited credentialing process to allow them to work in clinical areas. The night curfews meant longer shifts and more fatigue, because staff could not move freely at night and transport options were limited. In addition, staff could not travel to visit family during leave because the lockdown measures included a ban on intercity movement.

Voluntary services were organized for support functions to boost security and traffic flow outside the hospital, meal services for staff doing long shifts or for those who could not go home, and transport for staff. We began leave planning and implementation of staff redeployment from non-essential and less busy areas. More staff engagement sessions were organized and FAQs designed and circulated.

Acceptable levels of absenteeism were determined, and we modified our business activities to reduce face-to-face contact by having more Zoom meetings. I had never used Zoom before, and it was a brand new experience for so many of us at the hospital. We put in place staggered work hours, flexible worksites, teleworking and telecommunicating, and reduced travel, however, most of these measures did not apply for frontline workers. We continued clinics for staff and volunteers on self-care, which included immunity boosting tips. We also issued more staff ID badges and stickers, which facilitated their movement as essential workers after the 7 pm curfew.

Creativity and innovation

What helped us fast-track many of our digital strategic objectives? Covid19.

As part of our hospital's strategic agenda over five years, we had thought of our expansion plans into digital networks. This was fast-tracked, and for the first time we have online pharmacy delivery services. We activated telemedicine portals and implemented hotlines for ambulances to function around the clock. These were breakthroughs for us. We learned three important lessons *connectivity*, *adaptability*, and *flexibility*. At this time, it was so important to remain connected to what was happening on clinical platforms globally, adapt and adopt new protocols, establish new standards for patient safety, and be flexible in our approach.

What we were saying though media

Media houses around the world had plugged into every area to get the latest news out. Even after work ends, social media doesn't stop. No matter which site or app you go to, there is always something about covid19. It's hard to escape and to have a conversation without the virus. We streamlined the sharing of information to staff, clients, media, and the general public. We designed posters, to share information and help reduce stress and anxiety, which we circulated via digital platforms. Importantly, we encouraged people to stay in touch with elderly parents and relatives.

Accepting the new normal

After almost two months of the above measures, in May 2020 we decided to gradually start reopening the hospital. Our planning for resuming some of our operations was guided by our training, protocols, and standards, using the safe mode approach. We increased surge capacity and created additional patient rooms and initiated a red zone for covid19 patients, to protect the rest of the hospital from the virus. We established new guidelines for almost all clinical areas and prepared various checklists to create a safer environment. It was not ideal but life had to move on, and we have had to accept new ways of functioning.

Perhaps Kenya succeeded in flattening the curve. By August 2020, as a nation and we, as a hospital, were not overwhelmed by people suffering from covid19. Although there has been a steady increase in numbers, we, thankfully, have so far been able to manage. This has become the beginning of a new journey for all of us.

Challenges

Perhaps we should have seen it coming. The supply of PPE was under threat. The Kenyan manufacturing sector slowly woke up to the reality that we needed our own production lines to supply a steady stream of PPE and other equipment. In the interim, we managed to import these through the support of several well-wishers and donors. But stocks of PPE could be insufficient to deal with the pandemic if there is widespread community outbreak. The Ministry of Health has been helpful in providing direction and guidance, however the economic stimulus from the government did not cater for private hospitals.

PPE has become an expensive and rare commodity. There aren't yet many manufacturers of these in Kenya, and imports have been delayed due to lockdowns and reduced freight handling capacity in other parts of the world. This may be one of the most single defining factors in our fight against this pandemic. If the pandemic is not controlled, we will need regular and increasing quantities of supplies. Access to other medical equipment is also limited. The hospital has a short supply of oxygen, ventilators, and critical care capacity. We have a covid19 testing machine, but there is a critical shortage of kits.

How will things change going forward?

So, what will be happening in the next few months? Will things become normal, or what does normal now mean? And how does all this affect the healthcare sector? Perhaps patients will want healthcare that is more immediate yet remote, e.g. more telemedicine treatments but affordable.

What changes we make today will determine how resilient and relevant we will be. The new digital wave of doing business awaits us. We must all upskill and reskill. We – in Africa – do not want to be left behind.

We don't know how long it will take for a vaccine to be developed, but we encourage all health professionals to strongly reassure people about the need to continue washing hands, practicing physical distancing, and wearing masks so we each do our part to keep more people from getting sick.

We have built a covid19 recovery plan on the following themes:

- Resolve
- Resilience
- Return
- Reimagination
- Reform

Our achievements

When everything is uncertain, everything important becomes clear. It was heartening to note during this period that none of our staff was infected with the virus, and our patient mortality rate remained low. Most of our patients returned home in excellent health. Our teams made incredible efforts. All our staff are heroes. Something good comes out of every crisis. Policies and protocols were designed and will be adapted and reinforced going forward. We have learnt so much and experienced so many ups and downs and continue to learn. We will not let this crisis go to waste!

Provisional conclusion

The current situation is continuously evolving and challenging us every day. As we prepare and implement all envisioned processes and measures, we must be cognizant of the fact that the scenario could change in a matter of days or as per national directives. As I write this, our daily cases are still on the increase. All our preparations and plans may yet be tested to their fullest.

End note

Women, in all their diversity, bring fundamental contributions to governance and democratic spaces, but their role and input is too invisible. It is with this concern in mind that I take this opportunity to thank Langaa Research and Publishing for recognizing women leaders and providing us with this opportunity to reflect – on our practice, our lives, our communities – and to share in writing.

We stand united and with full intention and resolve at M. P. Shah Hospital to confront any problem to enable our position as a leading healthcare facility to be further fortified. Let us all come together and fight this threat with truth and science, not rumour and panic.

Let us trust and pray for The Almighty's Blessing and Grace in our endeavours.

Dr. Toseef Din *serves as Chief Executive Officer of M. P. Shah Hospital in Nairobi, Kenya. She was born into a humble family in Nairobi. She has three sisters and is married with three children. She brought her extensive management experience to M. P. Shah Hospital in 2011. She helped launch the new paediatric unit, bariatric surgery program, kidney transplant program, Diabetes Care Centre, and the cochlear implant program to address severe hearing loss. She has contributed to blood donation drives, anti-tobacco campaigns, community health camps, an affordable community dispensary, and efforts against the practice of female genital mutilation. In 2019, she launched the hospital's "go green" vision, which includes reducing the carbon footprint of the hospital, reducing waste and disposing of waste correctly, engaging in eco-conscious landscaping, and one day perhaps creating M. P. Shah Hospital forest. She is a certified Kaizen (change for the better) practitioner. She is a Fellow of the Association of Chartered Certified Accountants, United Kingdom (ACCA) and a member of the Institute of Certified Public Accountants of Kenya (ICPAK). She is a firm believer in equal opportunity and quality healthcare for all. She believes the voices of women need to be heard and that adding women in leadership and decision-making positions enhances the efficiency and operations of an organization. She is an advocate of mentoring, continuous professional development, and investing in the next generation.*

chapter 7

Covid in Africa: Keeping It Hopeful[1]

Margaret LoWilla

Covid19 only became a reality for me months after I first heard whispers about it. I did not bother to pay any mind to this virus that was coming from the Far East. After all, was it killing any Africans? Perhaps it would not travel this far.

As a young woman residing in Nairobi, Kenya, covid19 felt like a distant nightmare I might never have to experience. But as months went by, the virus began to spread, and more people died. "But is it killing Black people?" Denial!

On 13th March 2020, Kenya announced its first case. This was followed by a cessation-of-movement order by the President and a curfew initially instated from 7:00 pm to 5:00 am. One of the most immediate ways that the coronavirus and the measures established by the government affected me (and most people in Kenya) was the worry about food and other essential household supplies. So, similar to the American mania of tissue paper hoarding, residents of Kenya stormed supermarkets trying to ensure that their households were stocked up.

Nairobi scenery changed as well. Washing stations popped up at the entrances to businesses, restaurants, and markets. Nairobi residents no longer walked on the streets mask-free. Instead, we saw creativity showcased through *Maasai* and Ankara print masks. Many people started working from home. Some cohabitated with their loved ones, while others sought out virtual connections to ease the loneliness of solitude.

The coronavirus frightened me for several reasons. It was so far out of my control. I struggled with the helplessness of not knowing how to protect myself and my family, especially because they are scattered all over the place – with my mother, aunties and grandmother in South Sudan, my elder brother in Tanzania, and my sister-in-law and nephew in Uganda. How

[1] Copyright © 2020 Margaret LoWilla

LoWilla, M. (2020). Covid in Africa: Keeping it hopeful. In M. N. Kinyanjui, R. Thaker, and K. Toure (Eds.), *Covid stories from East Africa and beyond: Lived experiences and forward-looking reflections* (pp. 57-60). Bamenda: Langaa.

would I ensure a blanket of protection from this alien virus so that we could all be reunited sometime soon? The uncertainty was nerve-wracking!

This was the first time I had ever been directly confronted with my own mortality. Don't get me wrong, I am aware of death's imminence, but it suddenly became more apparent to me. The idea that I might contract a deadly disease from a subliminal act such as shaking hands or mundanely receiving packages from others was worrisome! However, in the midst of the uncertainty, I kept something in mind that one of my supervisors asked me to do while I was writing a paper on youth and covid19 in Africa – "Keep it hopeful!"

And I have! Not just in the tone of the paper I was writing, but in neutralizing my fears. Mother, Aunties, and Grandmother are together. They will look after each other no matter what! It is the safest place for them to be. Although my brother is separated from his wife and child at the moment, it is for their own wellbeing.

My mortality does not need to signify imminent doom, rather an opportunity to add value and acknowledge where value is being added.

In South Sudan, young people started innovatively spreading awareness via the blue messenger bicycle initiative. Trained volunteers ride these blue bicycles "mounted with megaphones, amplifiers and batteries to help pass information to people in the neighbourhoods of Juba" on covid19 and related matters, hoping to reach 60,000 people per day.[2]

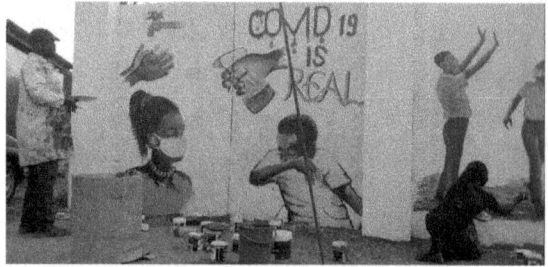

#AnaTaban street mural, South Sudan

Similarly, AnaTaban (meaning "I am tired"), started in 2016 by South Sudanese creatives to "support the tired people of South Sudan," launched the #WagifCorona or Stop Corona campaign. The youth movement, which is based on the values of solidarity, courage, citizenship, nonviolence, and

---

[2] "Resilience in organising during the time of covid-19 in South Sudan," by Michelle D'Arcy, 26 May 2020, www.impactcap.co/post/resilience-in-organising-during-the-time-of-covid-19-in-south-sudan

no political alignment, uses the power of the arts to sensitize the public about covid19, for example by painting murals around Juba.[3] [4]

In Kenya, Mike Oyola, based in Kawangware, Nairobi, has dedicated himself and his resources to distributing soap and water to various households. He says, "We can't do anything about the overpopulation here. Quarantine is not likely to work because people need to eat. So what we can do is focus on sanitation."[5] In Uganda, Olivier Nkunzurwanda runs the Refugee Innovation Centre in the Rwamwanja Refugee Settlement, which is home to nearly 70,000 refugees. He works with young people to help create awareness in the community about the virus. He also encourages community members to join WhatsApp groups in an effort to increase dissemination of information on how to prevent the spread of covid19.[6]

For me, the biggest lesson from this pandemic so far is that when you "change the way you look at things, the things you look at change."[7] I was able to change my perspective from being fearful to being hopeful. I urge everyone to try to do the same… Keep it hopeful!

Margaret LoWilla holds a bachelor's in Economics and Business Studies from the Australian Catholic University, where she worked with Josephite Community Aid in Australia, engaging with Sudanese refugee children to aid their transition into a new educational system. She is completing a master's in Governance, Peace and Security at Africa Nazarene University in Nairobi, Kenya. Margaret has worked with local civil society organizations in South Sudan on women's rights, women's political participation, and advocacy against child and forced marriages. As assistant project coordinator of Leadership Crucible in Juba, South Sudan, she focused on the mobilization of young women for peace rallies and community dialogues and conducted trainings on good

[3] www.facebook.com/**AnatabanSouthSudan**/posts/2639874846234315
[4] Source for photo of street mural:
www.facebook.com/AnatabanSouthSudan/**photos**/pcb.271458045543
0420/271457693
8764105
[5] "Here's how youth in Africa are creating rapid responses to covid-19,"
www.dotrust.org/africa-youth-covid-19
[6] "Find out how youth in Africa are creating rapid responses to covid-19," 30 July 2020,
www.theyouthcafe.com/covid19-and-youth/how-are-africa-innovating-rapid-responses-to-covid-19 and also see www.facebook.com/refugeeinnovationcentre
[7] "A conversation with Wayne Dyer," a self-help author and motivational speaker, in an interview with Ellen Mahoney for *NaturalAwakeningMag.com*, September 2009,
www.drwaynedyer.com/press/conversation-wayne-dyer

governance and the importance of democratic participation. Her research interests include women and the state in Africa, and the dynamics of conflict in the Horn of Africa. She is currently researching South Sudanese women's participation in peace processes after independence.

Adapting
to
new
realities

chapter 8

Coronavirus: Retracing Our Steps
Back to the Home[1]

Mary Njeri Kinyanjui

The home is being repositioned and refashioned as a haven: the space free from disease, the healing space, the secure space. The place protected from strangers who are likely to transmit the disease. Should we have left it? I am thinking about Karl Polanyi and the movement from home to the firm and the corporation. Is the virus forcing us to rethink those movements? The movement from work back to homeworking was rapidly put in place as a temporary stopgap measure to address the coronavirus pandemic. However, it gives us a chance to reflect on the possibilities of promoting homework. In this chapter, I discuss the spread of the coronavirus, the factors that contributed to the movement from home to work, and the pros and cons of working from home.

The coronavirus: Covid19

It started in the city of Wuhan in Hubei province in China. According to Bryner (2020),the first person known to have come down with coronavirus was a 55-year-old man who contracted it in November 2019. In December, the disease spread throughout the city of Wuhan. According to Bryner, scientists now suspect this coronavirus, SARS-CoV-2, originated in a bat and somehow hopped to another animal, possibly the pangolin, which then passed it on to humans. The disease is now spreading between people without any animal intermediary[2].

The disease spread like bushfire, especially in cities. By March 14, 2020, the disease had spread to almost all continents in the world through importation, and then it spread through rapidly accelerating local

---

[1] Copyright © 2020 Mary Njeri Kinyanjui
Kinyanjui, M. N. (2020). Coronavirus: Retracing our steps back to the home. In M. N. Kinyanjui, R. Thaker, and K. Toure (Eds.), *Covid stories from East Africa and beyond: Lived experiences and forward-looking reflections* (pp. 63-71). Bamenda: Langaa.
[2] Bryner, J. (2020, March 14). First known case of coronavirus traced back to November in China. www.livescience.com/first-case-coronavirus-found.html

transmission. In the United States, the first case was reported on January 20, 2020. States in the country with the most deaths from covid19 include New York and New Jersey, and the people of the Navaho Nation, spread across several different states, have been very adversely affected.

In Kenya, the first case was reported on March 13, 2020. By March 15, two cases were reported, and by May 20, 2020 there were 1,029 covid19 cases in the country. Here are the figures on coronavirus infections as of March 14 from the World Health Organization (WHO) daily report of the same day[3]. Globally 142,534 cases were confirmed and 5,392 deaths (437 new from the day before). In China 81,021 cases were confirmed (18 new) and 3,194 deaths (14 new). Outside China 61,513 cases were confirmed (9,746 new) and 2,198 deaths (423 new). The virus had spread to 134 countries. By May 19, 2020, the number of cases was 4,731,458, and 316,169 people had died from the disease. This called for quick responses by all governments to control the spread of the virus.

The measures taken to control the spread of the disease include personal hygiene, handwashing, covering the mouth while coughing or sneezing, sanitizing, physical distancing, wearing a mask, and avoiding crowds. The need for physical distancing has led to curfews and lockdowns and the closings of schools, churches, restaurants, theaters, pubs, and libraries. Supermarkets are almost the only public places remaining open. Most countries except Sweden and Tanzania were put on lockdown, as was the entire city of Wuhan. People are being encouraged to minimize travel. Flights have been cancelled. Sporting events have stopped, and national league activities have been postponed. Cinemas are closed. People are being told to stay at home and work remotely. Boardrooms and workspaces in corporations and factories are no longer safe.

The home is the only place where people are secure, safe, and free from the spread of the disease. It is also the healing space. This move has significant ramifications and implications for the transformation of the home into a working place.

In the 19th century, when the great transformation was taking place, people were encouraged to leave their homes where they did craftwork to work in corporations in towns and cities. The feminist movement has also

---

[3] World Health Organization. (2020, March 14). Coronavirus disease 2019 (COVID-19) Situation Report 54. www.who.int/docs/default-source/coronaviruse/situation-reports/20200314-sitrep-54-covid19.pdf?sfvrsn=dcd46351_8

been calling women to move from their workplace in the home to work in corporations, warehouses, government offices, and boardrooms. It is thought that participating in corporate and factory life and boardroom work outside the home frees women from ever-present distractions at home. These new spaces are the ones where women get paid; work at home goes largely unpaid. It was therefore a great moment when the understanding of homeworking shifted, and the office, boardroom, shop floor, and warehouse became ideal places for capitalist production.

But the virus has forced people to retreat to their homes to work from there, because it is considered safe, secure, and healing. What does this mean for women workers? A friend told me she is in self-isolation and working from home. She is also able to do boring jobs in the home that she usually avoids. So, is retracing steps back to the home going to be beneficial for women? How productive will they be in the midst of household responsibilities? It will not be the same for all women, but let us explore these questions.

Working away from home definitely gave many women many advantages. They could keep company with peers and adults. On the home front, they were used to living with children and working with pots and pans, brooms and mops. Working away from home has been important for women's socialization and mental health. They interact with people who are not family and engage in gainful production. It also saved women from routine tasks of cleaning, cooking, and nurturing. Outside the home, they have had the privilege of working with technology and machines. They use their brains in different ways. They learn new things and strategize in new ways. Experts at drawing on their emotional intelligence to nurture, they became experts on many other fronts as well.

Working outside the home also gave women a chance to be at work, just like men. It was a step towards equality, because the woman could also bring an income to the home and receive social protection such as health and worker injury compensation insurance. Working away from home also increased women's mobility. They could make journeys to work and to conferences in their hometowns or different towns or even other countries. This was different from when they were stationed at home. Working away from home also gave women visibility.

From home to work

The journey of women from home to work has taken place over a long time. It has involved political activism and education. In different countries, laws were passed to facilitate women's participation in work outside the home. Paid maternity and paternity leave, together called paternal leave in some counties, other family leave, and daycare facilities have been introduced. Activism has increased the number of women with formal education, which in turn has boosted their participation in work outside the home.

Women able to achieve balance between family and work are hailed as the greatest achievement of neoliberal feminism. Women such as Sheryl Sandberg have celebrated their ability to *"lean in"* in the masculine world of work and at the same time maintain happy families[4]. In spite of gains women have made in the world of work outside the home, there are still many aspirations that have yet to be attained. One issue is that the higher up the job ladder, the fewer the women. In most countries, women still earn less than men for the same work, and women have to cope with the double-day phenomenon. They may be doing two jobs, one at work and the other in the home. The coronavirus pandemic invites us to rethink working away from home and working at home.

The home was the center of production until the 19th century when the great transformation described by Karl Polanyi took place[5]. For women, great transformations came later with feminist activism in the 20th century. Now, at the outset of this second decade of the 21st century, working from home is being encouraged as a strategy for physical distancing that will help reduce human contact and thus limit the spread of coronavirus. The home is being repositioned and refashioned as a safe haven. It is the space free from disease, the healing space, the secure space. We are being forced to retrace our steps back to the home that is the secure, safe, and healing space.

The retracing of steps back to the home happened abruptly. There was no preparation for it or activism surrounding it. Beginning the week of March 14, colleges and universities in the Americas and all over the world started closing, and in-person instruction was halted until further notice. Faculty and students were unprepared for the closures, necessitated by

---

[4] Sandberg, S. (2013). *Lean in: Women, work, and the will to lead.* London: Ebury.
[5] Polanyi, K. (2001). *The great transformation: The political and economic origins of our time.* Boston: Beacon.

health and safety reasons to limit the transmission of covid infection from one person to another. Faculty were advised to start teaching remotely using Zoom, Google Meet, Moodle, Teams, Blackboard, and other platforms. In addition, email and WhatsApp are used by many educators and learners in Kenya. Also in Kenya, part of the Kenya Education Cloud has been reserved for online learning materials for technical and vocational education and training (TVET) and skills development. The TVET sector has borrowed online courses in mathematics from other education streams and put in place teams to design interactive online modules specific to the TVET curriculum. Some countries in Africa provide instruction via radio and television. In addition, UNESCO is exploring widespread use of off-line learning platforms such as digital libraries for communities without ready access to internet[6]. Instruction is thus communicated from a distance because face-to-face interactions are considered hazardous. So, with no preparation, faculty and students retraced their steps back to their homes.

The assumptions are that most teachers and students will have a regular supply of internet connectivity through broadband, that learners will be in the same time zones as their peers and teachers, and that in countries like Kenya they will have a reliable regular supply of electricity. There is also the assumption that everyone has adequate room space in the home for peace and tranquility that allows for learning, teaching, and other work. Most students, teachers, and other workers will also, it is assumed, have access to a smart phone, tablet, or laptop computer with the right settings, applications, and megabytes to support online teaching and learning and interaction. Online working will be a boom for tech companies as they sell their apps or charge for their use. Thank goodness for high-speed internet, because working from home is now easier than it would have been 20 years ago.

The environment has also been transformed in many homes in Europe and North America. There is the dishwasher, the vacuum cleaner, the washing machine, the food processor, and many other gadgets that have made it easier to work in the home. This gadgets shorten the time spent in doing household chores. There are also toys, games, and YouTube videos to keep children busy, which means one can concentrate. In Kenya, most

---

[6] See www.widernet.org for more information on the use of digital libraries and offline education platforms around the world.

households of working women are likely to have a domestic live-in worker who assists with housework. Does all this mean then that the home is the ideal place from which to work?

The home seems to be about the only option at the moment, but it is not necessarily the ideal site. People leave home to escape distractions, for diversity, or just because homes may not be that peaceful. Getting away from home allows for some, if only momentary, physical distancing from family. Dieng observes that working from home causes exhaustion and needs strategic collaboration and organizing[7]. It reinforces the old feminist question about the divide between social reproduction and production and who should be responsible for parenting. Parenting is work like any other and should be treated as a collective responsibility.

Lydia Gaitirira, of Amka[8] space for women's creativity, related the following to me. She met three women at Jeevanjee Gardens in the Central Business District in Nairobi, Kenya. The women were reading the Bible. She asked them why they came to Jeevanjee Gardens to read. They responded that it is the only place they can concentrate. In their homes, they do not have the peace and tranquility to read and discuss.

Two scenarios presented in the Kenyan WhatsApp social media space demonstrate the difficulties of working from home. One is a viral video depicting a broadcaster sharing the news from outside his house. After all, stereotypically, men do not spend time in the house. It is even said that a house is not for spending time during the day but for sleeping. Before a camera, the man was reading the news from a table under a tree. After a while, he noticed that one of his goats had gone astray. He stopped reading the news and called out to his workers to catch the goat. When they were not able to catch it, he abandoned the news reading and rushed to help. Of course, all that was captured on camera, and the video circulated around the world via social media.

The other scenario is a picture of a woman working on her laptop with a baby over her shoulder. What must have happened is this. The baby

[7] Dieng, R. S. (2020, April 22). Tired all the time: Caring, parenting and home working during covid-19. *Corona Times*. www.coronatimes.net/parenting-home-working-covid-19
[8] Amka is a feminist group in Nairobi that supports women's programs including reading and writing, civic education, and economic empowerment. Lydia Gaitirira is the Founder, and I am a member of the group. "Reading in unusual places" is carried out in bars, prisons, and gardens in Nairobi.

started crying and needed to be quietened. The woman picked up the baby, placed him over her left shoulder and continued working. She is seen in the picture holding a cell phone with her right hand to take a call, while staring at the computer.

These two scenarios, however gender stereotyped (could the roles have been the reversed?), depict some of the distractions on the home front. In the office, such distractions are minimal. Attendants take calls and clean and maintain the orderliness of the office. This is largely absent in homes. One has to do it all. One cannot ignore a crying baby simply because of professional responsibilities. One cannot ignore the clutter overtaking the home workspace. As if those difficulties are not enough, there are temptations to check what is in the fridge, make coffee, or remove or put clothes in the washing machine.

Working from home may also mean loss of visibility or loss of motivation. Supervisors and individuals who make decisions cannot appreciate the work ethic of employees in the same ways as in face-to-face relationships. People are less able to read body language, and some may struggle with punctuality, both of which are important for teamwork. There is the risk that morale is affected by a lack of companionship and comradeship that comes with working in a shared physical space. Colleagues who were sources of energy and benchmarking are now distant. Is it possible to be present for each other even when at a distance? Workers with little self-discipline or who cannot work without supervision are likely to suffer from procrastination.

In spite of distractions at home and the physical distance from colleagues, there are likely to be some benefits in working from the comfort of one's homes. It can be time saving. There are no journeys to work. I think of people in Nairobi who used to leave the office at 4 pm to beat UN, Thika Road, and Outer Ring Road traffic and then still get stuck. With fewer people on the road, traffic jams become a thing of the past. Without travel, savings are made on fuel and the wear and tear of the car. People who did not bring their lunches to work also make a savings, because they are not eating out. Workers work flexibly and worry less about dress codes. They are more independent in scheduling their work and can build in time to be with family close by. Supervisors rely more on output, which may mean their biases based on race, gender, and age are minimized.

While hoping that the virus will, eventually, be stopped, there are important lessons to draw from the forced retreat to working from home. This retreat has some advantages and some drawbacks. For example, Elisabeth Hannon, deputy editor of the *British Journal of Philosophy of Science*, observes that women's submissions to the journal have plummeted during the lockdown, while those of men increased[9]. Catherine Kyobutungi of the African Population and Health Research Centre, who remains very active professionally, tweeted with a picture of herself and her child: "Why are men publishing more than women during #Covid19? Me I am busy reclaiming top spot as baby's most favorite person. Papers?? Nah!"[10] She is sensitive to that fact that many women are facing challenges in combining research and work at home. There is also increasing evidence that domestic violence has increased around the world during the lockdown[11].

If women are not able to work from home, it might affect equality between men and women at their workplaces. It may also have a bearing on the norms and values of work and time allocation. For example, how does one combine housework with office work and other nurturing activities, or who will pay for the increased consumption of electricity and internet bundles and bandwidth? Another consideration is whether the day's work at home should be similar to the nine to five workday, or more flexible, i.e. working when everyone has gone to bed and there is peace and quiet. There are also issues of how one can stay motivated and disciplined in isolation. People just have to become creative, like having offsite meeting spaces, virtual chats over coffee, and Zumba workouts via Zoom or Google Meet to keep things moving and cheer each other up.

The important thing for me is how to make our homes secure, safe, and healing as they were intended to be. What kinds of spaces should housing have? In countries like Kenya, room size is often sacrificed to attract more money. Also, many people in the world live in two-bedroom flats and apartments without private studies. There is a need to rethink this type of

---

[9] *The Guardian.* (2020, May 12). Women's research plummets during lockdown, but articles from men increase. www.theguardian.com/education/2020/may/12/womens-research-plummets-during-lockdown-but-articles-from-men-increase

[10] See April 26, 2002 tweet at
https://twitter.com/CKyobutungi/status/1254472063596859392

[11] Bettinger-Lopez, C., and Bro, A. (2020, May 13). A double pandemic: Domestic violence in the age of covid-19. Council of Foreign Relations. www.cfr.org/in-brief/double-pandemic-domestic-violence-age-covid-19

housing. We must also rethink corporate structures and supervision. How are human qualities of work going to be integrated and reflected? If we are thinking about transforming the home into the future place for women's work, we need to consider many things, including technology, housing justice, performance assessment, and how to deal with distractions.

The impact of workers' mental health as they work in isolation is also something to consider. To finish a deadline, can a parent shun a child crying at the door? The transformation of work from home is a reality with which we shall continue to deal as a global community.

Mary Njeri Kinyanjui *is named after her paternal grandmother. Njeri is a single parent, and her father was a migrant labourer. She earned her PhD in Geography from the University of Cambridge in the United Kingdom and her master's from Kenyatta University in Kenya. She taught at the Institute for Development Studies at the University of Nairobi in Kenya. She has benefited from numerous awards and fellowships and been a guest scholar in development studies at research centres and institutes across Africa and Europe. She has also been a member of the Board of Governors of several secondary schools in Kenya. At the time of writing this chapters, she was a Visiting Research Associate at Five College Women's Study Research Center, based at Mount Holyoke College in Massachusetts in the USA, where she facilitated a seminar on Topologies of self-reliance and solidarity in African communities. She is author of the Langaa book* Coffee Time, *which is based on the experience of her family and is practically a treatise on development. Other publications include:* Women and the Informal Economy in Urban Africa: From the Margins to the Centre *(2014);* African Markets and the Utu-Ubuntu Business Model (2019); *and* The Sweet Sobs Response of Women to Anthropain *(2019).*

chapter 9

Covid Dating and Anti-Social Cues[1]

Nyawira Muraguri

> *Social cues (n): Types of indirect
> communication that inform or
> guide our interactions with others
> by influencing our impressions of
> and responses to them.*

Saturday, Quarantine Day 14

I stumbled into my first covid date. That's what we're calling it now: covid dating – loosely translated as "the act of attempting to do what is already difficult in an almost impossible situation." I'm not good at normal dating by any standards. I figured I couldn't be that much worse at covid dating. Maybe this could level out the playing field between me and all the annoying women out there who somehow seem to enjoy the dating process. Not forgetting the *extremely* annoying – those who not only enjoy dating but grow and become better at it through the process. They don't understand the struggle. How could they? When they're so good at it. Showoffs!

I didn't plan on it happening the way it did. I guess you can say I found myself agreeing to a set of actions that led me to a date. Don't get me wrong: I wanted to meet him. Let's call him Gabriel. Because I think giving him the name of an archangel will make him more likeable.

Back to the date.

I met Gabriel in what felt like a different time but was actually only a week before the Stay at Home measures were implemented by the Kenyan Government. I met him at a party. Remember those? As I sit in my house alone now, I often wonder why I turned down so many offers to attend these so-called parties before. I had taken it all for granted. Having the freedom to sit in restaurants and bars and dance to music in close proximity

---

[1] Copyright © 2020 Nyawira Muraguri
Muraguri, N. (2020). Covid dating and anti-social cues. In M. N. Kinyanjui, R. Thaker, and K. Toure (Eds.), *Covid stories from East Africa and beyond: Lived experiences and forward-looking reflections* (pp. 73-85). Bamenda: Langaa.

to other people. Sometimes I even treated it as a nuisance. In my defence, I had just turned 33, so I thought I didn't like crowds, or having to keep up with those dance moves that looked like someone was going through an exorcism.

He didn't speak to me at the party. Why do men do this? It's as if they don't know there might be a global pandemic. He got my number from a mutual friend afterwards and messaged me. This was after the measures had been implemented. I wish I had met up with him before that. That his first text would've come a week sooner and the first date would've made it into the realm of the normal. But that didn't happen. Timing is everything when used right. Otherwise it's really nothing more than a missed moment.

I had been messaging him for two weeks when he asked to meet. I was hoping to keep the WhatsApp conversation going until the covid19 crisis was over, so I could curate the date in the way I had always felt comfortable – dinner in a noisy place where the fact that we couldn't hear each other over the music would mask my anxiety. Where the lighting would be flattering regardless of the time spent on blending my foundation and, most importantly, where I could easily call an *Uber* home if the date went south. But I was caught in a weak moment and found myself agreeing to not only a walk in the park but also dinner (which I would make) at his house afterwards. I guess this was the covid dating definition of going Dutch – he would provide the accommodation and I would bring the food.

So here I was driving to his house, with *njahi*[2] packed in containers in my backseat, calculating the probability of him being a psychopath. We have mutual friends, so there's no way he's crazy – only a 50% chance. But I don't know our mutual friends that well – so 60% chance. I've spoken to him for a few weeks. I'm smart enough to tell if there were any red flags – back to 50%. But he's been in the house social distancing for two weeks, so maybe he's lost his mind – back to 60%. What if he's boring? Sometimes boring is worse than crazy.

"At the roundabout, take the first exit onto Oloitoktok Road." My google maps interrupted me. My destination was now only seven minutes away. I could always turn the car around. Feign a sickness.

---

[2] *njahi* are black beans, usually served in a stew or mash

"*At the roundabout take the third exit onto Githunguri Road.*" I hadn't told him I had left the house already, so he would never know. My car was braver than I, so I kept driving.

I remembered that in Kenya, femicide is perpetrated by young men thought of as normal, until they weren't. I thought of Ivy Wangechi and Monica Kimani. Did they see it coming? Were there any signs?

"*In 300 meters, your destination will be on the right.*"

It was too late, I had arrived.

I parked the car, confirmed the apartment number – 4D. I walked up the stairs, caught my breath, fixed my hair, nervously sanitized my hands, considered running back down one more time, and rang the doorbell.

He opened the door. He didn't hug me hello. He didn't even try to lean in for a peck. Maybe if I had situated my hand a bit closer to his, he would've taken it. But I didn't. Was he scared of me? I should've told him that I had heeded the stay-at-home call. That I never left the house and that I compulsively sanitized everything in my house.

I was so confused. Was he being respectful of my social distance needs? Or was it something else? None of my prior knowledge prepared me to decipher the meaning of all this. Maybe it was as simple as the smell of the sanitizer. Maybe I should have perfumed it. Maybe I should've leaned in for a hug. That would have been second nature to me in my previous world. I should have tried to hold his hand, somehow. Or even do that awkward elbow bump that I see people in churches doing. Would it have been worth it? I really didn't know him that well – what if *he* was the risk? It was too late now. The moment had passed, and I would never know who he was avoiding.

The novel virus or me.

I got home and couldn't shake the awkward feeling that had lingered through our interaction. That initial moment didn't feel right. It was like a first impression – without legs. Just arms. I realized how different the new world would be and how ill prepared I was for it. It occurred to me how all the social cues I relied on to read how an individual was feeling towards me were now somehow unavailable. I needed to find new strategies quickly. I picked up the phone and video called him.

He didn't answer.

Shit.

Monday, Quarantine Day 16

I logged into work early. As a self-confessed choleric and Capricorn, work has always been a welcome distraction when all the other aspects of my life are less appealing. For instance, when someone eats your *njahi* and then refuses to answer your call. That should be a civil offense. I should be able to take you to the Chief for that, at the very least. I was having a very productive morning, ticking things off my to-do list, and occasionally glancing at my phone so see if Gabriel had sent a message. I hadn't bothered to do my hair and still had it in *matutas*, or Bantu knots. I didn't have any calls that required video.

Or so I thought.

I glanced at my phone again, and when I turned back to my laptop a message from my boss had come in. "Are you available to catch up in five minutes?" he asked. I panicked. I knew he preferred video calls, but this time I wasn't ready. My house was a mess, and I was still in my pyjamas. I decided I would not turn my video on. He was my boss and it was Monday, but that didn't mean he was entitled to seeing me, my hair, and my house in this state. He very predictably asked me to turn on my video. I politely declined. I could hear the surprise in his voice as he carried on. "It's a Monday, and she reports to me," he must've been thinking.

I'm the kind of person who likes to keep my private life *private*. My dad says I'm secretive. I just think I'm guarded.

If I were to describe myself as a Zoom character, I would be far from those brave souls who take work video calls from their bedrooms (I don't care if your desk is there, nobody in the world wants to see your bed). I would also be better than those who never turn on their video. I would settle somewhere centre-left. Turning on video is acceptable only when the hair is presentable. It's an African affliction. Locating your camera in a way that invites unsolicited interior decorating advice is completely unacceptable.

Tuesday, Quarantine Day 17

To avoid being branded antisocial at work, I made sure I had pulled back my hair as far back as I could and was camera ready this time. I tied my hair so tight I had a headache before the call started. Headaches and work don't mix, I thought to myself as I turned on my video.

"Nyawira here – can everyone hear me? Good to see you all."

I noticed one of my colleagues was wearing a wig. A very good looking one at that. I had never seen her in a wig before, and I immediately identified with her tumult. The sisterhood of the bad hair day. I felt a kinship I had never felt towards her before. I messaged her.

Me: *"Hi Esther, nice hair!"*
Esther: *"Thanks. I had to. I was losing my mind with all these video calls."*
Me: *"Me too. My hair is tied so tight right now, I can't even think."*
Esther: *"I can send you their contacts, they're affordable."*
Me: *"Could you? They deliver, right?"*
Esther: *"To your doorstep. For 100 bob[3]."*

The key information was secured, but the call dragged on. I went to the Company's Instagram page and scrolled through pages of different wigs, acknowledging that I had entered a whole new world with which I was not acquainted.

I opened five google tabs on my computer: 1) What to look for when buying a wig, 2) How to tell if a wig is your size, 3) What is a lace front wig?, 4) Do all wigs need glue?, 5) How to make a wig not look like a wig. I took the leap. I got in touch with the Company, ordered a bob wig, paid via M-Pesa, and sent my delivery details.

Wednesday, Quarantine Day 18

The wig arrived. It looked better on the model on the website. Buyer's remorse creeped in. I shook the negative thoughts away, settled back into my computer, and started a three-hour binge session of YouTube videos showing dummies such as myself how a wig should be handled. It was a real education. I learnt that wigs are plucked. That you apply concealer on the parting and that the version I had bought was a lace front, therefore I could only wear it down. I followed the instructions carefully. After what felt like an eternity, I emerged – a new woman.

I took a few pictures of my new look and sent them to my "soft-ball" friends – the ones who are mostly supportive. But most importantly, these are the friends who I was sure had less experience with wigs so would be

---

[3] *bob* is slang for Kenya shillings

more impressed at my effort than how good it actually looked. It worked, they sent "like" and "clap" emojis.

That was all the confidence I needed.

I was ready to make my debut.

Thursday, Quarantine Day 19

I had a call scheduled with a Swedish client. He always put his video on, even if I didn't. I never understood it. I figured he was just being Swedish – uncomfortable with offending even those who clearly deserved it. So, to make up for the 50 times he had spoken to a black screen and kept his cheer in the past, I turned on my video.

"Hi, Lars, Nyawira here – good to see you."

"Hi, Nyawira, how are things in Nairobi? I hear the Government has passed a dusk-to-dawn curfew. How is that going?"

I was going to tell him how different Nairobi felt. How I couldn't feel her heart, her beating pulse. The kiosks that fed us were empty. I couldn't smell the usual *nyama choma*. I blamed it on the facemask I now had to wear. It blocked people's warmth. The social distancing had finally silenced the taxi drivers. The one metre rule had finally stopped the unsolicited stories in *matatus*. I couldn't hear the Friday night excitement. Nairobi may not have been the best before, but at least She was real, She was alive. Now the curfew and closures of public spaces had tied her hands. All I wanted was the old, annoying, frustrating version of Nairobi back.

Before I could say anything. He had a look in his eye. One I had not seen before. In that moment, I knew. I had been in enough conversations with white people to be able to see an unsolicited "black hair comment" coming. I blame it on my time in school in England. I had gotten used to lecturers announcing to the class that I had "new hair."

They thought it was a compliment.

Every. Single. Time.

It didn't occur to them why they considered it important enough to mention. I mean, Josie and Renata would change their hair colour and Seo-yeon would unsuccessfully try to change hers, and there was never any comment when they did. But as the only African woman in the class, all I had to do was hold my hair up and there was a comment. I came to dislike it, even dread it. Because no matter the intention, the outcome was always that of making me feel like an outsider.

"What have you done with your hair?" Lars interjected.

Here I was again. Feeling slightly intruded upon. As I debated how honest my answer should be, he continued.

"Did you use that thing? What you call it? Hair straightener?" He motioned with his hands. "We used that also when we were teenagers. Everyone, including the boys, wanted to have straight hair back then." He laughed. "It looks very nice," he said changing his tone. Realizing he had probably said too much.

I didn't know how to translate this information, so I smiled and with my most serene voice said, "Yes, I used a straightening iron."

Covid19 had turned me into a liar.

A wig-wearing liar.

Friday, Quarantine Day 20

I read the air wrong again. Another colleague, let's call him John (in keeping with the religious theme), scheduled a meeting in my calendar. I wrongly assumed I didn't need video for this. It was a brief call and one of the participants had a child. I thought we would spare him the embarrassment of us watching him parent. I joined the call, and all was going well until everyone, as if on cue, turned their video on. This was new-age peer pressure. I felt as if I were a teenager again, caught between smoking a cigarette and being true to my Christian Union vows.

The peers won, and I turned on video.

"Hi, Matthew, Mark, Ruth – good to see you all."

As was usual at work, I was the only African on the call. I had an animal print turban on. I knew what would happen next. I was the animal print elephant on the Zoom call. Much to my chagrin, my colleagues took the bait. It was university again, and nobody cared if Josie had dyed her hair red.

Was there a new covid manual where black peoples' hair was added to the "appropriate small talk list"? My version of the manual only had weather, curfew, lockdown measures, and flattening the curve as universally agreed upon chatter. Was there a premium version? Maybe I could add Caucasian beards and recirculate widely. I wondered to myself and smiled at the thought.

Sunday, Quarantine Day 22

I was enjoying engaging in my most recently acquired vice. While everyone else was being productive and learning a new language, I had taken to watching South Korean soaps on Netflix. The show, called "Crash Landing into You," was about a rich lady from Seoul who had accidently crossed the border to the North and fallen in love with a Northerner. As the two love birds were about to find out that their destinies were intertwined, my phone beeped.

It was Bumble – the dating app. You have a Match, it announced.

I was excited but also trying to talk myself out of the excitement. I had been here many times before. I would get a match, we would speak for two days, and the conversation would peter out. I didn't expect this to be any different. I appreciated the attention though, now that there were no parties, restaurants, or friends to distract me. Apparently, having a social life was in some ways bad for my love life. Who knew? Reports on CNN and in *The Economist* were showing an increase in the number of hours people were spending on dating apps, and the average length of people's conversations had increased. I told you this pandemic would level out the playing field.

He was a good-looking, interesting man, I came to find out. Let's call him Michael. A self-declared pessimist. We talked about the economy and how it would take decades to recover. I am a natural born optimist and have found that it is generally easier in life to think that things will get better because, that way, you only have to deal with one problem – the current situation. Pessimists, on the other hand, have to deal with both problems. The present and the future.

It was hard not to be a pessimist in this situation. After all, Kenya is a country where 80% of the economy is informal and where most people live off daily wages with little to no room for social distancing due to congested working and living conditions. We are a country where the Government had no fiscal space before all this began. Where corruption has left our economy close to ruin and where we did not need a global pandemic to expose our incompetence. The situation is akin to the day in school where you went to class, and the teacher announced a spot exam. It always happened in the subject you knew the least and at the time you had been paying the least amount of attention. That was Kenya, sitting at the exam, with no answers and no room for cheating. The last thing we needed was a global pandemic to expose our failures. Not only to the whole world but to ourselves. The low-income country with a body dysmorphic disorder. Seeing itself as a Middle-Income country.

Monday, Tuesday, Quarantine Days 23, 24

We discussed the possibility of a recession or even worse, a depression. We argued about what the post covid19 future would bring. There was that pessimist behaviour again – worrying about 2026 when it was already bad enough now. People were losing their jobs; others were taking pay cuts. The companies I worked with were revising their projections of future performance. Everybody was expecting the worst. I found solace in discussing the abstract – because no one knew if I was right or wrong. I prayed and hoped and prayed and hoped, but all the global indicators were pointing south. The US had lost over 30 million jobs in two months. We had no way of knowing what hit we should brace for in Kenya.

I hoped we could keep these intellectual discussions going on *ad infinitum*, but he wanted to meet. What's with people and wanting to meet in person? With the last negative encounter overshadowed by the optimist in me, I agreed to my second covid date.

I planned this date better than the last. First, I was not going to "waste" my food like the last time, so I asked Michael to meet me the following Saturday at a Coffee House in Kilimani. I was not going to make the mistake of meeting at someone's house again. The parking lot also served as a carwash making it a more casual location. The carwash business, it occurred to me, is an extremely resilient one. Come rain, shine, or curfew, men need somewhere to go during the day, to escape home life for a while.

Wednesday, Quarantine Day 25

Maringo[4] is a loosely used Swahili word that I grew up hearing a lot. It was always attributed to someone or other in Primary School. I never fully understood its meaning, but I was happy to go along and use it to describe anyone I did not want to like. In hindsight, I realize that the character trait it described was customarily attributable to females. I didn't see the word being thrown around at men. I never questioned it at the time. Blame the

---

[4] *maringo* translates to proud or boastful

patriarchy for the early indoctrination. All I knew was that every time I was asked why I never spoke to Girl A it would go something like this:

The World: "Why don't you talk to Girl A?"
Me: "*Ako na maringo*[5]."
The World: * free pass
Me: * winning smile

I'll try to describe what these people – these *maringo* people – did and then how they made us feel, in that order. They walked with an air of importance – that was a big part of it. If I were to break it down today, I would say they had proper posture. At the time, I suppose respect and reverence were directly correlated to poor spine alignment. These *maringo* people kept their hands to themselves and wiped down everywhere they sat or touched – acting as though the world was covered in germs or worse – a novel virus. They made others feel as though they were better than them. Unworthy of their words or physical touch.

These people, I realize now, had a head start. Having been unknowingly social distancing for years, I doubt these *maringo* people have had a hard time adjusting to this new normal. It's people like us, the average people pleasers, who are having trouble adapting. I spent over 30 years actively trying *not* to be that *maringo* girl. I went out of my way to shake people's hands, despite my view of their hygiene status. I touched people often, as a sign of acceptance and reassurance. I sat in uncomfortable situations to prove that I did not think of myself as better, even when I did. Especially when I did. Now a virus had ordered me to stop. To roll back all the years of conditioning. Now I could only say hello with my eyes. No hug or handshake. Just eyes, hand sanitizer, and smiles. No way of knowing if my eyes and smile convey the same humble orientation. Only time will tell.

The first time I saw hand sanitizer, I was a teenager in high school. A group of exchange students from the U. S. had arrived and would be spending a month at our school. A few of the girls had been spreading rumours that foreigners cleansed their hands every time they shook hands with "the natives." Most of us immediately took offense. Did they not realize that it was rude to cleanse your hands in full view of the source of

---

[5] *Ako na* means "She has"

the germs? Even the germs deserved a level of respect. I wondered if they thought malaria or HIV was passed on through handshaking. The rumour was confirmed when I saw them sanitize their hands after greeting a group of girls. I wondered whether they did this back home. Or if this was a new habit, formed for a new environment? It occurs to me now that these ladies, now in their 30s, must be fully in their element. Hailey and Elizabeth, the exchange students who came to Kenya in 2003, are probably never going to catch this virus.

Saturday, Quarantine Day 28

I arrived at the Coffee House at noon. I was half an hour late.

It was taking me a lot longer to get ready in this period. I was out of practice. I had been working from home for a month and hardly remembered the contents of my underwear drawer.

I had also picked up indoor exercise. It was so liberating working out without the judgement of others. Without the correction of others. Having the ability to have fun and injure yourself without others interfering was a good feeling. But these exercises always take longer than advertised. For some reason, the "30-minute Tabata session to burn 500 calories" on YouTube always takes 45 minutes and only burns half the calories it advertises. This was the other reason I was running late. I had miscalculated how long it would take to get my morning workout done.

He called me as I was driving, and I could hear the impatience in his voice. I could at least still read *that* right. I told him I was 15 minutes away. It was a lie – it would take me at least 20 minutes. But this was the Kenyan way. As a culture we assumed everyone knew that 5 minutes meant 10, 10 meant 20, and so forth. I sped up, jumped the lights at the *Dennis Pritt* junction and got there in 17 minutes.

I parked my car, fixed my wig, reapplied my lipstick and reached for my mask. As I walked into the restaurant, I wondered why I bothered with the lipstick. After all, I wore the mask over it and even worse – it would all be transferred on to the coffee cup and the bagel I was planning to order. The post-covid19 me would never forgive me. We were going into a recession and here I was, wasting essential female armour.

I saw him from the corner of my eye and tried not to look like I had. I walked over and smiled when we made eye contact. I think he could tell I was smiling but I was not sure. I had been told in the past that my dimples were my biggest charm and now I couldn't use them because of. This. Damn. Mask.

I smiled anyway – for me.

After a few awkward helloes, we were seated at a table on the pavement, about half a metre away from each other, deep in conversation. I enjoyed this. My now unmasked dimples were my first line of attack. We talked about everything from the impact of the pandemic on climate change to the impact of the pandemic on my edges. I was getting the hang of covid dating, I told myself. All I needed was a government-imposed curfew and some time to get it right. I ate gracefully. When I saw the thick red line on my paper coffee cup, I wondered how much lipstick was left on my lips.

I wanted to touch his arm, but I had to remind myself that we were living in a different time. A time that would shift the definition of consent forever. One that would make the #metoo movement appear victorian. We were stepping into a time when we would probably need to seek consent to be closer than 1.5 metres from someone. One where we would need to read the teacup right for the possibility of a handshake and where we would need written advance permission for hugs. Leaning in for a peck would be the new third base – reserved for those engaged to marry. Anything beyond that would only be possible after dowry was paid in full.

I got home and wondered if this was going to be any different. Would he call? Or was I back to square one? I asked myself why I agreed to meet him in the first place. Was it because I liked him, or because I did not want to spend the afternoon alone in my house? I didn't answer that question. It didn't matter. We were all coping with new challenges, and I wasn't ready to unpack the layers.

I turned on the TV and caught the News Update on CNN. Trump was being Himself; there were over 730,000 covid19 cases in the United States; Americans in various states were getting antsy and protesting for the end of social distancing. I rolled my eyes at the Americans and changed the channel to BBC. Hard Talk with David Miliband – discussing the world that would emerge when all this was over. I had been having so many of these conversations lately. I felt immediately tired. Tired about the things that I was recently worrying about that I was not used to worrying about. From the trivial like how to make sure my glasses didn't steam up when I was driving with a facemask on to the germane like what massive shifts we would see in the global economy in the next few years.

We're supposed to stay home.

When our hearts want to reach out. When we yearn for connection more than ever. When we want to go back to how we felt. How we loved (or not) and lived before all this began.

We're supposed to lean in.

When submerged with pain and fear.

We're urged to be stronger, to do the right thing. To know the statistics, to decipher the information. To work with a Government that has never cared. To have hope in the systems that were never there.

They ask us to be bigger than it all. When all we feel is small.

We're supposed to show resilience. Be better people. Build a better world.

Are inequality and social injustice the ingredients to a fairer world? Because that is what we are stuck with. Are these unfortunate scraps served to us sufficient to light the flame of change? I'm not sure.

We're supposed to know, to act, to move with bravery.

But we are just ordinary people, seeking peace, and strength to fight another covid day.

In this fight with our mortality, we need to remind ourselves to rest.

I saw a message come in from Michael and ignored it. I switched the TV off, turned my phone to Airplane mode and went to bed.

Nyawira Muraguri was born and raised in Nairobi. She is an impact investor by day and an avid reader and poet by night. Her work depicts life as she experiences it and centres around the process of empowerment and disempowerment that women go through in their daily lives and the ways in which they can learn who they are, grow, and emerge stronger through it all. She uses her work to reconnect with herself and pass on light-hearted messages of self-compassion.

chapter 10

The Girl Who Met Her Shadow[1]

Joanne Ball-Burgess

There was a monster outside. Something no one had seen before but that resembled other monsters from the past. It was a killer virus that caused people to lose their breath and their temperatures to soar. People cried out in pain until they wished their own life away. Townspeople prepared graveyards and waited for the next person to meet such a fate. It was likely that many of them would perish because the ravenous monster was hungry for human life.

In the face of this monster, humans retreated inside. There was no one to talk to outside except for the occasional chatty bird or swaying tree. By day, butterflies fluttered around aimlessly. At night, crickets chirped loudly to each other, exclaiming through their chirps how the air felt clean and the sky clearer. While humanity was on the brink of disaster, nature flourished once again.

And while the whole world ran with fright from this unseen, viral threat, she, was running from another, more sinister, much more powerful creature, which was also invisible.

For most of her life, she had known *it* was there. She often sensed its looming presence. She remembered watching the creature from the darkened corners of her room when she was around 11 years old. In her ear, it often taunted her with whispers of horrendous possibilities and heinous outcomes to situations.

Her heart would race. Sweat would pour from her forehead. The breath that usually flowed in and out of her youthful lungs without thought or effort became a struggle. Right when she thought she would surely take her last breath, the monster would vanish, and her world would return to normal. For a time.

---

[1] Copyright © 2020 Joanne Ball-Burgess
Ball-Burgess, J. (2020). The girl who met her shadow. In M. N. Kinyanjui, R. Thaker, and K. Toure (Eds.), *Covid stories from East Africa and beyond: Lived experiences and forward-looking reflections* (pp. 87-92). Bamenda: Langaa.

It was like those moments when the dark swirling sea becomes teal blue after a storm, or when wild, unpredictable winds, threatening to blow the roofs off houses, ease into a gentle breeze from the east, and the crackling skies brighten into a symphony of sunny smiles. In those instances, she was calm and could see clearly again.

But on this occasion, she could not see the ocean. Humans had retreated behind closed doors, and there was no one to talk with – except for when the darkness would return to claim its place in the empty corners of her room. Her heart would race with anxiety. Her chest would heave up and down with secrets as the gritty gloom seeped into the dusty corners of her dwelling.

Sometimes, when she had gotten enough sleep and was eating well, the unseen torturer would seem small. In those moments she could easily turn her head away from the lurking creature and continue with life as normal. When exhaustion had taken its toll, however, the savage beast would grow big in her eyes – feasting on her very fatigue. It was as if exhaustion were tangible nourishment for its insatiable appetite. The invisible monster dined on her panic as her courageous soul wasted away in fear. Its voice grew louder in her ears. Its stature expanded beyond its simple borders, no longer occupying only her darkened room corners but enveloping the entire room with its ugliness.

It was difficult to breathe, to think, to be. This darkness made life impossible to live. While all the world was afraid of losing their life to the viral monster outside, she, had almost offered hers up willingly many times before.

Her monster was not the one out roaming the streets. No. Others could not see what she had run from so many times before.

Like the invisible outside virus did, anxiety crushed her lungs and choked her breath, preventing air from flowing in and out easily. And like for the monster outside, there was no cure, no vaccine.

Alcohol was a quick remedy. It was like placing a colourful band aid on a wound oozing with pus and threatening infection. Magical juice that swallowed up problems whole. Like a pathological gambler, she had often placed all her hopes and insomniac dreams on this drink – rolling the sweet-bitter brew around with her tongue and swallowing its peppery vices down her longing throat. Those spirits calmed her spirit and silenced the monster. It became like a gallant prince charming whispering sweet nothings into her ear, and, for that moment, all would seem as it should be. Mmm... the magic juice.

Just when she thought that this magical brew was all that she needed, like a volcano erupting vomitous insanities, up burst the problems. They rose from the depths like a soul emptied from intoxicating loneliness. The tipple band aid had lost its grip, and the infection was showing. The monster had returned. And it was hungry, ravenously hungry. Again.

It is a new law: to wear a mask whenever leaving the house. Outside adventures were rare nowadays, but occasionally a shopping trip or visit to the pharmacy was required. When she fitted the mask onto her face for the first time and fastened it tightly at the back of her head, interestingly, the act did not feel strange. Somehow it felt familiar. How long had she worn a mask, not to protect herself from an unwanted deadly virus but rather to protect others from meeting her? The real her.

How long had she made herself invisible to the world through politeness, schedules, rules, and religion? Hiding behind multiple masks, she protected others from meeting the shadow she had tried so hard to bury beneath herself. "If they cannot see when the edges of my smile droop into bewildered sadness, I will be safe. If they cannot see the tears run down my cheeks because the mask has caught and soaked them up like a lonely handkerchief, then perhaps I am shielded," she thought. Safe from whom? The world? From what? The virus? Or herself? She didn't know. On some days it all felt the same.

Masks, which people were wearing to avoid breathing each other's air, to protect from catching the deadly virus, were familiar to many – who had practiced the art of shielding their hearts to protect themselves from those who might cause them pain. But *those* masks, unseen to the naked eye, also prevented the wearer from breathing in deeply of another's love and had left their souls sterile and untouched.

Before the outside monster arrived in town, work, family, friends, and travel were great distractions – from the invisible calamitous creature inside. As the pace of life quickened, in the hustle and bustle of daily life, she had all but forgotten about the beast that lurked beneath the bedsheets. It was easy to chalk those moments up to wild imagination, as long as she kept moving. And so she did.

This killer pathogen outside, though, had forced her to slow down. To all but stop and face the inside creature: the monster lurking in the corners.

The savage beast inside was her shadow. It was perhaps a far greater threat than what had already claimed thousands outside.

She peered, terrifyingly at the shadow. Trembling. Wondering what to do. Surmising that this shapeless form was much more powerful than she.

Somewhere outside, animals that hadn't seen each other before appeared out of the forests into the naked streets and stared at each other with curious wonderment. "Where are all the humans?" they perhaps wondered. Just as quickly as they appeared, they scampered back into the forest when a lone person wearing a mask came into sight. As the human walked by, the animals frolicked happily back into the forest. Camouflaged.

The animals flourished while horror roamed. More lives had been claimed. Some people were sick and didn't know it yet. This was the curse of the monster outside. Humans inside thought they were safe, but by the time they discovered that they were ailing, they would have already unknowingly inflicted others with the same sickness. Those who retreated inside had a higher chance of survival. Bur for her, for the one living with a secret monster inside, there was no guarantee. Sweats and panic came at night. Deafening silence screamed loudly. Worry and despair coupled with cries and pleas to flee her body – to whatever they call the afterlife. Fear: What if there was no afterlife? Who were "they" anyway? Worry, panic, despair… the cyclical anxiety continued throughout the night and sometimes into the day.

After nights like this, she exhaustedly dragged her tired body around the house, with nowhere to go, nowhere to escape. She could not flee this invisible villain with which she lived. It was louder than ever, gobbling up the little joy she had left, swallowing her every giggle, and anticipating every future laugh. It devoured these like pre-packaged snacks… and was still hungry.

Hungry for what? This venomous shadow danced in the corner of her bloodshot eyes. It followed her home and made it hard to inhale life itself, and as soon as she turned her head to look, it vanished like the wind. It often felt like the musty heaviness of an old Victorian dress with trimmings that suffocated. Bows and buttons that tamed and entrapped rather than beautified.

In these times of corona, yes, the monster outside had a name, although she did not; it was time to face the monster inside, who was also nameless. To introduce herself to it and it to her. To shake hands with the darkness.

To admit that the monster on the inside was staring back at her when she stared into the mirror. Was walking with her when she trudged around the house. It liked the same coffee that she did and revelled in the same television shows that were her favourites.

Slowly, she turned her head over her left shoulder and faced the monster. She noticed familiar, anxious, eyes staring right back at her as her body followed suit to face the somehow familiar creature. Her secrets, perceived faults, fears, anxieties, most sinister thoughts, and lustful ideas had been lurking and following her, suffocating her aspirations, and silencing her inner voice. This was the monster, deep within her own soul, taking up space within and without, that she was sure would kill her.

Instead of running away, she decided to sit with this monster and ask about its day. At night, she chose to say goodnight to this monster and then put up with its screams and tantrums rather than hide under the covers. On full moons when she thought it would surely kill her, she pacified the creature and reminded it gently that it could not exist without her. Its scared eyes would soften and mirror her gaze. Facing it caused her to discover that her personality and traits were so intertwined with the invisible beast that phrases like "It's just the way I am" or "I've always been like this" felt comfortable, even though she wasn't really sure these phrases were true.

But after a while, enough was enough. She had gotten to know this monster almost as well as herself. She thought she had pacified it, by acknowledging its presence and giving it space in her life, but this monster would never be pacified or satiated. It would always crave a piece of her. Then all of her. It would always wish to envelop her being and cause her to social distance from experiencing life's wholeness, even after the monster on the outside had left town. It would be so easy just to accept her fate. For her world to be consumed by hypotheticals and invisible fears.

But she was not a pacifier of the invisible monster. She was determined to be a warrior against it. She was not purposed to be lulled by the comforts of ignorant, blissful sleep. She was destined to fight against it. But how? She had thought that this monster was stronger than she and that by killing it, she would simultaneously kill herself. She was so tired. She did not yet know that she was like the moon. And like the moon, this darkness that caused her so much pain was also the light that would cause her to shine.

It was as if she were waiting for the moon to rise after a fiery sunset, so that she and all the other creatures of the night could join in with the celestial song of the stars, but her time to shine had not yet come.

So she sat. She would wait. She would live one day at a time looking for the moment when the light of the moon would peer through her shadowy world. When the outside monster would disappear for good. Her waiting was the war. Her patience and daily grace with herself were the weapons.

She sat, staring out of her window onto a lonely street. She pressed the tips of her fingers against the glass, knowing that on the outside, all was not yet as it should be. She determined that the monster on the inside would not be her demise. She was like the celestial beings of the night. She would use her pain as the darkened soil of her life. Her lonely tears like lively libations. And this fertile awareness would be the catalyst of the lunar essence that would cause her to shine for all the world to see, one day, soon.

Joanne Ball-Burgess *is a Bermudian, born and raised in Bermuda, of Afro-Caribbean descent. She has been living in Nairobi, Kenya for nine years. She is a dancer and educator as well as a writer. She wrote "An underworld education," published in* Take This Journey with Me: Bermuda Anthology of Memoir and Creative Non-Fiction. *She also wrote* The Lizard and the Rock: A Fable of Bermuda's Discovery *and* The Priceless Hogg Penny: A Tale of True Treasure.

chapter 11

Covid19 in Kigali, Rwanda[1]

Mirka Eikelschulte

Rwanda had not yet reported a single case of covid19 when one was first reported in the Netherlands in February 2020. My husband Jörgen and I had arrived in Kigali on January 10th and were scheduled to return back to Europe on March 31st. As February turned to March, the Netherlands was slowly but surely locking down whilst in Kigali life went on as usual.

The very first time we reflected on whether to stay in Kigali or return to Rotterdam was on my son's birthday, March 14th, when we still had another fortnight to go in Rwanda. It was not a small decision to make. The rationale for staying was clear: there were no reported coronavirus cases in Rwanda yet, temperature and humidity seemed less suitable for airborne transfer of the virus, and we were living rather isolated high up on a hill. The rationale for returning was equally clear: we would be closer to our family in Europe and if something happened, we could tap into a health system with which we were more familiar.

The decision quickly moved to a more emotional assessment, raising the questions: Where did we feel safer? Where did we feel more at home? To my surprise, I couldn't answer these questions in favour of either scenario. We felt equally safe and at home in Kigali as in Rotterdam, and so we decided to stay.

The announcement of a two-week lockdown was published a week later by the Office of the Prime Minister under the title: "Announcement on enhanced covid-19 prevention measures"[2] and with a mere five hours' notice. By midnight, unnecessary movements and visits outside the home were no longer permitted. Rwanda was among the first countries in sub-Saharan Africa to put in place a coronavirus-related lockdown.

---

[1] Copyright © 2020 Mirka Eikelschulte
Eikelschulte, M. (2020). Covid19 in Kigali, Rwanda. In M. N. Kinyanjui, R. Thaker, and K. Toure (Eds.), *Covid stories from East Africa and beyond: Lived experiences and forward-looking reflections* (pp. 93-100). Bamenda: Langaa.
[2] www.rbc.gov.rw/fileadmin/user_upload/guide/announcement%20on%20enhanced%20COVID-19%20prevention%20measures.pdf

Fortunately, we had shopped for food shortly before the lockdown was announced: the fridge and freezer were filled, and we figured that two weeks at home should be manageable. Little did we know that this shutdown would last for 42 days.

Although we felt comfortable with two weeks of being homebound, fear started to cast its shadow over us: we were in a country where we did not speak the language, and we realized that becoming sick was not a good idea because one wouldn't want to enter into the medical system.

On top of these complications was the issue of mobile money, MoMo. Mobile money is known and used throughout Africa but was alien to us. Entrepreneurs were quick to arrange for home deliveries, but all of them required MoMo payment upfront. We had no MoMo but realized that to take part in any economic activity, we needed to learn and adapt. We did, eventually. Although putting money on our phone still feels somewhat strange, we have become more familiar with it and gained trust that it actually works.

I read an article online[3] about Rwanda being "known for imposing draconian measures whenever crises happen." Both of us come from countries (Netherlands and Sweden) where governmental orders are considered as guidelines rather than outright instructions. We realized that it was a very different story here. Could we comply?

By March 16th, the Dutch national airline KLM announced a 70% reduction on all flights, and on March 25th a final flight was departing from Kigali to Amsterdam. This fact forced upon us another moment of reflection: did we really want to stay? The March 25th flight would be our last opportunity to return for an indefinite time. Had anything changed compared to when we had first decided to stay? No. Once again, we decided to stay in Rwanda. Our chance to return over the short term was gone.

At this point it is relevant to provide some more background on our living situation: we live at the edge of Kigali in Nyarugenge district, in an area called Kanyinya Hills, some 200 metres above the city centre. We own a house on land that seamlessly runs over into the property owned by our close friends, Bénédict and Alyssa, who live with three of their four children. Our houses are some 50 metres apart, and we share the

---

[3] "Coronavirus: Rwanda imposes Africa's first lockdown," *Deutsche Welle*, 22 March 2020, www.dw.com/en/coronavirus-rwanda-imposes-africas-first-lockdown/a-52878787

compound as an "extended family." Our rural living situation implies that we have no shops anywhere close to where we live. There are a few local kiosks where women and men sell basic items, but in general we need to drive the eight kilometres down to the city centre to buy what we need for a week or longer.

With the food we had bought (and no huge stock of toilet paper, which seemed to be a priority in Europe), we would manage for a while. However, after a week something totally unexpected happened: our friend Patrick texted us saying a surprise was on its way. The surprise was a mototaxi driver bringing us two cardboard boxes filled with potatoes, bananas, loafs of marble cake, banana bread, and other goodies. This gesture brought both of us to tears. We had no lack of money to buy food, yet Patrick and his wife Joan had felt they needed to support us. More important than the food was their gesture, which made it so very clear to us that we were not alone. There were people out there, thinking about us, caring, and being sensitive to the stress we might experience by staying in a country where neither of us was born or raised.

The weeks at home were a time of pure relaxation. We invested much time in learning Rwanda's very difficult language, Kinyarwanda. We read. We researched a variety of different topics on the internet. I finished the Swedish language course I had earlier started. I also attended my first-ever online funeral.

After 10 days, we felt we should gradually plan for some food shopping. We understood that the police were controlling the streets of Kigali, and we had met people who had been sent home. We had also heard that those without a good reason to move around had been sent to the local stadion to sit there for hours to reflect upon their misbehaviour. This was no encouragement to leave the house, and so we postponed it – day after day. However, on day 14 we really needed to go out. I admitted to Jörgen that I was scared. I was scared of being stopped and not being able to explain that we needed to buy food. I was afraid of what I might encounter in town. Or rather, of what I might not encounter in town, namely streets buzzing with people.

On the day we left home for the first time, I went to Alyssa and asked if she needed anything from town. Yes, she needed to replace her empty water canisters. We took them, happily, because we realized that two empty water canisters in the back of the car would prove to any police officer how urgent this shopping trip was.

When driving down the hill, we indeed saw many police officers along the main roads monitoring the traffic. They let us pass. Other police officers, standing on the sidewalks, were questioning pedestrians. I had prepared a few sentences in Kinyarwanda, expressing that we had been staying at home but now needed to buy food. We were eventually stopped. The fact that I understood the policeman's question "tugiye he?" (where are you going?) was the first small success on this first trip out of our home. And my ability to answer the question gave me the confidence that we just might complete our short expedition.

Upon arrival in town, the shops we visited were empty but not totally deserted. And the streets of Kigali? Empty indeed, but occasionally we did see people walking or driving around. Security guards were doing their duties as usual. Kigali was not buzzing with people as it normally is, but it had also not turned into a deserted moonscape.

The first two weeks of lockdown were extended by another two weeks and then yet another two. We then very much realized that each additional week of lockdown would start to have severe consequences for all those who depended on going out for their daily income and food. And indeed. It did not take long before the first WhatsApp message came in:

"Hello my friend Mirka, How are you doing nowadays? Here in Rwanda we are afraid of covid-19 because it is increasing day per day. We have 19 cases of coronavirus now. The government of Rwanda has published new measures to prevent this pandemic. We are told to stay at home at least two or three weeks without going anywhere for our protection. But here in region we used to get what to eat by going outside looking for tasks, then after you get wage as a casual worker. I call for help for anything to feed for children. Bank services and food shops are working but other activities are closed. Be further from covid-19 by staying under the Lord's feathers."

This first message was quickly followed by others from different people we know from throughout the country:

"Morning, just staying home but I wonder how long we can be staying home without foods. Hope you are safe with your husband."

"Morning dear, umeze ute? Can you help me in these bad days, even 2k [2 euros] can help."

"Hi, last month I got half a pay but worked the whole month. Next month there will be no pay at all."

"Morning, how are you there? Today is my kid's birthday for 2 years. You can help us to a present. God is with you."

Jörgen and I thought what to do. With quite some consultancy work coming in, we felt we needed to give back to the country. First, we decided to send some money to our housekeeper, Delice, who could not come to work due to the governmental restriction on taking mototaxis. We then complied with some of the requests above, putting some € 200 aside for support. Whenever we bought or received food – which Patrick and Joan were still sending to us via mototaxi –, the employees on our compound, Rosalin and César, as well as our friends Bénédict and Alyssa, would receive part of it. We gave Rosalin and César 1.5 kilogram packages of rice, fortified porridge, sugar, *biscuits*, juice, and vegetables. Some food also went to our night guards. We commissioned work in the garden to give some people in the village an income. We told our Kinyarwanda teacher, who had lost three quarters of her pupils, that we would increase our lessons.

Rosalin, a single mom to four children, had earlier caught our attention, as an employee of our neighbours Bénédict and Alyssa. She was helpful, incredibly hardworking, cheerful, and never seeking special benefits from us, unlike Bénédict and Alyssa's former employees who had circled around us to profile themselves. This had always made us feel uncomfortable.

Having to think about how to deal with domestic employees was very new to us. Hardly anyone in Europe has employees working for them on a full-time basis. Here, we soon came to realize that we *muzungus* are expected to hire people to help us with our domestic chores. Rather than doing the work ourselves, as we are used to, we are expected to allow someone else to have a job. I vividly remember the very first time I was down on my knees cleaning the balcony floor. When finished, I directly looked into the eyes of some five Rwandans watching and pointing at me.

We had observed Rosalin doing her job tirelessly, always willing to walk the extra mile. One day Alyssa asked if I wanted Rosalin to do extra chores in the house. Yes, I said, I would like that. And so Rosalin came to our house. On a temporary basis, because at some point Delice would return. But for now, she came, and I liked the idea that it gave her an extra income. It was she who decided on the timing, and once she was in, we jointly looked at what needed to be done. She enjoyed coming, I could tell. And while she was wiping the floor or doing the laundry, she constantly talked to me. Not that I understood much of what she said, but I loved listening to her voice and watching her smile.

One day I asked Rosalin whether she would like to be my "conversation teacher." With my hands, feet, and some words I managed to explain that I would want her to come twice a week for one hour to just talk with me. I would pay her for it. Initially Rosalin could not quite understand why I would pay her for sitting and talking. But once we started, she turned out to be a wonderful teacher. Her bubbly and talkative character really helped take my pronunciation to a new level.

Although my husband and I made regular and long phone calls to our biological families in Europe, we realized that our small community in Rwanda had turned into a family too. We had to help and support each other through this period of lockdown.

To occupy myself I started to do something I never thought I would do voluntarily: knitting. Alyssa had managed to arrange some balls of yarn for me, but no knitting needles. My creative husband took some wooden brochette sticks – or shashlik sticks – and sanded them. So here I was, knitting scarves under the African sky. The first one went to César, the second one to Rosalin. Rosalin wore that scarf day and night. Sometimes it was wrapped around her neck, other times she would tie it around her head. No matter how she wore it, she looked beautiful. Bénédict and Alyssa's children also got interested in my knitting activities, and before I knew it, I was sitting on the terrace one afternoon teaching them how to knit. That may not sound so special, but for me, who had had the lowest possible marks in the subject "arts and crafts" at school, who had started to knit a pair of socks that remained unfinished in my closet for years, it was quite something. For the children, the knitting was an additional activity, when schools had closed and the days at home were long.

One Friday evening, our extended family got together. It was a beautiful and warm night and sitting outside we felt fresh and energized. That one Friday evening became so popular that we decided to make Friday evenings a tradition, often doing a barbeque outside. Alyssa wisely said: "If we make it a tradition, the children will have good memories once this is over." They hopefully will not talk about "the terrible corona lockdown" but will just remember the wonderful Friday evening barbeques. Although the lockdown has meanwhile been eased, the Friday evening get-togethers still happen. It will not surprise me if we end up doing them for years to come…

Our family in Europe was initially surprised about our choice to stay in Rwanda. Was it wise? What if something went wrong and one of us needed to be hospitalized? Were we safe? We fully understood these questions. We appreciated how the Government dealt with the corona crisis. All visitors entering the country had to submit themselves to a two-week quarantine. Posts on social media were extremely positive about the quarantine: yes, you were to stay in a room for two weeks, but there was a wifi connection, the staff were very nice and polite, and the food was good as was the overall atmosphere. The number of coronavirus tests carried out per day was 800 to 1200, which was good for a small country. The testing focused on active tracing of possible infections rather than general screening. The Government also started to mobilize food handouts to the most vulnerable. Surging food and sanitizer prices were counteracted by the Ministry of Trade and Industry, which "directed retailers and wholesalers to avoid increasing prices of goods, whether imported or domestically produced[4]."

As I earlier mentioned, becoming sick was not something you wanted. It did happen that I felt a slight pain in my stomach, and I caught myself thinking: "Oh, I hope this is nothing serious." Days later, I got more obsessed, until I said to myself: "Stop it, Mirka. These are not helpful thoughts. You have never been sick, and you will not be sick." Miraculously the pain disappeared.

I spoke with a Dutch friend of ours who said he had been living in Rwanda with the knowledge that, if necessary, he would always be able to return to Europe within 24 hours. The fact that this was no longer the case scared him. I understood that feeling. My mother in Germany was in lockdown and so were my daughter in the Netherlands and my son in Spain. What if something happened to them? How could I stand by their side? "What if" was another unhelpful thought, which I pushed aside. We talked regularly with family abroad, and they were all careful and seemed to be doing well. WhatsApp calls became our lifeline for frequent and long conversations.

Our return flight, scheduled for March 31, moved to May 15, then to July 4 and eventually August 8. Two and a half months in Rwanda turned into seven months. If anything, this lockdown period has strengthened our

---

[4] "Rwanda: Traders warned against price hikes," by Julius Bizimungu, 22 March 2020, www.newtimes.co.rw/news/traders-warned-against-price-hikes

love for Rwanda and for living an "extended family" lifestyle. We have taken on board new activities, been part of the small community around us, had enough food, and been able to give a little bit of support to those needing it.

During the entire period of lockdown, we have felt totally safe and sheltered. This small East African country has not failed us for even a second. This difficult time of covid19 has shown us, once again, the importance of human relationships and how much we love the friendly and caring people of Rwanda.

Mirka Eikelschulte (57) was born in Germany but moved to the Netherlands at the age of 19, where she has lived ever since. In 2015 her Dutch company founded a food producing subsidiary in Kigali, Rwanda. This brought her to the country as Marketing Director, an opportunity which she and her Swedish husband Jörgen (68) wholeheartedly embraced. By the time her contract ended in 2017, they had both gotten so attached to the people of Rwanda and the beautiful country that they decided to make it their second home. The fact that they had built up a local network of close friends was the main driver of their decision. Ever since, they have been commuting between their home in the Netherlands and their home in Kigali. Officially retired, they are occasionally asked to provide consultancy services for local projects in the area of food and agriculture. If these fit their time and travel schedule, they are happy to take them on board.

chapter 12

No Hugs in Weeks[1]

Nyambura Nash Kariuki

The following story was drawn by Nyambura "Nash" Kariuki, an illustrator and animator living in Nairobi, Kenya. Kariuki says she is drawn to create around the seemingly small and quiet tragedies that the pandemic and its mitigation measures have caused in all of our lives, as well as the ways in which human resilience has triumphed over frustration and fears. She recognizes **Baraza Media Lab** for the grant to create the story.

2020 started like any other year.

Maybe even a bit more special as we were starting a new decade.

Resolutions were made and others were to be maintained.
Things felt hopeful and exciting.

1.

[1] Copyright © 2020 Nyambura Nash Kariuki
Kariuki, N. N. (2020). No hugs in weeks. In M. N. Kinyanjui, R. Thaker, and K. Toure (Eds.), *Covid stories from East Africa and beyond: Lived experiences and forward-looking reflections* (pp. 101-108). Bamenda: Langaa.
This story, under a different title, was published in *The Continent*, issue 13, July 11, 2020.

When the news on Covid-19 started filtering through, I didn't pay much heed. Who did really? .

It felt like the usual noise. In our lifetimes, plagues came, went and fizzled out. .

This one would do the same. It felt far away. We were busy.

2.

But the news kept coming. And getting worse. And confusing. I got annoyed by how I couldn't avoid it.

I tried muting it on my social media accounts.

We tried to carry on like it wasn't happening.

3.

4.

Until we couldn't anymore. Things changed overnight, literally.
Almost every schedule and plan I had was in shambles.
We know that life isn't ever assured, but this was overwhelming.
It felt like I had failed and the fault was that I existed.

5.

Slow chaos. A quiet disaster. On top of hearing stories of people dying and others risking their lives to save them, our own lives were unravelling..

Still, it didn't feel right to complain. After all, aren't you alive? And doing your part? Staying at home? Washing your hands? .

Even if your savings are steadily decreasing. And you haven't had a hug in weeks.   5.

Now what? I guess, you start stitching things back together. Sort of. What else could you do? We laughed because at least you weren't the only one that felt uncertain or disappointed.

6.

We comforted each other as well.
For all the loss that was happening,

people can be really nice when it counts.

People also adapt, even when they felt they
couldn't. There is no other way but forward.

7.

We're still moving. Humble, tired and resigned.
Not as excited or as hopeful, but with adjusted expectations,
not too bad most of the time.,

It sucks but oh well.

8.

Nyambura "Nash" Kariuki *is an illustrator, designer and self-taught animator living and loving in Nairobi, Kenya. She has always enjoyed and even found kinship in the zany worlds of various cartoon characters. She began seriously exploring the cartoon medium in 2015 and continues to self-teach to date. She has worked with various brands such as the Qai Qai doll, Joanna Kinuthia Cosmetics, Think Equal organization, and many others. She is currently freelancing as an illustrator and designer.*

chapter 13

Humanizing Covid:
Humor during a Pandemic[1]

Ukaiko A. Bitrus-Ojiambo

All of humanity found itself in a predicament in 2020. Stories emerged of a virus in China that was spreading around the world. People relied on different sources of information to learn about the new disease. Many people have shared humorous images and videoclips that express what they are thinking and how they are coping. This chapter discusses fifteen videoclips, memes, and images that have circulated in Kenya during the covid19 pandemic. It explores how humor helps people make sense of the pandemic situation. Humor and its expressions are cultural, yet humor is a universal coping mechanism, known to diffuse interpersonal and broader social tensions. It can bring insight and understanding, provide relief during moments of stress and strife, and bring cultures and people together. Through interpretive analysis of humorous texts, this chapter provides a perspective on how human beings communicate, stay connected, regenerate culture, and stay "human" during a global pandemic.

Bakhtin "carnivalizes the present because it is a hope for the future" and goes on to suggest that "surely we can discern at least a single voice that is still here to remind others how necessary to the pursuit of liberty is the courage to laugh."[2]

---

[1] Copyright © 2020 Ukaiko A. Bitrus-Ojiambo
Bitrus-Ojiambo, U. A. (2020). Humanizing covid: Humor during a pandemic. In M. N. Kinyanjui, R. Thaker, and K. Toure (Eds.), *Covid stories from East Africa and beyond: Lived experiences and forward-looking reflections* (pp. 109-128). Bamenda: Langaa.
[2] From the Prologue (p. xxiii) by Michael Holquist to *Rabelais and his World* by Russian philosopher and literary theorist Michael M. Bakhtin (1895-1975). See p. 256 for Bakhtin's description of the victory of the future over the past and how "Popular-festive forms 1135-141ook into the future" in ways that turn "the worse into ridicule."
More background information from the back cover of the book: Bakhtin "examines popular humor and folk culture in the [European] Middle Ages and the [European] Renaissance, especially the world of carnival, as depicted in the novels of François Rabelais. In Bakhtin's view, the spirit of laughter and irreverence prevailing at carnival time is the dominant quality of Rabelais's art." For both Rabelais and Bakhtin, "carnival, with its emphasis on the earthy and the grotesque, signified the symbolic destruction of authority and official culture and the assertion of popular renewal." Source: *Rabelais and his World* by Michael M. Bakhtin (translated by Hélène Iswolsky and published in 1984 by Indiana University Press). https://books.google.com/books?isbn=0253203414

Introduction

Who could have predicted that 2020 would be the year of a global epidemic turned pandemic? How many countries would have to navigate through the threat by coordinating policy and action, in concert with other countries? Many countries found themselves lining up to act and then falling, in a domino pattern. An early meme on breaking the chains of transmission of the covid19 virus suggested "stepping out" of line (physical distancing).[3]

Working with different nations' health ministries, agencies such as the World Health Organization have been providing daily statistics on the number of people confirmed to have contracted the virus and the number of people who recovered from it or died from it. As of June 17, 2020, there were over 8 million confirmed cases of covid19 globally and almost half a million deaths confirmed; there were 187,625 confirmed cases in Africa, with 3,860 confirmed cases and 105 deaths in Kenya.[4] The pandemic revealed personal and national strife, sacrifices, and global efforts to deal with it all. Different nations have had varied responses and outcomes.

In the beginning, many thought the virus would remain in China. However, being globally linked, it would inevitably show up in Kenya. In February 2020, the Government informed its citizens that three members of the public in two major cities who could have possibly contracted the coronavirus tested negative. The official message asked the public not to panic, advising all to maintain personal hygiene.[5]

By mid-March, the Government announced the first confirmed case of someone in the country who had contracted covid19. Public health and safety strategies included physical distancing and curfews and later lockdowns of ports and cities. The mandatory wearing of masks in public came later. Handwashing stations started appearing at the entrances to markets and malls. The Ministry of Education ordered all schools and

---

[3] "This artist couple's whimsical video artwork illustrating the power of 'social distancing' has gone viral – see it here," by Sarah Cascone, 16 March 2020, https://news.artnet.com/art-world/artists-viral-match-video-coronavirus-1805979

[4] "Coronavirus disease (covid-19) situation report 149," by the World Health Organization, 17 June 2020, www.who.int/docs/default-source/coronaviruse/situation-reports/20200617-covid-19-sitrep-149.pdf

[5] "Update on novel coronavirus," Republic of Kenya Ministry of Health press release, 2 February 2020, www.health.go.ke/wp-content/uploads/2020/03/Corona-2nd-Feb-2020.pdf

institutions of higher learning to physically close. Many, however, quickly began using educational technologies for distance and online learning. Although special data bundles were made available to students through telecommunications companies, this has not responded to the needs of learners without smartphones. Through the Ministry of Interior, all places of worship were instructed to halt physical gatherings.[6] Eventually, religious communities learned to meet the needs of the faithful remotely, and even funeral services went online. What adaptation!

Many youths and working-class people around the world, including in Kenya, have social media presences, occupations, and/or preoccupations. Kenya is a country of 54 million people, and it is reported that about 77% of the population consults social media for news. The most preferred social media platforms for news are WhatsApp (67% of social media users), Facebook (66%), YouTube (51%), Twitter (40%), Instagram (26%), and Messenger (21%). The same platforms are used for other purposes: WhatsApp (90%), Facebook (82%), YouTube (83%), Twitter (56%), Instagram (56%), and Messenger (48%). Kenya is reported to have an 87% internet penetration rate, and, like elsewhere in the world, fake news, misinformation, and disinformation are rampant.[7]

In recent years, the integration into daily life of technology has extended and disrupted social interactions. We now access information and learn through traditional media (radio, TV, newspapers) and new media (via mobile phones, including smartphones, and other devices). Despite the different epidemics of our time, such as SARS[8] and Ebola, coronavirus has left us feeling as if *we have never been here before*. We could not imagine how interactions would shift, continue, and thrive technologically.

With the curtailment of physical interactions, technology infused private and public spaces in new ways. We adapted quickly to doing the

---

[6] "Churches and mosques shut in Kenya after covid-19 surge," by Fredrick Nzwili and Munyaradzi Makoni, 25 March 2020, www.thetablet.co.uk/news/12632/churches-and-mosques-shut-in-kenya-after-covid-19-surge
[7] *Digital news report: Kenya*, by Reuters Institute for the Study of Journalism, 2020, www.digitalnewsreport.org/survey/2020/kenya-2020. An alternate source claims that active social media users as a percentage of the total population in Kenya is only 16%; see *Digital around the world in 2019*, https://digital4africa.com/data/#:~:text=Kenya. Another alternative source reports that the internet penetration in Kenya stood at 43% in January 2020; see *Digital 2020: Kenya*, https://datareportal.com/reports/digital-2020-kenya#
[8] severe acute respiratory syndrome (SARS)

same things differently. For instance, meetings, seminars, funeral services, exercise classes, thesis defenses, and lectures have been conducted virtually. Webinars are everyday occurrences – to the point of webinar fatigue. This all happened within demographics that had not used technology in such dynamic ways.

Vocabulary like *new normal* and *novel coronavirus* have been normalized. Everyday language is filled with medical terms and reference to safety protocols, for example: isolation, social distance, six feet/1.5 or two metres, work from home (WFH), quarantine bills, personal hygiene, frontline workers, testing kits, contact tracing, flatten the curve, and personal protective equipment or PPE.

Similarly, new narratives are emerging in Kenya and neighboring countries. The new narratives connect to previously existing realities and take on new dimensions in light of Covid. They explore topics such as police violence, gender-based/domestic violence, and food (in)security. There are prominent and less prominent – and absent – voices in the newly constructed narratives, including on mental health, cybercrime, terrorism, and the needs and rights of people living with a disability.

In this new normal, people started sharing "corona" content on social media. For example, a video that circulated via WhatsApp showed an African diasporan in the kitchen claiming how she "cures her family of cold. We have the cure. The whole family uses it…" The "cure" involves submersing oneself into a steam bath of lemons, spices, and herbs. The video is no longer available.

The corona content being circulated among family, friends, and colleagues includes jokes – about the deadly virus. I started asking myself about the significance of the jokes. In this chapter I explore the meaning behind the sharing of such content and argue that the humor in it is a mechanism for understanding, questioning, and dealing with the uncertain, stressful, and sometimes scary times brought about by the covid19 pandemic.

I first discuss Bakhtin's thinking about "carnivalesque" humor and consciousness, which will help frame and bring insight to this reflection. Then I present descriptions of humorous videoclips, memes, and images that have been circulated through social media. Finally, I discuss some emerging, crosscutting themes. By the time we reach the conclusion, I hope readers will have gained cultural insights and a deeper understanding of the importance of humor for humans, especially in times of crisis and change.

Bakhtin's carnivalesque

The thinking of Bakhtin (1895-1975) can help us understand the role of humor, including satire, during Covid. Bakhtin humorously uses metaphors to critique an oppressive political regime of his time in Russia and is fascinated by how Rabelais, in the first half of the 1500s, during the European Renaissance period, explores laughter and folk culture, in stark contrast to bourgeois Europe's literary creations (Bakhtin, 1984). Dimitriu (1994) draws on Bakhtin' work to explore how Breyten Breytenbach, imprisoned for his resistance against apartheid in South Africa, uses humor in his writing to "subvert the external pressure to which he was constantly subjected in prison" (p. 130). All three authors – Rabelais, Bakhtin, Breytenbach – critique totalitarianism and promote openness, transgression, and plurality through their writing and their use of humor.

In his metaphors, Bakhtin uses carnivalesque analogies to reflect what happens during human and societal interactions and cultural processes. The first area, *grotesque*, comically distorts or overturns reality in ways that can be thrilling, shocking, extreme, and even vulgar. The second is the space of *carnivalesque* itself, where "the spirit of laughter and mockery" as a mental attitude along with inner defiance and sometimes irreverence is a "power of rebellion," often in opposition to official culture (Dimitriu, 1994, p. 131). Players or actors use various means to tell their story or mock authoritarianism. Third, *ritual spectacle* allows one to view one's life as if from another realm, looking in. Fourth, the *trickster* defies convention and finds a way out of a situation in which they are trapped by exploring their identity and role though playacting.

Bakhtin's *carnivalesque* is endowed with destructive and creative powers that help humans survive, bear witness to struggles, and continually regenerate culture; it is not about laughter and irreverence merely for the sake of cynicism or nihilism (Dimitriu, 1994). Laughter is the "social consciousness" of people (Bakhtin, 1984, p. 92). Laughter suspends fear or terror; it is omnipotent and metamorphotic (Lachmann, 1989).

Below, briefly, are insights into humor, texts, and storytelling.

Humor

Although humor is not easily defined, its expression is common in life. In this chapter, humor is generally considered as "jokes."

> Jokes are numerous and do not have authors; they are invented by, improved by and circulated among large aggregates and networks of individuals. Jokes are a true spontaneous product of the imaginations of and a good reflection of the tastes of ordinary people. (Davies, 2008, p. 157)

Jokes bring laughter. Laughter is transtemporal, lifting us beyond our physical context and placing us in a liminal space (Lachmann, 1989), giving us a sense of freedom, despite our real situation (Bakhtin, 1984). We look for jokes, others close to us point them out, or we create jokes ourselves. Jokes, and humor more generally, punctuate our discourse and are meant to be uplifting, aesthetic, political, ludicrous, or even derogatory or a have a combination of objectives. Humor conveys deep information about the types of relationships we have with others and the nature of relations in our society.

Texts

Handwritten artifacts have been shared across time and space for millennia. Today the internet allows for the instant sharing and movement of data. The interconnection of people provides a receptive audience and also propels information more and more quickly, i.e. making it *go viral*. This apt phrase, coined from the medical term "virus," referring to an infective agent that multiplies only within the living cells of a host, in techno-social terms means the fast spread of information among groups.

In this chapter, I refer to videoclips, memes, and images as "texts." The texts include data that is verbalized (orally, through song, through writing) and/or pictorialized (drawn, dramatized). Such texts are a form of pop art and can be analyzed, especially in relation to social context (Jensen, 2013).

Embedded in the texts are messages and layers of meaning – manifest and latent. It is sometimes comfortable to remain at the anonymous uses and gratifications level in relation to information received, i.e. "This is funny" or just wishing to share a good laugh. Probing deeper into meanings is sometimes hard because it reveals histories, pains, and the state of the world. Justifications to quickly move on to the next text may include the following: "Why take a joke seriously?" or "What does it have to do with me?"

Storytelling

Human beings are storytellers. Through storytelling, we connect deeply with ourselves and others. Storytelling reveals the essence of our humanity and implies a willingness – on the part of the tellers and the listeners – to be vulnerable. When people share their stories, we feel like "we know them." We share what we have experienced, (over)heard, or were told; what we remembered, dreamed, or imagined. Stories allow us to (revisit and) deal with trauma (Pendzik et al., 2016; Sharf & Vanderford, 2003). Also, stories inspire, letting us "dig deeper" into our humanity. Stories allow us to bond at the deepest level of communication, akin to a religious act (Smith, 1992).

African storytelling has been used to pass on observations, encouragement, warnings, and insights from and about common people. Today, these stories go beyond folklore to include urban myths, videoclips, images, memes, jokes, and vignettes. We combine culture, language, context, and technology to develop stories out of current life issues (Pendzik et al., 2016). Resharing these stories releases them from hegemonic positions.

Presentation and analysis of the texts

In this section, 15 texts are presented and interpreted within Kenyan and broader African sociocultural and political contexts. The contexts in the selected texts include home, school, neighborhood, church, and hospital. Participants include couples, children relating to others such as a teacher, health workers and patients, clergy and congregants, and law enforcers and members of the general public. The texts depict how people are adjusting to a "new normal" and thinking of life beyond the pandemic, even as they may be nostalgic for life before Covid. I analyze and discuss the texts in relation to each other and related media content, African cultures, my own sense of humor, and Bakhtin's carnivalesque.

These texts are among many that were sent to me on WhatsApp, from March through June 2020. For the most part, the texts represent Judeo-Christian realities of formally educated, urban Africans. This exploratory reflection paves the way for broader scope and analysis of African representations of other themes in pop culture, social media, artifacts, and art.

I analyze the texts knowing that the readers, based on their perspectives and experiences, may perceive different nuances and discern other manifest (i.e. evident or obvious) and latent (i.e. hidden or below the surface) meanings. The goal of textual analysis is not to achieve one meaning. In fact, it helps reveal the multi-layered nature of texts.

I will present five videoclips, five memes, and five images. I first present a name for each text and then describe the text: the participants, where the action or interaction if any takes place, and the relational context. Then I describe how humor is being used in each set of texts as a way to cope in the face of Covid. In the subsequent discussion section, I discuss different themes that emerge.

Videoclips

1. Laundry room prayer

In the laundry room of a home, a woman is doing chores and praying. Through her prayer, we learn that she is from a "big house" rather than a "small house." "Big house" alludes to polygamy or extramarital relationships. Even though she and her husband still do not speak much, due to Covid, they "spend time together" and "We are even helping each other with household chores because he has nothing to do, no sports, no more lies."

2. Church communion service and offertory

We see a seated congregation, facing a pulpit during a church service. The congregants and the clergy, as is customary, occupy separate spaces. The scene possibly is captured early during Covid when much less was known, because face masks are not worn. However, some semblance of physical distancing is present.

3. School rollcall in 2029

This animation depicts a classroom in the future where social space is demarcated by "teacher in front" and pupils, in rows and columns, "facing the teacher." The teacher initiates rollcall, indicating power and distance. On the board, one can read the date: 23 March 2029.[9]

4. Heading home past curfew
A person is walking outside past curfew time. The video shows tensions between civilians and law enforcers, who are indirectly referenced though the sound of a siren.

5. The pallbearers[10]
At a funeral in a field, along with mourners, are pall bearers and a band. The pallbearers and band members entertain those gathered. This was filmed before Covid. Memes or spinoffs of this clip have since emerged.

The praying woman (in clip 1) uses spiritual dialogue to cope in a dysfunctional relationship. It could be significant that she is in the laundry room – putting dirty laundry in the public space while she "performs" and simultaneously brings order to disarray through her speaking, praying, dancing, and cleaning. The listener hears her acknowledge: "Covid is bad, but good." Good because it has brought her couple back together. The dancing, speaking in tongues, and exaggerated movements (Bakhtin's carnivalesque verging on grotesqueness) humorously distracts the viewer from the seriousness of the message. The viewer is aware that the woman is aware of her "acting" role while she is being recorded. The scene is quite theatrical, with the viewer drawn into its intimacy.

The church service (in clip 2) shows a "new era." In a performative way, bread is hurled and juice is squirted at congregants during communion. A giant spatula (grotesqueness) is used to receive the offertory gifts from congregants, rather than passing around an offertory bag or basket. Humor is displayed, in what is a usually a contemplative and sacred event, when receivers awkwardly catch (or try to catch) the hurled elements. Note that the hand throwing the bread is not sheathed.

During school rollcall (in clip 3), the squeal and misuse of the term "pregnant" is a malapropism by a student who meant to use a similar sounding word with a different meaning: "present." The teacher's

---

[9] "Covid-19 class roll call," Joe Wise TV, 7 April 2020, https://youtu.be/nhs43Bf-Hrk
[10] "Ghana's dancing pallbearers," BBC Africa, 27 July 2017, https://youtu.be/EroOICwfD3g

confused reaction is brief, as he continues the rollcall. The students are named after new terms from the pandemic, making humorous connections to African naming systems based on events, not sparing Covid. The names are emphasized as captions with capitalization, e.g. COVID Ncube, CORONA Bebe, and QUARANTINE Vuzugena.

Walking home (in clip 4) and adopting camouflage behavior shows how people are "creative" while breaking the curfew imposed to contain the spread of the coronavirus. The person jumps into the bushes at the sound of the siren, thus becoming "invisible" to official powers. The person recording the video laughs, which distracts from the seriousness of the situation. The person recording becomes an actor in the scene. The laughter of the person recording mixes with the laughter of the viewer(s), establishing connection.

The pallbearers (in clip 5) break the norm of sadness and solemnity to "lift the mood" of mourning during a funeral – in a performance meant to celebrate and entertain. They dance with the casket on their shoulders, while the band plays. Subsequent clips by meme creators show a person engaged in an extreme behavior, such as standing on the edge of a cliff, about to lose their balance. Or Trump making fun of Biden for wearing a mask. At that instance, one sees the Ghanaian pallbearers and hears the exact song as in the original clip produced by BBC. The dancing pallbearers are a novelty and allow mourners to "send their loved ones off in style." The memes using the original clip introduce gaiety into solemn circumstances and allow viewers to smile, even laugh, and decompress. Though the original clip was produced in 2017, it became very popular after the onset of the covid19 pandemic and inspired covid-related memes.

Memes

Memes are "jokes passed across social media" in the form, for example, of image macros (digital media featuring an image superimposed with text), GIF images, which are often animated, or videos.[11] Slight

---

[11] "The *Wired* guide to memes," by Angela Watercutter and Emma Grey Ellis, 1 April 2018, www.wired.com/story/guide-memes

variations, through human imagination and creativity, are added to an original idea.[12] I present five memes here.

1. Woman at church
A woman is shown, seated in a pew, with others in the background. The woman is peering over her bifocals, exploring private thoughts.[13]

2. Subscription renewal
This text meme with emojis is based on today's subscriptions culture. It demonstrates waiting for information that would bring good news: the end of lockdown. "Dear Kenyans, your subscription to the 21 days daily curfew service has been renewed successfully" (followed by three or more grotesque smiley faces).[14]

3. Does anyone know?
This is text-only: "Does anyone know if we can take showers yet or should we just keep washing our hands?" The relational dimension is personal, asking how far personal hygiene extends.

4. I did not use it
This meme shows a senior citizen in her headscarf. She is seated with a detached spirit of "you may not be interested, but—"[15]

---

[12] "Richard Dawkins on the internet's hijacking of the word 'meme,'" by Olivia Solon, 20 June 2013, www.wired.co.uk/article/richard-dawkins-memes

[13] "Next time when they shout 'something big is coming your way in 2020' don't just shout 'I receive!!'. First ask 'what is that?'" From the Facebook pages of "I've heard this joke before" (3 April 2020) and "Laughter is the perfect medicine" (5 April 2020), respectively at
www.facebook.com/Ineverheardthisjokebefore/posts/2847036032078195?   xts   and
www.facebook.com/1494411220685296/posts/next-time-when-they-shout-something-big-is-coming-your-way-in-2020-dont-just-sho/2716260508500355. As of 4 October 2020, the first post had 41 funny comments and had been shared 330 times.

[14] For example, like here, from 16 May 2020:
www.facebook.com/ModernCorpsKenya/posts/dear-kenyans-yoursubscription-to-the21-days-daily-curfewservice-has-beenrenewed-/164318045112616

[15] "I'm not adding this year 2020 to my age i did not use it" with image, 13 May 2020, https://twitter.com/Xmasterpz/status/1260393515458183168

5. I'm a politician

Depicted is a hut, indicating a hospital, located in a rural area. A politician is on a stretcher, being taken to the hut. Health workers in personal protective equipment (PPE) ignore his pleas to not take him to the hospital in a hut.[16]

The woman at church (in meme 1) addresses the practice of "crossover services" on the eve of December 31, which are common across Africa, including Kenya. Congregants repeat declarations and receive blessings for the coming year. This meme invites us to reconsider what we often unthinkingly say (see the footnote associated with the presentation above of "Woman at church" for details).

The "subscription renewal" meme (2) is a light way of sharing bad news. The subscription is for a renewed 21-day curfew. Many Kenyans have subscribed to services, like mobile money loans and internet phone service, which come with automated messages to one's phone. The "subscription renewal" resembles these automatic messages. However, the sense of grotesqueness in the smileys shows the reader it is not authentic, while poking fun at the very real extension of the curfew.

Personal hygiene messages have flooded different media channels and are posted at handwashing stations at entrances to public spaces, like markets and shopping malls, and to restaurants and offices. The "Does anyone know?" meme (3) refers to and mocks the incessant messaging about correct handwashing procedures using soap and running water, which, taken very literally, could suggest that personal hygiene concerns only the hands.

The woman's private thoughts (in meme 4) are unexpected (see the link in the footnote above) due to her age and status as a senior citizen. The reader – whether youth or senior – through the statement above her image can share in and relate to her private thought about not including the year 2020 in her age.

---

[16] The "I'm a politician meme" is available on a Twitter feed, 26 March 2020, https://twitter.com/mukulaa/status/1243138459356856320. One of the comments from the same day is as follows: "It's a lesson to our leaders to invest more in the health sector. At the moment one can't run to Europe to seek better treatment in case he/she fall victim of #COVID2019 pandemic. I'm imagining of a situation where the most powerful sharing rooms with peasants at Mulago" (hospital).

The politician's predicament (in meme 5) points to the debate about the state of healthcare facilities and politicians' inclination to go abroad for medical treatment, which is not possible because of the closure of the airspace as a measure to limit the spread of the coronavirus. The meme is a humorous critique and satire of power and authority at a stressful time – when politicians discover the everyday challenges of ordinary life among their citizenry.

Images

1. The landlord increases the rent
This image is of a landlord who has been beaten due to having raised the rent. Many people have lost their regular income stream, due to the covid19 situation, thus the focus on the absurdity of a rent increase and the reaction of the tenants in causing bodily harm to the landlord.[17]

2. Loaf and tea
The location is ambiguous. It could be in a home or office. However, the relational element is the ritual and social act of having tea.

3. Boy on a slide
The boy playing on a slide shows normal play behavior. However, the slide, punctuated with perforations, looks like a grater. That he cannot get off the slide parallels the year that we cannot escape, that we must move through.[18]

4. Tanzanian president
The President of Tanzania is shown speaking formally. He is the leader, speaking to his followers through what looks like a nationwide broadcast.[19]

---

[17] "Landlord beaten by tenants after hiking rent in the midst of coronavirus pandemic," by Kai Eli, 28 March 2020, https://breakingnews.co.ke/landlord-beaten-by-tenants-after-hiking-rent-in-the-midst-of-coronavirus-pandemic

[18] "If 2020 was a slide," https://ahseeit.com/?qa=22924/if-2020-was-a-slide-meme

[19] A screen capture was taken from a newscast similar to the following and edited to create the image that was circulated and is commented in this paper. "President Magufuli questions Tanzania's covid-19 numbers citing sabotage by lab officers," Kenya Television Network (KTN) prime, 4 May 2020, www.youtube.com/watch?v=dYfSqMult6c

5. Swiss Alps

A scene in the Swiss Alps depicts being free – outdoors with nature. In the background is a group of friends and an officer pointing. In the foreground, an individual is being held and taken away while seeming to resist.[20]

In image (1) about increased rent, a person whose swollen face looks beaten is shown. The heading indicates that a landlord in Kisumu, a port city on Lake Victoria in western Kenya, increased rents, which led to tenants beating him. Though not humorous, it demonstrates spectacle. The display of violence simultaneously evokes pity, lack of justice, and vindication.

Having tea in Kenya is a tradition inherited from the British colonizers. The super-sized loaf of bread (in image 2) is humorous. It could express the desire to make up for all the teas that didn't happen due to the physical distancing. The size of the loaf of bread could also suggest how some people who are staying at home, to isolate themselves from others, may be overeating.

The boy on the slide (in image 3) is shown learning a tough life lesson of "grin and bear it," because he can see the dangerous perforations in the slide but cannot get off it. The slide could also represent a threshold, between one life and way and being and another.

Humor and irony are used (in image 4) when a political leader takes a surprising standpoint of "Covid is Satanic" – to encourage isolation and social distancing.

In the Swiss Alps (in image 5), there is a "Hills are closed" sign, and a young woman is being escorted off the hills, showing how the daily pleasures of life can no longer be enjoyed.

Discussion

The various texts – videoclips, memes, and images – reveal different predicaments, feelings, dynamics, and dimensions of human relationships and existence. Each viewer can recontextualize and reinterpret each text, in relation to their knowledge and lived experiences, especially in relation to

---

[20] A meme similar to the one I saw is available at the link that follows here (the background is different but the foreground similar). "Hills are closed" is a "pandemic version of the sound of music, laughter is good medicine," www.pinterest.com/pin/407223991309537004/?nic_v2=1a52mF3ij

living in this "new normal" Covid reality. The authorship of the texts is diverse and, in most cases, unknown, but they all have a shared historical timeframe and shine a spotlight on different realities of coping with Covid.

Texts such as the ones analyzed in this chapter often reveal stories about which mainstream media are silent, or they bring other angles to issues. The laundry room prayer (in videoclip 1) provides insight into African marital practices, role expectations, and power dynamics. The clip alludes to deeper social issues. Kenyan media narratives on gender-based domestic violence typically frame the woman as perpetrator and the man as victim (King'ori & Bitrus-Ojiambo, 2016). Professor Mombo further explains that humor (as in videoclip 1) can convey a woman's fears and aspirations regarding her relationships,[21] in ways the media cannot. The scene suggests the carnivalesque of Rabelais, as explored by Bakhtin, in which the "censored, unofficial consciousness moves outwards" and "internal speech becomes external" in an almost Freudian way (Lachmann, 1989, p. 145). On the "horizontal level in the carnival," which "replaces the vertical hierarchy of official culture," the woman through her prayer in the laundry room is "bringing forth the repressed" and "publicly exposing that which is concealed" (p. 142). Her body "transgresses its own boundaries" (p. 146) and becomes a vehicle of self-expression.

The politician's reaction to the state of health facilities (in meme 5) shows social stratification, limited and differentiated access to public services, and power dynamics. One grand narrative of global leaders is the need not to overwhelm medical systems. The meme highlights the politician's disgruntlement with the dismal state of the healthcare system, when he is the one that needs to be served by it. The meme demonstrates grotesqueness or absurd reality (à la Bakhtin) and irony. Prior to air borders being closed, the wealthy and those who could manage to raise personal funds traveled to other countries for medical treatment. India, for example, had become a popular destination for medical tourism. This meme spotlights (under)development and, indirectly, (scandalous) projects meeting personal agendas, at the expense and neglect of communities' needs and wellbeing.

---

[21] As part of a virtual public lecture series on "Covid19 as Exile," Prof. Esther Mombo of St. Paul's University in Limuru, Kenya on 4 June 2020 shared on gender and humor during Covid.

African socio-political dynamics and cultural practices are shown in the school rollcall setting (in videoclip 3). The emphasis on the children's names reflects how African naming conventions can be based on an occasion or an event.[22] African names are integral to our identities and personhood. The surprising response "pregnant" (due to using the wrong word, sounding similar to the one the student intended) suggests the deeper problem of girl children having to drop out of school because they were impregnated. During the writing of this chapter, it was reported that 3,964 girls in a Kenyan county – on average 28 girls per day – had been impregnated within the first five months of the year, with the number peaking in March, when schools were closed because of Covid. Mainstream media narratives blame this phenomenon on the migration of girls to rural areas where they live with limited supervision and are subject to "sex pests."[23] The emphasis on the activities of the girls and their grandparents rather than those of likely male perpetrators of sexual violence shows the unequal, patriarchal society in which girls and women navigate and the media's agenda-setting and framing roles. Media framing simultaneously unveils societal issues, for example childhood pregnancies, and masks them, for example covering up the criminal act (King'ori & Bitrus-Ojiambo, 2016). The clip brings another angle to the media stories, in that we actually hear the voice, however briefly and softly, and can sense the anguish and shame of a girl – who may have been raped by a community member, even a family member, teacher or classmate.

The various texts presented provide an insider's view to someone's experiences. This is rich in that we get to perceive others' thoughts and allow them into ours. Via social media, people have multiplied the vicarious sharing of experiences of life. This blurs space-time dynamics because the private and sacred become public and asynchronously open for viewing, spectacle, and interrogation (Bakhtin's carnivalesque). In both church services (in video clip 2 and meme 1), the humor, whether

---

[22] "African naming traditions," by Adelaide Arthur, 30 December 2016, www.bbc.com/news/world-africa-37912748 and "Power of names," by Mia Sogoba, 11 February 2019, www.culturesofwestafrica.com/power-of-names explain how circumstances and events are used to name children in Africa.

[23] "Alarm as 3,964 girls impregnated in Machakos County in five months," by Pius Maundu, 17 June 2020, https://nation.africa/kenya/counties/machakos/over-3900-girls-impregnated-in-machakos-731184

overt and laughable or more subtle, is apparent – in acts and private thought – in spaces deemed sacred.

That humans have had to adapt to a new world is evident in the texts. Situations are depicted humorously, and sometimes with overt critiques of power structures (as with the politician at the rural hospital in meme 5, the landlord in image 1, and the political leader in image 4) or latent critiques (as in the woman's prayer in videoclip 1 and the school rollcall in videoclip 3). It is interesting that critiques concerning the situation of girls and women are latent (hidden below the surface) and critiques of the situation of men more overt or manifest. This deserves further exploration.

The curfew-breaker (in videoclip 4) makes fun of what would happen if one is not home by curfew. The curfew-breaker can be seen as a trickster, à la Bakhtin, finding the way out of a precarious situation. At the beginning of the curfew period, Kenyan news stories showed how the police in the coastal region harassed (even before the actual curfew time) people who were trying to board a ferry to get home.[24] Some were shown being beaten and/or taken to quarantines centres (for which they would have to pay out of their pockets). Similarly, a *boda boda* (motorbike) rider was beaten by police, leading to his death, after attempting to return home, past curfew, after taking a pregnant woman to the hospital.[25] The videoclip of the curfew-breaker makes light of what can be quite serious while simultaneously warning and critiquing law enforcement systems.

Reusing the theme of the dancing pallbearers (in videoclip 5) in other videoclips shows the interplay between different texts, as the humor from one situation is creatively incorporated into other stressful situations to bring some comic relief. Even texts not authored in Kenya and not even representing African contexts (i.e. the Swiss Alps) can resonate in Kenya because they address understandable situations and social relationships having to do with the challenges of life during Covid and the need to adapt and cope.

---

[24] "In Kenya, security forces attack ferry passengers trying to make coronavirus curfew," by Eyder Peralta, 27 March 2020, www.npr.org/sections/coronavirus-live-updates/2020/03/27/822559830/in-kenya-security-forces-attack-ferry-passengers-trying-to-make-coronavirus-curf

[25] "Kenyans under brute attack amidst coivid-19 curfew," by Saida Ali, 6 April 2020, www.indepthnews.net/index.php/the-world/africa/3439-kenyans-under-brute-attack-amidst-covid-19-curfew

The texts show a desire and anticipation of things returning to normal, in the longing to roam the hills (image 5), have tea (image 2), and reach home without the impediment of a curfew (videoclip 4). The boy on the slide (in image 3) must certainly wish, with a sense of nostalgia for the past, that the slide (representing daily life) were not filled with perforations (representing crisis) that make what he is so used to doing so scary. This is an example of Bakhtin's ritual spectacle, i.e. viewing one's new corona lifestyle from multiple perspectives.

Sense-making continues for the senior citizen (in meme 4), who is part of a population particularly at risk regarding covid19. Though she says she did not "use 2020," she nonetheless (in some iterations of the meme) tries to be useful by providing unsolicited advice to members of younger generations. There is a carnivalesque sense of regeneration via the younger generations to which the elder is bound. A likely latent meaning is that she empathizes with the struggles of people looking for work at a challenging time and encourages them to persevere, in a spirit of intergenerational support and solidarity.

In general, the texts employ a sense of Bakhtin's carnivalesque to resist the all-encompassing and all-consuming totalitarian nature of the coronavirus. They also provide different perspectives, through the use of humor, showing how people cope during challenging times. At a broader level, they raise questions about the nature of social relations, for example, in families, worship experiences, and educational settings, in normal and in unprecedented and changing times.

Conclusion

Humor has served serval functions in the Kenyan context during the covid19 pandemic. First, humorous texts have been profusely circulated via social media. This has facilitated the sharing of thoughts and feelings by proxy – about social structures and relationships, including those outside mainstream media depictions and about which individuals and communities may feel powerless.

An issue that arises in the texts is the *novel* ways in which humans have had to adapt to life, continue living it, and maintain social connections – despite physical distancing, renewed curfews, and mandatory lockdowns. The texts also allude to deeper relational and social issues during a pandemic, including domestic and gender-based violence, patriarchy, ageism, classism, joblessness, childhood pregnancy, and police violence. The texts often challenge or complement how mainstream media frame issues.

The analysis and discussion of the 15 selected texts – videoclips, memes, and images – align with literature discussing how humor can bring cathartic release, assist humans in coping with tension, nourish community connections, and regenerate culture. Indeed, the promulgators of these texts are able to "ridicule" the virus and maintain a sense of shared humanity. All the analyzed texts show human agency, resilience, and creativity – that humans are "woke" to what is happening around them.

African storytelling, which used to take place mostly face-to-face and is passed on through generations, is today also practiced online, via contemporary textual formats that verbalize, memorialize, and unveil stories about local and global predicaments. This new form of communication contributes to the ongoing development of identities and the evolution and sharing of values and perspectives. Culture is far from frozen in time... it is in movement, continually being interrogated and de- and re-constructed.

In the face of an invisible, powerful, and deadly virus, creating and sharing humor shows that people do not choose to take the position of powerlessness. With humor, we turn situations upside-down and inside-out. Through the circulation of the texts, the "victim" is both actor and spectator in the tragedy (à la Bakhtin, 1984, and Dimitriu, 1994). The use of humor demonstrates the human resolve to "keep going" in the face of adversity and uncertainty and the desire to be free to express thoughts, fears, frustrations, joys, desires, and aspirations.

References

Bakhtin, M. M. (1984). *Rabelais and his world.* Bloomington: University of Indiana Press. https://books.google.com/books?isbn=0253203414

Davies, C. (2008). Undertaking the comparative study of humor. In V. Raskin (Ed.), *The primer of humor research* (pp. 157-182) Berlin: Gruyter.

Dimitriu, I. (1994). The trickster and the prison house: The Bakhtinian dimension of "the carnivalesque" in Breyten Breytenbach's *True Confessions of an Albino Terrorist. Literator 16*(1), 127-138. https://doi.org/10.4102/lit.v16i1.598

Jensen, K. B. (Ed.). (2013). *A handbook of media and communication research: Qualitative and quantitative methodologies* (2nd ed.). London: Routledge.

King'ori, M. E., and Bitrus-Ojiambo, U. A. (2016). Newspaper framing of gender-based (domestic) violence of women-on-men from Nyeri County, Kenya. *African Multidisciplinary Journal of Research, 1*(1), 4-35. http://journals.spu.ac.ke/index.php/test/article/view/16

Lachmann, R. (1989). Bakhtin and carnival: Culture as counter-culture (translated by R. Eshelman and M. Davis). *Cultural Critique, 11* (Winter, 1988-1989), pp. 115-152. https://doi.org/10.2307/1354246

Pendzik, S., Emunah, R., and Johnson, D. R. (2016). The self in performance: Context, definitions, directions. In S. Pendzik, R. Emunah, and D. R. Johnson (Eds.), *The self in performance: Autobiographical, self-revelatory, and autoethnographic forms of therapeutic theatre* (pp. 1-18). New York: Palgrave McMillian. https://doi.org/10.1057/978-1-137-53593-1_1

Sharf, B. F., and Vanderford, M. L. (2003). Illness narratives and the social construction of health. In T. L. Thompson, A. Dorsey, K. I. Miller, and R. Parrot (Eds.), *Handbook of health communication* (Chapter 2, 26 pages). Mahwah: Erlbaum.

Smith, D. K. (1992). *Creating understanding.* Grand Rapids: Zondervan.

Ukaiko A. Bitrus-Ojiambo *is a communications instructor at St. Paul's University in Kenya. Her scholarly contributions and interests are in media and cultural studies, autoethnography, and the role of language in communication. Ukaiko has experience in faculty development and quality assurance in higher education. Born in Jos in Nigeria, she has lived in Kenya for over three decades. Ukaiko is undertaking doctoral studies in human communication at Daystar University in Kenya.*

chapter 14

Nahya's Best Ramadan Ever[1]

Marloes Hamelink
Nahya Khamis Nassor

Nahya truly enjoyed Ramadan this year. She lives with her mother, brothers, and nieces in Zanzibar. Ramadan, the most sacred month in the Islamic calendar, fell in 2020 from the end of April until the end of May. Muslims abstain from food and drinks during the daytime, and spend more time praying and being with family and friends. Due to corona, Nahya spent much more time with her family this Ramadan and had the chance to study the Quran much better than in any previous year. In other years, she enjoyed breaking the fast with family members and friends and eating in big groups. This year, she saw only the family members with whom she lives. She made the most of the situation and learned a lot about religion through YouTube, and she enjoyed sharing all the information with her mother and brothers. Her social life is suffering due to covid19, and she cannot wait to be in touch with more friends and family again. Because they could not meet physically, Marloes and Nahya spent two long evenings on the phone catching up on how life is for Nahya at the moment and which challenges she is facing. Those conversations became this chapter.

"It is not like in other countries where there are a lot of rules and restrictions due to covid19. At least that is the impression I get, judging by messages on my phone. The world is so affected by this virus. This news is really stressing me out. It is good to go outside and see life is still pretty normal out there. Earlier on, I was worried about everything. I was worried about going out of the house and basically doing anything. I am less worried now, but it is important we protect ourselves. I think I now understand a bit better what is actually going on, and I feel safer. Everyone wears a mask outside and uses hand sanitizer a lot. There are a lot of buckets with water and soap at different locations, so people can wash their hands all the time.

---

[1] Copyright © 2020 Marloes Hamelink and Nahya Khamis Nassor
Hamelink, M., and Nassor, N. K. (2020). Nahya's best Ramadan ever. In
M. N. Kinyanjui, R. Thaker, and K. Toure (Eds.), *Covid stories from East Africa and beyond: Lived experiences and forward-looking reflections* (pp. 129-134). Bamenda: Langaa.

I feel safe. I still travel by dalla-dalla (minibus), and most of the time it is pretty full.

"I go grocery shopping at the market, which is quite a different experience, if you compare it with other times. It is much quieter than usual, and people keep more distance. The government did a really good job at that. I don't get pushed by anyone when I am at the market, which is really nice. The prices of some items have changed a lot. Some products, like rice and meat, are much more expensive now. Meat was 8,000 Tanzanian shillings before, and now 10,000 shillings for the same piece. Other foods are cheaper, especially the foods normally eaten by tourists in hotels. At the moment, there are no tourists, and many products don't get sold. For example, lobster is very cheap now. We eat differently than before, mainly more seafood.

"I still go out to work, even though my schedule has changed a bit. We are kind of on a holiday schedule due to corona. We make sure there are not too many people at the office at the same time. I go in only two or three times a week. Due to Ramadan, we work seven hours a day; normally we work eight and a half.

"We are all at home much more. My mother hardly goes out, and my brothers are also at home more often than usual. My two cousins live in an apartment closer to town but are staying with us at the moment. The girls are three and six years old, and there is just more for them to do around our house. It is safer here because they don't have to be in touch with so many people. Normally they play outside a lot, and in our house it is easier to entertain them inside. I help them with their homework and their exercises. I enjoy teaching them mathematics, English, and Arabic. They have some issues with math, so I am creating games for them to have more fun learning it.

"This is the best Ramadan I have ever experienced in my life. We spend a lot of family time studying the Quran. We learn things we never knew before; I learn something new every day. I know for example how to pray the usual prayers, which we pray five times a day. During Ramadan, there are special night prayers, which I never learnt how to do before. This year, I had the chance to learn those prayers through YouTube. I follow a lot of online classes, and I am so happy I finally have time for this. My mom does not understand English very well, so my brothers and I translate the YouTube videos for her into Kiswahili. Her Quran is also in Kiswahili.

Mine is in Arabic. I studied Arabic as a child and can read the entire Quran in Arabic. I understand every Surah, every verse. This year we have a competition in my family to complete reading the entire Quran during Ramadan, within thirty days. My younger brother just won a few days ago, and I am about to finish today.

"We have more time to focus, which really helps with reading the Quran and learning about different prayers. Ramadan is a good time to learn about religion; it is the month the Quran was sent to Prophet Mohammed. Many Muslims try to read the entire Quran during Ramadan. Normally I don't have time for that, but this year we have a lot of time. Before, I would go to the mosque in the evening during the month of Ramadan. During other months of the year, I would sometimes go to the mosque if it happened to work out. In town there is a mosque which allows women, and if I was there around prayer time I would go. This year, due to corona, we don't pray in the mosque at all. Even my brothers don't go. They pray at home, but normally they would go to the mosque every day. Everyone prays in their own room. We don't pray together at home because everyone is busy with their own things. There is one prayer we are supposed to pray together, but I didn't study it properly yet. Hopefully, I will be able to do that next year…

"I feel my relationship with God has become much closer during this time. I am changing. I am even wearing the niqab, a facial cover that covers my nose and mouth. I started wearing it this Ramadan. I put it on top of my mask when I go outside. It feels good. I don't want to stop wearing it. It makes it harder for people to recognize me, which makes it easier for me to be outside. Social distancing is so much easier when I cover my face. Everybody knows me in town, and they would always come and talk to me. Now that I cover my face, nobody comes up to me which is safer and saves me a lot of time. I can just get my groceries and go home; there is no need to talk with everyone. The niqab for me is more about corona than about religion. It is okay for women to show their face and hands in public. In religious terms it is absolutely fine either way – if you wear the niqab or not. It doesn't really matter. But at this time, with covid19, it is nice that people stay away. If I look around in the street, I don't really see more women wearing a niqab. Maybe it is just me that really likes it. I think it is particularly good to wear it during Ramadan. It keeps men from staring at me. Ramadan teaches us that we need to change. It is not only during Ramadan that we are supposed to change, but we can start changes that remain for the rest of the year.

"This Ramadan has changed me to become a better person. My dress style is better. I am covering myself in a nicer way. I look more grown up. I wear my buibui (my abaya) in a different way. It shows less of my body. But most importantly, the biggest change is inside my heart. I have changed so much. I feel happier and closer to God. It is a really good feeling. I feel peace, and I feel very strong. It is important to maintain the strong feelings you might get during Ramadan. For that reason, it is good to change from inside. Your dress style you can easily change back after Ramadan. But when you change from the inside, it will stay with you. I know I have changed, and I will never go back to the way I was. I have grown. I will read the Quran, ask myself questions, and behave like it will be Ramadan for the rest of the year. The holy month this year has brought me closer to my family. It has brought love and peace.

"Around four o'clock in the afternoon, I go to the kitchen to cook iftar, the meal to break the fast. This year we cooked for six people every day. Normally we always cook for more because you can get visitors any time. This year nobody is stopping by. On the days that I am home, I cook something nice for the family. I like to cook biryani, rice and chapati. Things like that. Breaking the fast is a happy moment. Everyone enjoys the food. It feels like we have Eid every day. During this Ramadan, we often cook two dishes per day and exchange with my aunt, who is our neighbor. Now I am cooking mandazi and rice, and I make spice tea and juice. Everything I make we share with our neighbors. Whatever they cook, they share with us. This means we always have several dishes.

"Normally we put everything on a big plate in the middle, and everyone shares from the same plate. This year we didn't do that. My older brother called us and explained that we are not supposed to eat from the same plate because of covid. Now we each have our own plate. I miss sharing food from one plate. Even if you don't really have a good appetite, you will get it by sharing food. It is so much nicer. It is new for me to not have friends or family over for iftar. Usually we have a big iftar for the entire family. I really miss that moment. I don't know how many people we would usually have at home, but we have a big family. Maybe eighty or a hundred, but I really don't know. We are many, that is for sure. Everyone would cook a certain dish and bring it over. We have one place where all the men sit, and another place for the women. It is a lot of fun. This Ramadan is very quiet.

"At the moment I don't see any friends. I really miss them. At work, I see a few people. These are the only people, apart from my direct family and neighbors, I see these days. I talk with my friends through the phone, but it is really not the same. Normally I see my best friend every Sunday. I find it really difficult not to see her anymore. She is a doctor and is very busy these days. Usually we discuss our week, how work is, and life in general. Now she is so busy we can hardly communicate. She has nightshifts and her schedule changes, so I don't know when I can call her. Her work is very demanding during this time. It will be a while I think before we can meet in person again. She needs to be very careful with her patients. My other friend is in lockdown. His father doesn't want him to go out. He is just at home; we sometimes talk on our phones. He wants to go out and finds it really difficult to be stuck at home. He told me he misses the sun. Nobody I know is really going out just for fun here in Zanzibar. It is such a different life we live at the moment."

Two weeks later, a lot of things changed for Nahya. Nahya is very busy, but via WhatsApp we found a time when we could both sit down at home to properly catch up by phone. Marloes is in Dar es Salaam, and Nahya is in Zanzibar. People in both places seem much less homebound than when the arrival of the coronavirus in Tanzania was first announced. Even though the virus is still with us, the streets are slowly starting to look different: more people, fewer masks.

What brought about a big change in the life of Nahya is that after Ramadan, the house of her aunt and cousins burnt to the ground, and the family lost all their possessions. The electricity in the area fluctuates a lot, and this caused an electric shock to the main switch, which started to burn. Someone knocked on the door of the house and told the family there was a fire. The family was at that point not yet aware. Everyone managed to leave the house in time, while everything they owned burnt. Fortunately, no one was physically hurt. Nahya's aunt and her family are staying with Nahya and her family at the moment.

"We suddenly received a lot of visitors, people wanting to see my aunt and cousins. Everything changed really quickly for us. Things are much more back to normal now. I still go everywhere with my mask and sanitizer. I only saw one friend so far. I went to pay my respects because she lost her husband. I didn't even shake her hand. During Eid I was scared people would be celebrating and forgetting about physical distance. We just stayed home this Eid. I really missed going around and saying hi to everyone. This was our first Eid out of town, having moved to the suburbs four months ago. If it weren't for corona, I would have gone to town and seen my aunties, uncles, neighbors, and friends. This time around, we couldn't do that. We were too scared and decided to stay away from everyone. We just talked by phone. I don't know when I will meet up again with my friends. For my best friend, it depends on her schedule at the hospital, and how safe it is. And with my male friend, it depends on his dad. I really want to hug them. I am looking forward to the day I can see them again. I also look forward to going out again. I want to go to town. I want to meet up with people and see everyone. I want to go to Forodhani Parc for pizza."

Nahya Khamis Nassor *works at the Zanzibar Health Research Institute and lives with her mother and two younger brothers in Kianga in Zanzibar. During the covid19 outbreak, her two younger cousins came to stay with them. She normally works full time, but her office hours were reduced due to the outbreak.*

Marloes Hamelink *is a cultural anthropologist and journalist. She invests in hearing and sharing life stories of people. Currently she is doing research on the online lives and morality of Muslim women in Zanzibar. Her research themes include gender, social media, and religion. She lives in Dar es Salaam with her husband and two children.*

chapter 15

Neema Trades her Books for a Broom[1]

Marloes Hamelink
Neema Rubaba

"I really miss my life in Dar. I miss my daily routine and my life as a student. I miss hanging out with my friends who mainly stay in Dar." The daily life of Neema changed completely with the arrival of covid19 in Tanzania. Schools and universities closed down, and she received two days' notice to move out from the campus of the Hubert Kairuki Memorial University in Dar es Salaam, where she is in the fourth year of her medical studies. Neema moved back in with her family in Kigoma, a town and lakeport in northwestern Tanzania, where she lives with her mother, brother, and niece. At home with her family, she is responsible for most of the household chores. "Normally my mom has a house girl, but now she has to help out in her own family. My mom and brother still need to go to work. I am responsible for the work around the house. My life here is very different from my life as a student in Dar.

"In Dar es Salaam I spend my days at the University, with lectures and studying. On weekends I have some time to relax with friends. Normally I spend a lot of time studying. I really miss it, I never expected that I would miss it this much. I miss going to class, seeing my friends, spending time on my studies. The normal things I was so used to. It is difficult if your daily routine suddenly changes. Before Uni I was in boarding school in Bagamoyo. The focus of my daily activities has really changed. I would rather focus on becoming a doctor. I will be the first doctor in my family, if I graduate safely and healthy. That will make me feel very proud. When I was growing up, I wanted to be a pilot. When I shared my dream with my mother, she said she would always be worried about me if I were flying. My dad always called me doctor Neema, and he wanted me to become a doctor. After a while I thought, this is a great idea, and I decided to focus on the

---

[1] Copyright © 2020 Marloes Hamelink and Neema Rubaba
Hamelink, M., and Rubaba, N. (2020). Neema trades her books for a broom. In M. N. Kinyanjui, R. Thaker, and K. Toure (Eds.), *Covid stories from East Africa and beyond: Lived experiences and forward-looking reflections* (pp. 135-141). Bamenda: Langaa.

right subjects that would get me into medical school, even though it was challenging due to the hard competition. I am looking forward to a comfortable life once I will be a doctor."

Neema sits in her room in Kigoma, while she shares her story by phone with Marloes. Neema is at her desk, at the same spot from where she does her coursework. She is happy with her own room in which she can focus. Marloes sits in front of her laptop in the study of her apartment in Dar es Salaam. She is happily surprised with the good connection, which helps while they cannot have a conversation in person. She managed to set up most of her work life online and realizes that is not the case for everyone. They continue to talk about Neema's experience with online studying.

"We have been told we do courses online. But it doesn't really work. A lot of students don't manage to come to the courses. Normally there are around 130 students in our class, but in an online lesson only around 30 of us join. People cannot afford to buy an internet bundle, or they don't have electricity. It is not easy for everyone to make the time to join. Some classmates have chores to do during class time. I have attended almost all the classes. I don't find them as effective as the real-life meetings though. In an actual class, I can ask the teacher a question and will get an answer. During the online lessons the teacher often doesn't see the question, or he doesn't fully understand it, so I don't get the answer I am looking for. Normally, I could ask a student who sits next to me if she understands, and she could explain something to me. In this situation, you just may miss out on your answer." Neema feels that she and her fellow students are not ready to do all their studies online.

"Some of our classes take place in a virtual classroom where the teacher posts questions, and the students post answers. It is a lot of work for the teacher to go over all the answers, and you don't always get feedback. It is hard to get a lot of information out of such a class. We also have video meetings. It has been okay; I have been lucky that the connection is usually not too bad. If the connection is good, the video lessons work quite well. We either see the teacher talk, or he shares his PowerPoint presentation through his screen with us. I know from conversations with other students that the video classes are a challenge. If you get in late or the connection is bad, it is really hard to follow them. The lessons are shorter online, 1.5 hours instead of 2 hours or more. And we have fewer classes. I think when school starts again, we will start where we left off in March. We are supposed to have two classes, but one of the teachers doesn't manage to teach us online, because he is busy with other courses. Our graduation will be delayed, probably for the same amount of time universities are closed. I am not sure what effect this will have on our tuition."

Neema's phone plays a big part in her online studies, and this is sometimes challenging. "I join the classes from my mobile phone. This works; I can follow classes and meetings through video. I am not sure if every student has a phone that is good enough for these things. I find it much harder to focus on the lesson through my phone, though, than in a normal classroom. When I turn on my data people keep calling and texting, which is very distracting. At University, I put my phone away. We are not allowed to use our phones during classes, and I often turn off my data so I don't get any messages or calls. But for distance classes, I need the data. Fortunately, I have managed to join most of the classes. My mom takes over my household chores if I am occupied with classes. I had to miss a class twice so far when nobody was around to help. My mother wasn't able to be home at that time. Cleaning and washing of clothes for example needs to be done in the morning. The chores need to be done at specific times, otherwise everything piles up and it just becomes impossible to catch up. Classes are usually in the morning, and for many students this is a challenge because it interferes with household chores. That is one of the reasons so few students are joining the courses online at the moment."

Neema manages to deal with most of the challenges of online studying, but practice at the hospital becomes a real issue. "As soon as the pandemic was announced, no students were allowed in the hospitals. All hospital rotations were postponed. I should have been continuing my rotation at this time. From the practicums, we get to really learn what the profession means. In school we learn the theory, and I really enjoyed bringing that into practice during the work at the hospital. We were just starting. I was at the department for internal medicine for three weeks. You get patients with diabetes, hypertension, and other similar diseases. As students, we got to talk with the patients, ask them why they came to the hospital, and ask what their symptoms were. We are supervised by a doctor who discusses the diagnoses with us. We were taking turns presenting a case in front of the senior doctor and our fellow students. We were just starting; I didn't get my chance to present. I am sad to miss out on the hospital practice. I miss the contact with patients. It keeps you focused and up to date with studies.

Once we continue, they will cut down the rotation from eight to five weeks. I am not sure how we can learn everything in that time. It will be a challenge, but we have to adapt. I don't talk a lot with my fellow students now. It is very different normally in school. There you run into each other and have discussions. Most of my friends live in Dar es Salaam, so we don't get to see each other now. It takes an overnight bus to get there. I miss my friends from campus."

Neema and Marloes talk about the challenges Neema and her family are facing during this time. Business is not continuing as usual. The global spread of the virus and measures to contain it are impacting the local economy. "It is challenging for me to not go to University, and for my family, business is a challenge due to the coronavirus. My brother is a computer engineer. He works at an office but does not have as much work as before. He works for schools for example, and now they are closed. If he doesn't have work, he goes to the shop to help out my mom. My mom runs a shop. In this area we depend a lot on people visiting from the neighboring countries of Burundi and DRC. Most of the hotels are closed at the moment, however, because people can't travel. My mom's shop depended on the staff from those hotels as clients, and other people who are now without a job. She sells household items like soap, cleaning products, and also some food items such as peanut butter and vinegar. Just soap and tissues still get sold; for most other products we hardly have customers. We used to purchase at wholesale shops in Dar es Salaam. I would send the products to Kigoma by transport. At the moment, we don't have that option. This means we are missing out on products like air freshener, olive oil, and lunch boxes. Now we can only offer the products we order directly from the factory."

Neema and Marloes talk about church. The president of Tanzania requests people to pray, and Marloes shares her worries about bringing too many people together. Neema has a different view on this and feels church has a positive impact on her life and on controlling the spread of the virus. "We go to church every Sunday; my mom even goes every day. They take a lot of precautions at church, so it is safe to go. The mass is shorter, and there is no singing anymore because there is no choir practice at the moment. Just normal prayers, and we go home quite quickly after. It is always important to go to church, so for me that hasn't changed in these times. I am happy I can still go to church. It is the only time I am reminded about spiritual things that are important to me. It feels good that I am able to attend. In Dar I sometimes went with friends and sometimes alone. We used to have a priest on campus; otherwise I'd go to another church close by. It is nice here in Kigoma to be able to go with family. There used to be two masses on Sunday, but now there are more so the church does not get crowded. We used to sit with six or seven people on a bench, but now we are only two or three to a bench. If the church gets too full, people have to leave and come back for the next mass. The priest pays a lot of attention to safety and teaches the community about it.

"When I first moved back here, I saw that people refused to frequently wash their hands. They would give each other hugs, shake hands, and talk for a long time without keeping any distance. The priest keeps reminding us what needs to be done. Everyone washes their hands before entering the church, and the masses are shorter. There used to be one person to open and close the tap, so not everyone had to touch it. Now there is a paddle. Church used to be a more social event. We would chat with people we know. I still see people there that I know from primary school and the neighbors, but we don't stay to talk. Now we just go to the mass and straight back home. Whenever I leave the house it is with a purpose. We don't talk to people as much as before."

This time is not like a holiday for Neema, and her experience is quite different from her usual visits to her family. She spends much more time on household chores now, and the entire family is going out less. "I do get a lot of time with the family now. Everyone is home most of the time, and business has slowed down a lot. Usually I go home twice a year over the breaks to stay with my family. It is different now because I have less time to relax. The household chores are a lot of work; we don't have help now. This morning I did the laundry. I do it by hand; it is a lot of work. I don't enjoy it. I would happily hand the laundry over to the house girl when she is back. I also cook for the family twice a day. I do enjoy the cooking. This afternoon I cooked ugali, peas and dagaa, which are sardines. After my studies, it is time to cook dinner; we like to eat early. I will probably cook rice tonight. My mom will tell me later what she wants me to cook. At University, I always needed to see how much money I had and what I could get for it. Here, it is easier; I can cook a dish I enjoy. I also enjoy the extra family time. Normally everyone gets home late and is tired, and after night prayer it is already time to go to sleep. We go in and out, and everyone has their own activities. During this time, we are all spending much more time at home. We talk a lot these days. My brother tells about his business, I share how the day was at home, and my mom tells us if something happens at the shop. There is more time to share the stories about our daily lives, which is really nice.

"People still go out here; we are not in a lockdown. Most people have business to do or their work to go to. They just take their precautions. Everyone wears a mask; every shop has a bucket and soap. I don't know that many people in this area, so it is hard to say if many people here get sick. I have not been scared. I just wonder why schools closed if other businesses are going on. I wish they had stayed open. At the same time, I would also be worried if we had to go to the hospital at this time. If we would had had to go to Amana Hospital, we would have been in touch with patients who had the virus. My niece is staying with us at the moment. My sister, her mom, lives in Dodoma. She is very scared. In the beginning of the virus, she took her annual leave to stay with my mom with her daughter. She had to go back because of work. My mom really had to calm her down because she is so worried for her child. Now she is feeling a bit better. She says the situation is worse in Dodoma. I am not sure if that is the case or if she is speaking from fear. It is different there though. People have a lot of contact with each other and go out a lot. There are a lot of people on the street; it is difficult to control the virus. I am not sure if things have changed, or if my sister just got used to the situation.

"When I go back to school, I will miss home. I will truly miss being home. I will miss spending time with my mom and my brother. I am looking forward to seeing my friends though, and to getting back to classes. I am curious how everything will be and what will change."

Neema Rubaba *is a medical student at Hubert Kairuki Memorial University (HKMU) in Dar es Salaam, Tanzania. During the closure of her university due to covid19, she is staying with her family in Kigoma and helps out with household chores. She previously lived at the University Campus in Dar es Salaam to focus on her studies. She is President of the Rotaract Club of HKMU.*

Marloes Hamelink *is a cultural anthropologist and journalist. She listens to and shares people's life stories. Currently she is doing research on the online lives and morality* *of Muslim women in Zanzibar. Her research themes include gender, social media, and religion. She lives in Dar es Salaam with her family and is a board member of the Rotary Club of Oyster Bay as the director of the youth department with a special focus on education.*

chapter 16

Collective Voice on
Working and Showing Solidarity from a Distance[1]

Chimwemwe A. Fabiano
Essa Njie
Ikran Abdullahi

Balancing work and life during covid19
Chimwemwe A. Fabiano

Covid19 measures have affected the world of work. Many people who work in formal and informal sectors, especially women who are small traders, have been affected by covid19 and the measures to prevent its spread. In the formal sector some employees have been laid off, and others fear that with time their services could be regarded as nonessential.

In this short reflection, I briefly share some thoughts from three "urban professionals" from Malawi about working from home. Their experiences reflect some of the dimensions of adapting, managing, learning, and innovating in the covid19 context, alongside developing strategies for resilience and remaining human. Their thoughts also provide insight into widespread changes taking place in the world of work.

Though a lot of people have lost their jobs, most white collar workers who can work remotely using digital devices are now working from home. A friend who was at odds with working from home is now enjoying it. However, she fears that her job may in the long run be considered non-essential, that the employer may opt to outsource the work of her department, even though she has managed legal services for the company for over four years. This friend is a mother of four, including twin babies.

---

[1] Copyright © 2020 Chimwemwe A. Fabiano, Essa Njie, and Ikran Abdullahi
Fabiano, C. A., Njie, E., and Abdullahi, I. (2020). Working and showing solidarity from a distance. In M. N. Kinyanjui, R. Thaker, and K. Toure (Eds.), *Covid stories from East Africa and beyond: Lived experiences and forward-looking reflections* (pp. 143-152). Bamenda: Langaa.

Working from home for her has opened a whole new world of work-life balance.

For another friend, a mother of three children with two under the age of five, the option of working from the office in spite of covid19 gives her the freedom and opportunity to be effective in her workplace outside the home and as a mother and wife.

A civil servant reflected in a conversation with me on how the work-from-home arrangement has made her department more efficient. Their small department adopted a new mode of working where they can have only one person in the office per day. Given that their work involves physical and confidential paperwork, they cannot completely do away with office visits. However, with the one-person-in-the-office-per-day approach, the speed of the workflow has improved. Staff have become more organized and output-oriented. The woman reflected that she has more time to do other things, including her side hustle, and questioned the logic of the traditional 9 to 5 working hours.

Work-life-balance requires personal discipline, especially if you are working from home. Finding and adapting a suitable space for work in the home is a first step. Then on a daily basis, time management is important, including learning to multitask between care work and paid work. At the same time, one must remain professional, even when internet connectivity is poor.

Mental health, domestic disputes, and domestic violence can be challenges. These issues have always been there, even when people worked mainly from their offices, and they impact morale, productivity, and the quality of work. Working from home may present a new and morbid reality for some people: locked down in one space, and maybe a difficult space, where they are expected to live and work and somehow remain productive. The office may have been their gateway and avenue for access to much needed services and help.

There are other downsides to working from home. There is the risk of overworking and a potential lack of demarcation between work time and space and personal time and space. This could expose children to unhealthy working habits. There can be a lack of privacy when colleagues see your home and family, say during a zoom videocall. This may cause or exacerbate stress and tension in the family. For some people the balancing acts at home increase productivity and job satisfaction, while others would prefer to be back in the office.

Many employers have become flexible in the covid19 context, focusing on work outputs and the welfare of employees, including their mental health. Some organisations are developing more empathetic cultures, with the realization that their employees are core to the organization's survival and relevance during and post covid19. Some employers have recognized that it is less costly to retain and motivate their current employees than to hire and train new ones later. As a result, some employers are providing facilities and support to their current employees that they did not provide before, for example, furniture for home workspaces and financial support for internet access. I worked at an organization that allowed work-from-home arrangements, in recognition of the need for work-life balance, and so it is interesting to watch the world slowly catch on.

In April 2020 in Sierra Leone, the Minister of Education attended a zoom meeting with his ten-month-old baby strapped to his back. The picture generated a lot of positive comments on Twitter. He drew attention to the reality of many parents, particularly women, who have to balance paid work and care work on a daily basis. In contrast, in August 2019 a female Member of Parliament in Kenya was removed from parliament for bringing her baby to work, as if to say she cannot be both a Member of Parliament and a mother in the same time and space. It is my hope that the empathy and valuing of work-life balance demonstrated by the Minister of Sierra Leone becomes normalised and institutionalised. I envision a post-covid world in which we value and make clear provisions for work-life balance and flexible work arrangements, drawing on models that have been organically emerging during this crisis.

The current work-from-home arrangements are a sneak peek into the future of work. Covid19 demands that we reimage and rethink the ways in which we do things and the ways in which we organize our lives and communities. Companies and organizations are re-examining human resource management, people and talent management, job design, leading and managing remotely, labour policies and relations, and much more. Maybe for those who like working from home, we can have our cake and it eat too.

Chimwemwe A. Fabiano holds a bachelor's in Social and Political Philosophy from the University of Malawi and is pursuing a master's in International Cooperation and Humanitarian Aid with the Kalu Institute in Spain. Chimwemwe has worked in Malawi, Mozambique, Zambia, and Somaliland, on issues at the intersections of gender and transformative leadership within the development and humanitarian sectors. She has worked with World Renew, ActionAid, and the 50:50 Campaign. Her research interests include feminist theory applied to the politics of knowledge production and to the practice of leadership in peace and security. Currently, she is researching youth leadership in peacebuilding in South Sudan.

Still bound together in The Gambia, despite physical distancing
Essa Njie

When the novel coronavirus emerged in the Chinese city of Wuhan in December 2019, many observers underrated the strength of the virus and the possible catastrophe it could pose to humanity. Some people considered it a mere flu that could be treated and cured within a matter of days. Others, especially medical and public health experts, were mindful of what was about to strike the world. In late January 2020, the World Health Organization declared the crisis a global health emergency. The virus spread quickly, especially in Europe, and the global health body declared in its March 11 media briefing the first pandemic caused by a coronavirus.

It is a fact that the world continued to ignore the novel coronavirus and the alarming rate at which it was crisscrossing and spreading through countries and continents. While the United Kingdom was busy with its seemingly unending Brexit process, U. S. President Donald Trump was engaged in his "we built China" rhetoric.[2] The so-called trade war continued to attract the attention of economists and political analysts – examining the possible impacts of the Washington-Beijing rift on the global economy.

However, deadlier financial, political, and socioeconomic impacts were waiting to be posed by the novel coronavirus. Covid19 knows no boundary. Economies have been affected, peoples' social interactions restricted, local

---

[2] "'We built China': Trump claims country 'took advantage' of US in false claims about tariffs," by Alex Woodward, New York, 10 April 2020, www.independent.co.uk/news/world/americas/us-politics/trump-china-tariffs-us-white-house-briefing-who-coroanvirus-a9460236.html

and international travels minimized, and jobs lost. Every village, town, and city around the globe has felt the devastating effects of covid19. Communities across Africa have had their share of challenges.

In my home country of The Gambia, anxiety grew. With the country's susceptibility to the devastating impact of the virus due to its poor healthcare system and economic weaknesses, it was a foregone conclusion that the emergence of cases was going to create a serious health crisis. In short, the country was not prepared to handle the covid19 pandemic, despite previous experience preparing for Ebola.

Measures were desperately needed to curb the virus in a society where social interaction is high. With regard to social distancing measures, Gambians found it inconceivable in the beginning to respect them because sociality is part of being Gambian and part of our daily lives.

One major impact of covid19 in Africa is the loss of jobs. This has affected many households whose breadwinners have no alternative source of income. This is evident and highly felt in Gambia's tourism industry where employment is seasonal. With many employees laid off temporarily due to the limited number of tourists, other sources of income were needed. A seasonal hotel employee revealed to me that he would have to look for an alternate source of income to meet the financial needs of his struggling family during the period of the pandemic.

Remittances from abroad are a source of livelihood for many families in The Gambia. With providers of remittances out of work in Europe and elsewhere, many Gambian families have had to endure months without receiving their usual remittances. For the Muslim feast of Eid ul-Fitr (Koriteh), which marks the end of the fasts of the holy month of Ramadan, families receive money to buy new outfits. This year's festive occasion was different though. Many people had to celebrate without new outfits. Due to physical distancing measures, the feast was also marked without the traditional congregational prayer offered in the morning. Consequently, the feast of Eid ul-Adha (Tobaski) was observed in small groups in neighbourhoods without the usual village or town congregational prayer.

Social interaction constitutes one of the fundamental values of Africa. Arguably, social interaction binds people together. Because covid19 preventive measures include physical distancing, handshaking was called into question and had to be minimized or even eliminated. It was hard to promote such concepts when some people in The Gambia believe that covid19 is a hoax designed by the West. In the beginning, people who adhered to the measures were stigmatized.

Most Gambians could not recall a time when places of worship had to close. People could no longer go to mosques and churches for prayer. We struggled to come to terms with these new and unknown realities. For Muslims in The Gambia, special night prayers are offered in mosques, for men and women, during the last 10 days of Ramadan. The year 2020 did not see such gatherings. At beaches and other public places as well, regular visitors had to adapt to the new practices – staying home, else facing law enforcement officers.

In early August, there was a peak in The Gambia in new daily cases of covid, and by mid-September, the country had reported over 3,000 infections and about 100 deaths. These figures are of course incomparable to those reported in other countries owing to Gambia's infinitesimal population of just over 2 million people. It would seem that the growing number of reported cases of people who had contracted the virus would serve as a lesson to adhere to physical distancing measures. Instead, we remain bound together in our homes, marketplaces, and neighbourhoods, with some people still convinced that the virus is a hoax.

People started to take the measures more seriously when the government promulgated the covid19 regulations, including compulsory facemask wearing and observance of physical distancing in all public settings, and later, a daily curfew from 10 pm to 5 am. These measures remain in place, and people are adhering to them, at least to some degree. Non-adherence can lead to sanctions such as court rulings against violators.

Because markets remain accessible with certain regulations on opening and closing times, some Muslim scholars called on the government to equally open mosques. Subsequently, new regulations led to the opening of mosques and churches, but with strict adherence to physical distancing measures. However, imagine how hard it is to respect them when handshaking and close proximity communications are the norm. Schools and universities remain closed, with digital lectures ongoing.

From market to worship places, neighbourhoods, and social gatherings such as naming and funeral ceremonies, Gambians remain bound together, despite the physical distancing regulations.

Essa Njie is a fellow of the African Leadership Centre. He earned a master's in Security, Leadership and Society from King's College London. He also holds a master's in Human Rights and Democratisation in Africa from the Centre for Human Rights, University of Pretoria. His research interests are in post-conflict and post-dictatorship democratisation in Africa in the context of security sector reform and issues of elections, conflict, security, and human rights. Essa earned a bachelor's in Political Science from the University of The Gambia where he works as a lecturer in the Political Science unit, teaching courses in International Relations, Peace and Conflict Studies, and Gambian Politics, among others. Essa has experience working as a conflict monitor for the Economic Community of West African States (ECOWAS) in The Gambia, reporting on security-related threats and broader issues of governance. His recent research is on the Community of Sant'Egidio in relation to the conflict in Senegal's southern region of Casamance, to understand the role of leadership and of faith-based organizations in conflict resolution and peace processes.

Showing solidarity from a distance in 2020
Ikran Abdullahi

The Muslim community is known for close-knit large families and frequent religious gatherings which have taken place for centuries. However, Muslims all around the world have had to adapt their customs and practices in the face of the covid19 pandemic. The holy month of Ramadan, for example, which is a source of identity and spiritual motivation, was celebrated very differently in 2020.

Ramadan, a month-long religious celebration, is the third of the five pillars of Islam. It commemorates the revelation of the Holy Quran. It is observed through practices such as fasting, prayer, and the reading of the Quran. Islamic practice attaches a significant reward for congregational rather than solo worship, but congregational worship and the need for physical distancing are mutually exclusive. One hundred years ago, during the Spanish influenza, congregations of different faiths had to cancel services and quarantine, like now, despite the anti-congregational nature of isolation. Theology professor Robert Franklin is quoted as saying,

"However, all of our traditions aim for a sense of right relationship with the holy."[3]

The hallmarks of the Ramadan period include the need to show solidarity, for example by engaging in social activities such as family reunions, contributing to families in need, and travelling in groups to holy sites. However, in 2020, the majority of Muslims in Kenya celebrated the holy month of Ramadan and Eid (Festival of Breaking the Fast) in April and May at home rather than in the traditional festive ways.[4]

Mosques close and new ways of worshiping emerge

One of the largest mosques in Kenya and East Africa, the Jamia Mosque, was closed on March 18, and all congregational prayers were suspended in compliance with government directives. This obliged people to be innovative, for example through virtual prayers via YouTube.[5] There were prayers but no gatherings, which dampened the spirit of celebration.[6] However, the Muslim community has been quick to point out "...how Islamic scripture has specific guidelines on what people should do during a pandemic or plague. 'Any place that is under quarantine, you shouldn't go in. And if you are inside you shouldn't come out.'"[7] The new normal of prayers at home and virtual prayers has indeed helped mitigate the spread of the covid19 virus. The adoption of virtual religious services shows the agency of the faithful to innovate when up against a challenge to humanity.

---

[3] "Virus forces the faithful to improvise, observe holidays in isolation," by Gary Fields, 1 April 2020, www.timesofisrael.com/virus-forces-the-faithful-to-improvise-observe-holidays-in-isolation

[4] "Muslims mark Eid ul Fitr amid virus containment restrictions," by Julie Owino, 25 May 2020, www.capitalfm.co.ke/news/2020/05/muslims-mark-eid-ul-fitr-amid-virus-containment-restrictions

[5] "Under lockdown, mosques in Kenya offer virtual prayers for Ramadan, " by Halima Gikandi, 18 May 2020, www.pri.org/stories/2020-05-18/under-lockdown-mosques-kenya-offer-virtual-prayers-ramadan

[6] "Lockdown dampens Eid celebrations in Kenya's Eastleigh neighborhood," 3-minute video produced by Jason God with Amon Wangwa on camera, 25 May 2020, www.voanews.com/episode/lockdown-dampens-eid-celebrations-kenyas-eastleigh-neighborhood-4301351

[7] "Under lockdown, mosques in Kenya offer virtual prayers for Ramadan, " by Halima Gikandi, 18 May 2020, www.pri.org/stories/2020-05-18/under-lockdown-mosques-kenya-offer-virtual-prayers-ramadan

The erosion of alms for the needy

During covid19, the holy month of Ramadan heavily affected the poor.[8] It is advised in the Islamic religion to help the needy by giving food and clothing. This is based on the Quran, which inspires Muslims to be generous to kin and treat the elderly with compassion. Many mosques traditionally prepared Iftar packages to support the needy in breaking their fast. However, government restrictions, including the curfew in Kenya, had significant impacts on Muslim well-wishers and on communities assisted. Street vendors and livestock traders in markets where Muslim faithful gather during the end of Ramadan also suffered financial hardship. Despite the harsh economic situation, many Muslims still showed generosity to the less fortunate and some even tapped onto the power of social media to run crowdfunding campaigns to ensure that they reached out to the most vulnerable in society.[9]

Eid celebrations during covid-19

Muslims around the world used social media as a way to share their Eid celebrations with their loved ones. The Eid celebrations, celebrated twice a year, were affected by the coronavirus because people had to maintain social distancing and limit mobility. Eid al-Fitr was celebrated in May and Eid al-Adha at the end of July and the beginning of August. Young women and girls were not able to visit salons to do their henna ahead of the celebrations. This year, Eid celebrations for the most part were celebrated from home, with fewer family members and less fanfare.

To conclude, covid19 has forced a rethink of Islam's congregational nature due to the need for physical distancing to curb the transmission of the coronavirus from one person to another. Nonetheless, religious practices continued through online services and individual prayers at home – instead of at mosques. The provision of alms to the needy was creatively carried out as well. Ultimately, the covid19 pandemic has been a reminder that believers should be flexible in the face of obstacles, especially when

---

[8] "No gatherings as Muslims mark Eid," by Harrison Kivisu and Alvin Mwangi, 25 May 2020, People Daily Online, www.pd.co.ke/news/national/no-gatherings-as-muslims-mark-eid-37973
[9] "Help feed the needy in Kenya during Ramadan," by Abdullahi Mohammed Abdulle, 17 April 2020, www.gofundme.com/f/feed-the-needy-in-kenya-in-ramadan

there is a threat to life, because it is sacred and must be protected. The foundations of faith have been maintained to ensure suffering is alleviated. Allah expects people to be generous with their wealth.

Ikran Abdullahi *holds a master's in International Relations from the United States International University-Africa in Kenya. She worked with Somalia's Ministry of Constitutional Affairs on the constitutional review process. Before that she consulted for the International Committee of the Red Cross in Somalia and worked with Social-life and Agricultural Development Organisation (SADO) on gender equality awareness and empowerment projects, which have benefitted thousands of women affected by gender-based violence. Her research interests include gender and social inclusion, post-conflict reconstruction in the Horn of Africa, the crossroads of human rights and peacebuilding, and the role of youth in sustaining peace, security, and development. Currently, she is investigating leadership issues arising from the use of customary law approaches to addressing sexual and gender-based violence in Mogadishu and Garowe in Somalia.*

Working
with
the
most
vulnerable

chapter 17

By the Roadside in Kilimani
Waiting for Work[1]

Mary Amuyunzu-Nyamongo
Diana Kinagu
Catherine Muyeka Mumma

Many households in Nairobi are managed by women who are variously referred to as house helps, house girls, maids, house managers or "mboches." The contractual arrangements differ: full-time and resident in their employers' houses, full-time and commuting from their homes, or part-time employees working several days a week or when work is available, for example to clean clothes and houses.

Since the onset of covid19 in Kenya in March 2020, household members seriously considered what to do with their house helps. Some were asked to stay for the time being, while others were asked to leave until the corona situation stabilizes. Some employers are supporting the house helps financially from a distance, while others are not providing any support (maybe due to the difficult times all around), especially if they were part-time and paid only for days worked.

As a result, there is a new crop of women who have no work and no income, or have at-risk income. However, like in most households, they still have rent to pay and children to feed. These women will not be found in the records of the Ministry of Labour and Social Protection, which is responsible for cash transfers to poor and vulnerable families, because in ordinary circumstances they would be working. Furthermore, they may not be well known by local administrators because they spend most of their days in their employers' compounds and only return to their rented homes in the evening or over the weekend.

[1] Copyright © 2020 Mary Amuyunzu-Nyamongo, Diana Kinagu, and Catherine Muyeka Mumma
Amuyunzu-Nyamongo, M., Kinagu, D., and Mumma, C. M. (2020). By the roadside in Kilimani waiting for work. In M. N. Kinyanjui, R. Thaker, and K. Toure (Eds.), *Covid stories from East Africa and beyond: Lived experiences and forward-looking reflections* (pp. 155-161). Bamenda: Langaa.

We three women – two anthropologists and one human rights defender – as part of our effort to understand the impact of covid19 in our community, spent a day visiting with a group of women in these circumstances in Kilimani, an affluent neighbourhood of Kenya's capital city of Nairobi. We visited with these women along Muringa Road, which runs east from Ole Dume Road for a kilometre, ending at Menelik Road, which, going south, connects to Kindaruma Road which continues east into the neighbourhood of Upper Hill. We present here stories the women shared, which stories reveal some of the human predicaments in the face of this enormous crisis.

One woman walks east from Wanyee to Kilimani daily, a distance of about seven kilometres one way. She sits by the roadside waiting for work and any support that may come her way. Prior to the covid19 pandemic, one would find some women, perhaps a quarter of the current number, waiting to be hired to clean or wash for residents in the neighbourhood. When we saw the women, they were sitting silently wearing masks, observing the recommended 1.5-meter physical distance from each other, watching cars and passersby, and waiting.

At the time of our visit in April 2020, at 10:30 in the morning, there was a light drizzle, but the women stayed in their various spots. We spoke with a dozen women there, seeking to understand how covid19 was affecting them. At first the women were wary, but they eventually opened up to us, perhaps to help pass the time or because we explained how their sharing might help shape response measures. Or just out of a sense of hopeful and sisterly solidarity. Maybe they hoped we would be philanthropic after all and make their roadside waiting worthwhile.

We introduced ourselves to each woman. We indicated that we were concerned about their welfare and keen to hear their views on covid19 and its impacts on women like themselves. We sought each individual's consent before continuing the conversation. Each of the three of us spoke to one woman at a time, separate from the rest. We assured each woman we would not share her personal details, like real name or place of residency, as a means of ensuring their anonymity.

Several of them explained that the number of women along Kilimani Road would swell in the afternoon to more than double. On Saturdays and Sundays, the numbers tended to be higher. One woman, let us call her Kajina, stated that even the neighbours were complaining about the increased numbers of women along the road. She went on to explain that the larger numbers are a challenge sometimes for the women, especially when people offer aid which has to be shared equitably amongst them. She was quick, however, to point out that they do not send anyone away because each needs livelihood support.

We sought to learn whether these women were regulars in this location or newcomers, following the announcement of the first covid19 case in Kenya (on March 13, 2020). We also sought to know from them how their efforts to find casual work were paying off.

The common thread in all our discussions was that these women were not being offered work.[2] They nonetheless gather at the roadside almost daily, hoping to get some work. No one picks them up to go wash or clean, as used to happen before the onset of the pandemic. One woman opined, "They are afraid we will bring them the disease." One reason they continue to gather at the roadside is in the hope that a philanthropic person will pass by and offer them cash and/or food. They have been lucky a few times. They reportedly received maize flour, bread, masks, and some cash donations from people who felt touched by their plight. Some women told us they were once offered money by police officers who then advised them to go home.

It is clear that the number of women gathering on the roadside has exponentially increased during this covid19 period. Though the women know that no one will offer them any work, they explained that they have a higher chance of getting donations on that roadside compared to sitting at home or in other parts of the city. They explained: "The donations that come to the settlements never reach us. We are usually excluded and told that the support is for widows, or for one group or another that is on the list of the chief or local administrator, or on the list of the government. Some of us have given our names to many groups to be considered for social support, but we have not received that help. Sitting along this road is better because people can see us here."

---

[2] See similar conclusions in a 31 July 2020 article by Kwamchetsi Makokha titled "What washerwomen would say on a webinar: Regular Kenyans try to survive the economic fallout from the coronavirus," https://africasacountry.com/2020/07/what-washerwomen-would-say-on-a-webinar

Daily worries

After learning why these women sit by the roadside day after day, we conversed with them about their family responsibilities. Out of the 12 women with whom we spoke, nine are single mothers who are responsible for their households. Their rent is about 2,500 to 3,500 Kenya shillings ($25 to $35 US). They could no longer afford their rent and were not sure, at the time of the interview, how long their landlords and landladies would be patient. One woman mentioned that she last paid rent in February 2020. In terms of household sizes, on average each woman has four children or dependents. Since schools closed, the children are at home with little to eat. Sometimes the children reportedly go to bed hungry. Mariamu explained, "Before covid19, when I didn't get much, I would pass by the sukumawiki stalls (vegetable stalls) to pick the bad sukuma (collard greens) and cabbage leaves that were not sold for the day to cook for my children. I have never seen it this bad. Even the bad leaves of cabbage are not there anymore. The stalls are very dry. This disease had better end quickly."

The women complained that their school-going children are not being taught because they do not have access to smartphones or laptops for e-learning. Neither do they have access to TVs or radios. Wanjiru, a single mother of teenage children elaborated, "My *mulika* (simple) phone is the only one we have. I cannot give it to my children because I need it to write names and numbers of people who might promise me a job or a donation." In order to make ends meet, two women explained how their children had to join them in raising income through casual labour. Atieno illustrated the challenges they are going through; she asked her son to seek piecework at a construction site, but even those opportunities have dwindled.

The mothers of adolescent children were worried that their children could be taken advantage of during this period. Many men are at home, and the lack of food in informal settlements may make it easy for young girls to be enticed into sexual activities for food and/or money. One of the mothers, Kalekye, said: "I just talk with my children and tell them to stay at home. It is a difficult time for us who have adolescents, but we, mothers, just have to go and look for food." Two women were taking care of their children plus grandchildren from their adolescent daughters who dropped out of school when their pregnancies started to show. One of the women's daughters was made pregnant at age 14 by her teacher, and she had to drop out of school. "I have tried to pursue justice in this matter. The chief keeps telling me he is following up, but my grandchild is now two years old." Some mothers, especially those with teenage girls, were worried about leaving them at home on their own. One woman explained that she fears for her young girls in the small densely populated area where she lives and where some people have different thoughts and ideas about sex. However, she said she can't stop going to sit by the roadside because her young girls need food and she has to pay rent. She indicated that her only option is to pray for their safety.

Several of the married women reported that their spouses had also stopped working and were at home or looking for income through hustling. The inability to generate income is frequently a cause for domestic conflict. Constant tension at home can easily escalate into violence if provoked, and this extends to the children. Some women opted to live on their own to escape violence from their spouses, who in turn refused to support them with childcare. Many said they were worried about managing the quickly-piling-up monthly bills.

Asked how they found themselves needing to sit by the roadside, they cited changes in their fortunes. Some lost their jobs without notice, and at the time of our discussion they did not know whether they would be paid any wages. One woman was employed on a monthly salary but was asked by her employer to stay home until the covid19 crisis ends. She was paid a prorated salary for the 12 days she worked in March, but she does not know if she will be paid anything after that. Although they are back in their homes in the informal settlements, some women said that they are denied support by officials delivering aid, because they are considered young and do not fall into the category of "poor and vulnerable people." This is despite the fact that many of them are heads of their households and need all the support they can get. Muhonja, one of the respondents, expressed fear about her future and being able to feed five children.

A few weeks after the interviews, one of the authors of this chapter received a call from the lady taking care of her 14-year old's child: "I am calling to tell you that I have had enough. Do you remember me telling you about my daughter who was made pregnant by her teacher? I have just learnt that she is pregnant again, and she is only 16. I don't know what to do. I called the boy who made her pregnant to come and take her and marry her. He insulted me and told me I raised an immoral child. I am tired. I feel like running away and leaving her with her children. What do you think I should do?"

What are some of the things these women would like to see happen?

The women opined that the government should intervene on rent and facilitate their inclusion in social protection schemes. They reasoned that a lot of pressure would be relieved if their landlords/ladies would allow them to continue residing in their abodes without harassment. When asked if they preferred donations of cash or foodstuffs, they noted that both would work, however, they are usually in need of cooking fuel, cooking oil, and other items that are often not donated by well-wishers.

Covid19 and the response to it has created a new cadre of needy people in Africa and beyond. The women we met along the roadside in Kilimani were needy before the pandemic, but they were managing. Now, they and their families are needier and exposed to a multitude of new risks. These women may not be listed by Government in existing support system databases. They are also entering a pool of poor and vulnerable people which has expanded rapidly, implying that they will be competing with people who may be considered more vulnerable. The question is: How will we, collectively, ensure these women and all families are supported to be able to care for themselves and their children and live in dignity?

__Mary Amuyunzu-Nyamongo__ earned a PhD in Social Anthropology from the University of Cambridge in the United Kingdom. She is the Founder Director of the African Institute for Health and Development (AIHD). She has over 30 years of experience in social development with a focus on health, social safeguards, social protection, and poverty alleviation. With regard to covid19, her focus is on identifying and mitigating the social impacts in the immediate, medium, and long term.

__Diana Kinagu__ is a third-year student at the University of Nairobi undertaking a bachelor's degree in Anthropology. She is a keen researcher who wants to understand the human context of development.

__Catherine Muyeka Mumma__ is a human rights lawyer and defender who has served on the Commission for the Implementation of the Constitution and the Kenya National Human Rights Commission. She is part of the human rights teams that have championed *the right to health in Kenya including HIV/AIDS-related rights and is keen to see the poor and vulnerable not getting further disenfranchised by this pandemic.*

chapter 18

When Home is Not Safe:
Covid19 and Domestic Violence[1]

Sarah Nasimiyu Sikuku
Mary Amuyunzu-Nyamongo

Coronavirus (covid19) as a global pandemic has affected all spheres of life. As families quarantine together, rates of domestic and sexual violence are unfortunately increasing, affecting men, women, and children, however, women are most affected – as we will see later in this chapter.

In this chapter, we draw on our experience and encounters in the context of our professional work and community engagements to share stories that have been shared with us, and to reflect on domestic violence in Kenya during the coronavirus pandemic and what can be done.

The Kenyan government has adopted strict measures to counter the spread of the covid19 virus, and these measures are impacting women and girls, for example by elevating incidences of gender-based violence.

Here is a story of a woman named Karimi that we met in the course of our advocacy work.

Karimi (not her real name) is a middle-aged woman who resides in Nairobi. She is a stay-at-home mother of five children aged between 2 and 17. She narrates a recent experience of how covid19 suddenly affected her family life.

"I had never seen my husband so distraught when he came back home from work. He didn't give me the usual warm hug. Instead, he brushed me aside and said he was tired and needed to rest. I let him be. Later in the evening, as we sat at the table to have dinner, he shoved a letter to the side of the dining table and asked me to read it. I was reluctant to open it. I however took it and was hit by a disturbing headline: 'We are sorry, but we have to let you go.' My husband had recently gotten this job after years of searching.

---

[1] Copyright © 2020 Sarah Nasimiyu Sikuku and Mary Amuyunzu-Nyamongo
Sikuku, S. N., and Amuyunzu-Nyamongo, M. (2020). When home is not safe: Covid19 and domestic violence. In M. N. Kinyanjui, R. Thaker, and K. Toure (Eds.), *Covid stories from East Africa and beyond: Lived experiences and forward-looking reflections* (pp. 163-175). Bamenda: Langaa.

"I have been unemployed for five years, and it has been tough for us and our five children. Covid19 has changed the trajectory of my once flourishing marriage. My husband has become cold towards me. He is always at home, and that frustrates him a lot. For the first time, my husband slapped me, and things have slowly escalated into bitter arguments and even beatings. I am afraid for my life and those of my children. This once beautiful and serene home and family are no longer safe."

Karimi found out that she could seek support via the national gender-based violence tollfree helpline 1195, staffed 24 hours a day by a dozen tele-counsellors.[2] The counsellors coordinate and facilitate access to information, resources, and services. Karimi also learned that she could report her case to the gender desk at her nearest police station as well as to advocacy organizations.[3] However, it is worth noting that the restrictions imposed in response to the covid19 pandemic are "likely to make it harder for survivors to report abuse and seek help and for service providers to respond efficiently.[4]"

People have been obliged to *stay home* as a measure to mitigate the spread of covid19, alongside washing or sanitizing hands and wearing a protective mask. The situation has become a nightmare for many people as pressure and anxiety mount. Some people have lost their jobs. Some have lost loved ones to the disease. Some are very ill-equipped to deal with the psychological trauma, fear, and uncertainty that the virus brings. On top of all that, families are suffering from different forms of gender-based violence. The "stay home" phrase was initially seen as a safety measure but does not have such a positive ring anymore, because for some people, behind closed doors lurks another enemy, in the form of an intimate partner. Where then will we go if home is not safe?

Here is a story about Martha and her family, who we met in the Gataka neighbourhood of Nairobi.

---

[2] "Nairobi, Kisumu GBV hotspots, report reveals," by Kamau Maichuhie, 6 July 2020 www.nation.co.ke/kenya/gender/nairobi-kisumu-gbv-hotspots-report-reveals-1445592
[3] Advocacy organizations such as the Centre for Rights Education and Awareness (CREAW), the Coalition on Violence Against Women (COVAW), the Federation of Women Lawyers (FIDA Kenya) (their tollfree helpline for counselling and legal aid services is 08-00-720-501), or the Kenya Female Advisory Organisation (KEFEADO)
[4] "Tackling Kenya's domestic violence amid covid-19 crisis: Lockdown measures increase risks for women and girls," by Agnes Odhiambo, 8 April 2020, www.hrw.org/news/2020/04/08/tackling-kenyas-domestic-violence-amid-covid-19-crisis

Martha (not her real name) is in standard 8. She is supposed to be studying for her end-of-year exams in early November of 2020, because the Cabinet Secretary for Education indicated that national exams would go on as scheduled, despite disruptions caused by covid19 and measures to prevent its spread.[5]

Martha lives in a household with a history of violence. Her mother, let's call her Jane, who was taking me around Gataka, looked a bit troubled when she came to meet me. I asked her about her family and especially her husband. She said that she did not know where or how he was. *"Sijui kama ameenda kunywa ama ameanda kazini?"* (I do not know whether he has gone to take alcohol or to work). I asked her to expound on this observation. "He locked the door on us last week, on Thursday evening. I am now staying at my friend's house." Jane has five daughters ranging from 7 to 15 years in age. She and her daughters, a total of six people, left their one-room house to squat in someone else's one-room house.

I was curious to know what transpired that Thursday. Martha's older sister told me that their father came home in the evening drunk. He sat on the bed while the children were watching TV. He picked on Martha and asked her why she was staring at him. She wasn't. When she did not answer, he picked up the coffee table intending to hit her with it, but Martha's older sister blocked the table and, in the process, hurt her hand and foot. In addition, the father pulled and tore her dress. He broke the TV that Martha was using for her studies – because the Ministry of Education airs some lessons on TV. He then chased his wife and daughters out of the house and locked the door. He yelled after his two older children (ages 15 and 13) that they were ripe for marriage.

Martha wants to do her exams so that she can go to boarding school next year. I asked her how she was preparing for her exams. She explained how her mother has a phone on which she has downloaded some math lessons. Jane observed that she has neither credit nor data bundles for her children to access teaching materials. Before the lockdown, Martha could leave her home to study with other children. Now she lacks access both to her peers and to educational materials, while others have access to computers, internet, phones, TVs, and review materials.

Martha's home environment, where she is witness to emotional and physical abuse, was not conducive to home schooling. How will she continue her learning now? Will our response to covid19 expand socioeconomic divides, with the poor inordinately suffering the consequences of the virus? What measures can we put in place to ensure that children in informal settlements get access to quality education while we wait for schools to reopen? And what can be done about domestic violence, which is damaging people, disrupting studies, and tearing families apart?

---

[5] Note that the exams have since been postponed.

When asked about her most important wish, Martha said: "I want to stay in a place where I can learn in peace." She wants to pass her exams and, according to her mother Jane, she is very committed to her studies.

Understanding gender-based violence

Associate Professor of International Relations Fatuma Ahmed Ali writes that women are often the main victims of violence because of the patriarchal system in Kenya. She explains further that:

> Violence against women and girls has been acknowledged as a violation of basic human rights and a form of discrimination against women, reflecting the prevalent imbalance of power between women and men. This is because violence against women and girls is a universal phenomenon that is both a cause and consequence of gender inequality.[6]

In 2016, Sicily Kariuki (then Kenya's Cabinet Secretary for Public Service, Youth and Gender Affairs), Siddharth Chatterjee (United Nations Resident Coordinator in Kenya), and Stefano Dejak (then European Union Ambassador to Kenya) united to declare: "It is time for every man to start doing something to end the scourge of violence against women and girls in their homes and communities."[7]

Gender-based violence is violence experienced by a person "due to stereotypes and roles attributed to or expected of them according to their sex or gender identity.[8]" There are various forms of gender-based violence; among them are domestic violence, rape, incest, defilement, wife inheritance, female genital mutilation (FGM), forced marriage, confinement, bigamy, and femicide.[9]

---

[6] "Women's agency and violence against women: The case of the Coalition on Violence Against Women in Kenya," by Fatuma Ahmed Ali, in *African Conflict and Peacebuilding Review*, 2017, volume 7, issue 1, pages 51-65, https://covaw.or.ke/womens-agency-and-violence-against-women-the-case-of-the-coalition-on-violence-against-women-in-kenya

[7] "Let's unite to end violence against women in Kenya," Kariuki, S., Chatterjee, S., and Dejak, S. A., 25 November 2016, www.ipsnews.net/2016/11/lets-unite-to-end-violence-against-women-in-kenya

[8] https://plan-international.org/ending-violence/gbv-**gender-based-violence**

[9] See Kenya's "National Policy for Prevention and Response to Gender Based Violence" (2014), https://gender.go.ke/wp-content/uploads/2019/10/National-Policy-on-prevention-and-Response-to-GBV.pdf, **and** Kenya's "Protection Against Domestic Violence Act" (2015), http://kenyalaw.org/kl/fileadmin/pdfdownloads/Acts/ProtectionAgainstDomesticViolenceAct_2015.pdf

According to the World Health Organization (WHO):

The term "domestic violence" is used in many countries to refer to partner violence but the term can also encompass child or elder abuse, or abuse by any member of a household. "Battering" refers to a severe and escalating form of partner violence characterized by multiple forms of abuse, terrorization and threats, and increasingly possessive and controlling behaviour on the part of the abuser.[10]

"Sexual and other forms of violence against women have devastating consequences […] including serious physical, mental, sexual, and reproductive health problems, including sexually transmitted infections, HIV, and unplanned pregnancies."[11] For instance, the *Daily Nation* of the 17th of June 2020 reported that in Machakos County, Kenya, 3964 teenage girls in the county had become pregnant between January and May 2020.[12]

Inside the perpetrator's mind

There are multiple reasons why someone perpetuates harm against their partner. A big reason for abuse and violence is the expression of power and control. Perpetrators may have been exposed to violence while growing up and believe violent behaviour is the mark of control within the family unit. Gender-based violence can also be attributed to the fact that society does not promote and protect the dignity of the person. Covid19 fans a fire that is already burning, making underlying personal struggles all the more combustible in the household.

A case in point is Karimi's husband, who did not know how to cope with the stress of losing his job. The thought of being unable to cater for his family clouded his judgment. He began to see his wife as a burden. She thus became the object of his wrath rather than the supportive partner she could have been during the crisis. People like Karimi's husband need help

---

[10] "Understanding and addressing violence against women: Intimate partner violence," by the World Health Organization,
https://apps.who.int/iris/bitstream/handle/10665/77/432/WHO_RHR_12.36_eng.pdf
[11] "Tackling Kenya's domestic violence amid covid-19 crisis: Lockdown measures increase risks for women and girls," by Agnes Odhiambo, 8 April 2020,
www.hrw.org/news/2020/04/08/tackling-kenyas-domestic-violence-amid-covid-19-crisis
[12] "Alarm as 3,964 girls impregnated in Machakos County in five months," by Pius Maundu, 17 June 2020, www.nation.co.ke/kenya/counties/machakos/over-3900-girls-impregnated-in-machakos-731184

to learn to manage stress, otherwise they may turn to heavy drinking, scapegoat people, or rage violently against family members. These actions can also lead to criminal charges.

Societal perceptions of domestic violence

Based on the authors' perceptions and observations, gender identities and relations are complex. In some communities in East Africa and beyond, there is a conviction that violent men make good family protectors. We have heard some extended family members say that if a man does not beat his wife, then he does not love her. Some people go so far as to consider a woman as one of the children in the family and expect that she should receive "equal corporal discipline" for disobedience. We have known some women that even provoked their men to prove their prowess and masculinity. In extreme cases, where there is loss of life, the attitude is to parry the incident by blaming the deceased for bringing the plight on themselves.

To further confound things, domestic violence is considered a private matter, and neighbours or family members often refrain from interfering. A lady that chose to be anonymous disclosed to us how she stayed in an abusive marriage for years, believing that by staying she was being respectful and maintaining harmony in the home and fulfilling her husband's wishes.

These negative and discriminatory values and practices have been passed on from one generation to another. Violence in relationships and in society becomes accepted, and abusive situations are normalized. Some forms of violence have even been celebrated with much pageantry, for example when girls are circumcised, when men marry girls, or when wives in abusive marriages are beaten by their husbands. With the rise of advocacy and human rights movements, these violent cultural practices are being challenged and in some cases shunned.

What is really happening?

Even before covid19, it was difficult in many instances to provide evidence to substantiate allegations of domestic and sexual violence. Empirical data is required to convince the police and justice system to enforce existing laws that prohibit and penalize violence in the home. In Kenya, we have also had the release of petty offenders to decongest prisons to promote physical distancing. The reintegration of these members of society may not have been well thought through. Those released from incarceration who did not have a source of livelihood were likely to become dependent on relatives or friends on the outside who may have already been financially strained. This could exacerbate violence at family levels. A lady recently released from prison, let's call her Asumpta, in a phone conversation disclosed to us how she along with her children had been chased away from her matrimonial home by her husband after she returned home from prison. Prior to her being chased away, she was a victim of physical and emotional abuse by her husband.

Does empowering women help? What are some of the challenges?

Gender-based violence is partly addressed by empowering women to know their rights and to gain economic opportunities. Many women's empowerment programs focus on three key areas:

1. Empowering women to be economically self-sufficient. If an economically self-sufficient woman were to need to move out of the home, finances would hopefully be available. However, with limitations on physical mobility and partial lockdowns in some areas, moving out may not be a ready option. In addition, businesses have been hard hit, and some women no longer have a reliable source of income.

2. Building women's confidence and their ability to negotiate for their rights in the household, workplace, and community. The covid19 context negatively affects employment, which can diminish the confidence and pride of either partner in a household. The negotiating power of individual members in the household can decrease with loss of work or a major pay cut.

3. Supporting women in learning how to have control over their bodies, their time, and their movements, including freedom from violence. With covid19, movement has been temporarily clipped. Women's control over their bodies becomes a bigger challenge. For example, some women procure birth control while their husbands are outside the home. With husbands home, some women are going without their birth control choice.

Despite efforts to empower women over the years, reports of domestic violence are increasing during the covid19 pandemic, suggesting increases in domestic violence. How can we realize freedom from violence? Women's rights organisations in Kenya "petitioned the government to set aside at least 30 per cent of the Covid-19 emergency response fund to address gender-based violence in the country. [13]"

Breaking the cycle

In Kenya, women and girls suffer from domestic violence. According to the 2014 Demographic and Health Survey, 39% of ever-married women compared to 9% of men age 15 to 49 "report having experienced spousal physical or sexual violence." Among those, 39% of women and 24% of men sought assistance to stop the violence (physical or sexual) they experienced. [14] People who have suffered from domestic violence have feelings of shame and guilt and often suffer depression and anxiety disorders. Many of them feel trapped, not knowing what to do. Because of the belief that domestic violence is a private matter, women are inhibited from talking about their experiences so as not to shame their partners. Men face stigma for allowing themselves to fall prey to their partners.

Whether it is men or women or children suffering from domestic violence, knowledge is the first step: knowing where to legally report the violence (even if, as we said earlier, the lack of convincing evidence can prevent law enforcement from acting), where to seek refuge, which rights are being violated.

Hotlines are a good first step in this direction. Information about the Healthcare Assistance Kenya (HAK) Sexual and Gender Based Violence Rapid Response System and Helpline 1195 is available at HAKgbv1195.org. But are a dozen hotline counsellors sufficient for a country of over 51 million people? Counselling services and experienced professionals need to be available to support cases of separation and divorce. Counselling services should also include support for mental health and trauma, not only for survivors of gender-based violence but also for all members of the general public. Accessible and relevant psychosocial support can help people through challenges and reduce the incidences of gender-based violence.

---

[13] "Nairobi, Kisumu GBV hotspots, report reveals," by Kamau Maichuhie, 6 July 2020 www.nation.co.ke/kenya/gender/nairobi-kisumu-gbv-hotspots-report-reveals-1445592
[14] Kenya Demographic and Health Survey 2014, https://dhsprogram.com/pubs/pdf/fr308/fr308.pdf

Is there hope?

The women's movement succeeded in putting the fight against violence against women as a priority issue on the world's agenda. International conventions like the Universal Declaration of Human Rights, the Convention on the Elimination of All Forms of Discrimination against Women (CEDAW), and the African Charter on Human and Peoples' Rights have been ratified and efforts made to translate the provisions into policies, programmes, services and ways of thinking, living, raising children, and interacting.

Legislation, regulations, and policies exist and are being developed and also need to be implemented These elaborate how the rights articulated in the international conventions mentioned above can be understood and, for example, used to protect against domestic violence during and after covid19. Although Kenya and East African countries more generally have signed onto these conventions, there is still need for systematic action as per local legal frameworks on human rights to support survivors of domestic violence to exercise their rights in all spheres of economic, social, cultural, and political life.

Shifts in cultural norms are also necessary. We need to educate each other about equality between the sexes and raise children to treat all people with dignity, regardless of their sexual identity and other identities. Intimate partner violence should not be normalized as an acceptable cultural practice. Sexual violence cannot be accepted as a way of putting women in their place or punishing them. We need to address attitudes and structures that perpetuate violence in the household. We need to develop shared norms supportive of nonviolent behaviour to eliminate domestic violence. We also need to enforce laws and policies that make violent behaviour an offence.

Strategic responses in the wake of covid19

The Kenyan government has taken notable steps to address the situation of gender-based violence, for instance by making the existence of the 1195 hotline well known; however, these measures must factor in the unique and practical needs of diverse groups of women and girls of Kenya and the realities under which they live and operate.

Joanne Kobuthi-Kuria, the communications and membership manager at Amnesty International Kenya, wrote in early May 2020:

> Intimate partner violence is on the increase now more than ever, with two in three women experiencing violence as compared to one in three before Covid. This precipitated a nudge to all governments by UN secretary general Antonio Guterres to put women's safety first as they respond to the pandemic.

She goes on to explain that the "correlation between epidemics and violence has not been adequately documented," but we know that lockdowns "are not cozy, especially when you have to chill with a perpetrator." Thus, the government "must exercise the capacity to think beyond the epidemic and urgently incorporate a gender lens in response mechanisms." [15]

Agnes Odhiambo, a senior researcher in the Women's Rights Division of Human Rights Watch, observes that violence against women and girls is a crime. Women and girls "have a right to be protected even when the government is preoccupied with a pandemic." The government should enforce the existing laws to the fullest extent, prosecuting abusers for assault and for causing bodily harm. Protection orders should be initiated, enforced, and monitored. Odhiambo calls for public awareness campaigns that "highlight the risk of domestic violence and give detailed information on how victims, including those infected with coivd19, can access services." The government "should treat services for women who experience violence as essential" and "ensure these services have the resources they need." Furthermore, she explains, alternative accommodation should be made available if shelters are full. [16]

Jane Anyango, a community organizer in Nairobi's Kibera neighbourhood, has been recognised for her work supporting the creation of cultures of peace at the community level. For years, she has documented cases of gender-based violence and, with others, advocated for the rights of women and girls. She deplores how children suffer when parents start to

---

[15] "Domestic violence: The shadow pandemic," by Joanne Kobuthi-Kuria in her personal capacity, May 2020, www.amnestykenya.org/domestic-violence-the-shadow-pandemic

[16] "Tackling Kenya's domestic violence amid covid-19 crisis: Lockdown measures increase risks for women and girls," by Agnes Odhiambo, 8 April 2020, www.hrw.org/news/2020/04/08/tackling-kenyas-domestic-violence-amid-covid-19-crisis

physically fight. "Most conflicts are happening in the night or late in the evening so the kids cannot even run out" to avoid the violence, she explains, because of the curfew. She recognizes the importance of partnerships and networks in fighting the scourge of gender-based violence to create a better tomorrow.[17]

In March 2020, the United Nations Population Fund (UNFPA) issued a statement that highlighted how the pandemic "will compound existing gender inequalities, and increase risks of gender-based violence." It is imperative to prioritize the "protection and promotion of the rights of women and girls."[18] The World Health Organization provides answers to questions like what to do if the home is not a safe place, if someone is worried that somebody they know might be in an abusive relationship, or if one is worried about harming a partner. It also explains who is most vulnerable:

> Women who are displaced, who are migrants or refugees, and those living in conflict-affected areas, older women and women with disabilities are particularly at risk of violence and are likely to be disproportionately affected by violence during covid-19.[19]

The media has participated as a whistleblower to bring attention to the rising incidences of domestic violence during the covid19 pandemic. However, there are gaps in national data, capacities to respond, and systems to monitor trends and prevalence rates. The government has a responsibility to protect women and girls against violence during the pandemic. In Kenya, this responsibility was given to the Ministry of Interior and Coordination of National Government.[20] In addition, community-

[17] "Jane Anyango – community activist mobilises slum women in peace building," by Odhiambo Orlale, 1 December 2014, https://kw.awcfs.org/article/jane-anyango-community-activist-mobilises-slum-women-in-peace-building, and "Kenya activists fear spike in violence against women during coronavirus," by Rael Ombuor, 20 April 2020, www.voanews.com/covid-19-pandemic/kenya-activists-fear-spike-violence-against-women-during-coronavirus

[18] www.unfpa.org/resources/gender-equality-and-addressing-gender-based-violence-gbv-and-coronavirus-disease-covid-19

[19] www.who.int/emergencies/diseases/novel-coronavirus-2019/question-and-answers-hub/q-a-detail/violence-against-women-during-covid-19

[20] "National 2019 novel coronavirus contingency (readiness and early response) plan February-April 2020," Kenya's Ministry of Health, January 2020, www.health.go.ke/wp-

based organizations and nongovernmental organizations, some decades old, are collaborating to advocate for the protection of women and girls from gender-based violence during this crisis.

For effective integration of domestic violence responses into mainstream efforts, national covid19 response and recovery plans must be gender responsive and contextualized to different community realities. The action plans designed to address domestic violence must be backed with human and financial resources to support immediate practical and longer term strategic needs. Without such intentionality, situations permitting the progression of violence will persist.

Karimi and her children, Jane and her daughters, and hundreds of others – including women, men, and children – have suffered from domestic violence in Kenya during the covid19 pandemic. The crisis has magnified the structural violence and inequalities that the most vulnerable in society, including women, youth, and children, have had to endure. Some have reached out for support. Some suffer in silence. The reported incidences of domestic violence are on the rise in the country.

Together, we can bring attention to this issue, ensure that psychosocial support and care as well as other practical support is available to survivors of domestic violence, and contribute to important shifts in our households, communities, and nations toward cultures of equality, mutual respect, and negotiation rather than violence. We must put an end to stereotypes and discrimination based on one's sex, reduce the stigma associated with those who have suffered from domestic abuse, and build safer, more inclusive, and more resilient communities and societies.

Sarah Nasimiyu Sikuku *is a master's student in Monitoring and Evaluation at Daystar University in Kenya. She has over eight years' experience working in the development sector. Currently, she works at Clean Start Solutions, a social enterprise working to build the agency of women and help restore dignity and hope for the successful reintegration of women and their children impacted by the criminal justice system.*

---

content/uploads/2020/06/National-2019-Novel-Coronavirus-Contingency-Readiness-and-Early-Response-Plan-February-April-2020.pdf

Mary Amuyunzu-Nyamongo *earned a PhD in Social Anthropology from the University of Cambridge in the United Kingdom. She is the Founder Director of the African Institute for Health and Development. She has over 30 years of experience in social development with a focus on health, social safeguards, social protection, and poverty alleviation.*

chapter 19

Collective Voice on
Wanting to Feel Safe and Secure[1]

Nyawira Wahito
Ibrahim Mohammed Machina

Imagine... if you were 15 and could not feel safe
Nyawira Wahito

Imagine sitting in a one-room house, using a candle because you do not have electricity, trying to move closer so that you can get a glimmer of light to reflect on the book you are reading – to ensure you are not left behind by your classmates when schools reopen.

Imagine your father, who is trying to sleep in the next part of the room partitioned with a cardboard or a bedsheet, asking you to stop wasting the candle because now that there is lockdown, he has no money to buy another one.

Imagine blowing that candle off and promising yourself to try again tomorrow, and while you go to put the book away, your father grabs you and takes advantage of you in the bed...

Imagine your mother trying to reason with him to let you go, but before she can finish the sentence a huge slap lands on her cheek.

Imagine your father emptying his sperm on you and threatening to kill both you and your mother if you dare say a word to anybody. You are 15.

Imagine....

This is the life of many young adolescent girls in Kenya during the covid19 pandemic. As if their pre-covid existence was not difficult enough, covid has disorganised their lives and multiplied obstacles to healthy and

[1] Copyright © 2020 Nyawira Wahito, and Ibrahim Mohammed Machina
Wahito, N., and Machina, I. M. (2020). Wanting to feel safe and secure. In
M. N. Kinyanjui, R. Thaker, and K. Toure (Eds.), *Covid stories from East Africa and beyond: Lived experiences and forward-looking reflections* (pp. 177-181). Bamenda: Langaa.

safe daily living. The ban on large gatherings means that many shelters and safe spaces, usually accessible to girls, are closed. Curfews imposed due to the ongoing pandemic are an additional obstacle that hinder victims of sexual crimes from accessing justice. Additionally, the patriarchal nature of the Kenyan society, coupled with the high number of untrained police officers and a long chain of access to justice manned by patriarchal or untrained gatekeepers, lengthens the justice process even further. Covid19 then becomes a contagion which deeply exacerbates the issue further than in pre-covid times.

The elite-centric state in Kenya that put measures in place during covid without a gendered perspective has cost many girls their lives, their childhood, and their dignity. The increase in human rights violations in the form of rape, early and forced marriages, female genital mutilation, and teenage pregnancies is horrific and appalling.

As a country which has ratified many treaties and protocols in support of gender equality, Kenya needs to do better by her children, especially women and girls, not only during this pandemic but also any other situations, with or without crises. Milestones that Kenya has realised through the strategic but backbreaking efforts of women's rights organisations and activists are being reversed and washed down the drain. Girls must be protected through policies and their implementation, political will, safe spaces, and accountability – all working together to ensure that girls lead safe and self-fulfilling lives in society.

A shift has to happen in behaviours and attitudes. As a country, we need all of us to call out and move away from toxic cultures perpetuated by patriarchy and toxic masculinities. We need to do this in our organizational cultures, in our spaces of worship, in our politics, and in society at large. Leaders and systems need to work for the greater good of all in society. We the people cannot stand for sexual abuse by our leaders or the perpetuation of abuse in families and broader society. The Government of Kenya has to ensure that rules apply to all, from the top down, so people in society do not feel invincible after defiling children and raping girls.

Those who came before us did their best using all their capacities to ensure better futures for our communities. Now we owe it to future generations to create safe and more human futures for them, where everyone will thrive.

Nyawira Wahito *holds a bachelor's in Sociology and Philosophy from the University of Nairobi and is pursuing a master's in Security, Leadership and Society at King's College London. Nyawira is a feminist young women's rights activist with over eight years' experience working, most recently via the Resource Center for Women and Girls in Kenya, with adolescent girls from disadvantaged and underserved backgrounds.*

Mobilising responses to covid19 in North East Nigeria
Ibrahim Mohammed Machina

While working in North East Nigeria, I observed and experienced the violence perpetrated by the violent group *Boko Haram*, which caused a large-scale humanitarian crisis[2] in the region. The crisis has led to the displacement of people, food insecurity, and violations of human rights. The situation is further worsened by the coronavirus (covid19) pandemic and the measures imposed by the government to manage and contain its spread. As per World Health Organisation (WHO) and Nigeria Centre for Disease Control (NCDC) guidelines, Nigerians were directed to stay at home and practice physical distancing and personal hygiene.

I have no doubt that these measures are necessary to prevent the spread of covid19 among the populace. However, the situation has exacerbated existing structural vulnerabilities in communities in North East Nigeria and impacted the livelihood of millions of people, especially people who have been displaced from their homes and communities (internally displaced people, IDP). The number of people in dire need of humanitarian assistance in North East Nigeria rose from 7.9 million at the beginning of 2020 to 10.6 million since the outbreak of covid19.[3]

With no known vaccine, containing and managing the spread of covid19 relies largely on human behaviours. However, public health measures are only effective when large proportions of the population adhere to them. What has been running in my mind is that, while many people in North East Nigeria would be happy to stay at home and keep

---

[2] *An NGO perspective on the response to the humanitarian crisis in northeastern Nigeria*, mission report by InterAction, May 2016, https://reliefweb.int/report/nigeria/ngo-perspective-response-humanitarian-crisis-northeastern-nigeria-march-28-april-9
[3] Nigeria situation report – highlights, UN Office for the Coordination of Humanitarian Affairs (OCHA), updated 23 September 2020, https://reports.unocha.org/en/country/nigeria

179

their distance as well as practice regular personal hygiene, the question is: How?

- How many people can afford to stay at home and eat nothing?
- How many people can afford to wash their hands regularly with no access to water in their homes let alone in the IDP camps?
- How many people can afford to buy luxurious items like soaps or hand sanitisers?
- How many people can practice physical distancing when living in densely populated communities?

Asking people to stay at home and wash their hands with running water when they lack access to portable drinking water is a challenge. Asking people to stay at home when their sources of livelihood depend on informal businesses and daily wages is another challenge.

Do you want them to die of hunger? Furthermore, living conditions in most communities and the IDP camps make it difficult to practice social distancing. For example, how can you physically distance when 8 to 10 people share a small makeshift shelter? While many families during the lockdowns in the global north were busy stockpiling tissue paper, many families in North East Nigeria could not even stock up on foodstuffs due to hikes in food prices.

Despite these challenges, the resilience of these vulnerable communities in North East Nigeria is evident. People remained active and organised themselves during the pandemic: from sewing facemasks and producing bar soaps and other locally made products to using multi-coloured plastic kettles to wash their hands regularly to contain the spread of the virus.

Young people who drive motorised tricycles, popularly known as *keke*, and now take only two passengers instead of the normal four, pasted on their vehicles stickers and posters with information on how to curb the spread of the virus.[4] Town criers have also been seen and heard spreading covid19 prevention messages across communities in North East Nigeria – using loudspeakers mounted on *keke*. The town criers reach many

---

[4] Keke drivers in Maiduguri are spreading COVID-19 prevention messages throughout the city, even as the virus threatens their hard-won livelihoods," by Usman Kundili Bukar, 24 June 2020, www.icrc.org/en/document/maiduguris-keke-are-spreading-covid-19-prevention-messages

communities and IDP camps, without exposing themselves to risks of contracting the virus or contaminating others.

Local organisations have developed radio jingles to disseminate information on covid19. In addition, local and religious leaders have been offering psychosocial support and hope to their community's members, to help them cope with the stress and shocks associated with the pandemic. Community-based organisations and individuals also assisted many households with food items to cushion the effects of the pandemic.

The experience of previous disease outbreaks such as the Ebola epidemic in West Africa has shown that leadership is needed from both the state and society to effectively mobilise the whole-of-society in times of crisis.

I call on leaders in formal positions of authority to recognise the resilience of the communities in North East Nigeria and work with them to respond to their needs and aspirations. A significant challenge to the response to the crisis in North East Nigeria is the lack of trust between the government and the citizens. A legacy of mistrust, corruption, and unresponsiveness to the expectations of the citizens has weakened leaders' capability to address the *Boko Haram* insurgency, let alone successfully mobilise and respond to the covid19 pandemic. Leaders need to show transparency and accountability to cultivate trust and build effective partnerships with vulnerable communities in North East Nigeria.

Ibrahim Mohammed Machina *holds a master's in International Relations and Diplomacy from Nile University of Nigeria, Abuja and is pursuing another master's in Security, Leadership and Society at King's College London. Ibrahim has taught courses in International Law and Diplomacy and in Nigerian Government and Politics for undergraduate students of political science at Federal University, Gashua in Yobe State in North East Nigeria. His research interests include peace, security, and development in Africa, community resilience to violent extremism, and the role of young people in countering violent extremism. His current research has to do with sustained societal mobilisation in response to covid19 in Nigeria and leadership in crisis situations.*

chapter 20

African Women at Work during a Pandemic: Case of Muundo Barakoa[1]

Aguere Yilma Bultcha
Frannie Léautier
Eléonore Immaculée Nyamwiza

On March 4, 2020, at 2:43 pm, an email arrives from the Human Resources Director at our company. He announces that all non-essential travel will be suspended or postponed, and that no employee should travel to countries, territories, or areas with high risk of transmission of covid19, which at the time were limited to China, South Korea, Iran, Italy, and Japan. Further guidance: When on essential travel, one must observe recommended precautionary measures during the duration of the trip (e.g. avoid large crowds and public transportation) and upon return to the duty station may be required to self-quarantine for two weeks.

That message sparked a series of dramatic transformations in our lives. We are a decentralized team with colleagues located in multiple offices, and our team meetings started to become mostly virtual. All business meetings with third parties or partners were also conducted virtually rather than face-to-face. Anyone exhibiting the signs of a common cold (e.g. runny or stuffy nose, sore throat, nasal congestion, mild fever) was encouraged to stay home until the symptoms disappeared. Those having symptoms such as a headache, fever, cough, or difficulty breathing were encouraged to immediately seek medical assistance.

Things started to change. We were constantly watching the news and reading alerts and updating each other. The traditional close greetings were gone because we avoided close contact with each other. Strange looks were exchanged when someone did an everyday thing – like sneeze. The mood

[1] Copyright © 2020 Aguere Yilma Bultcha, Frannie Léautier, and Eléonore Immaculée Nyamwiza

Bultcha, A. Y., Léautier, F., and Nyamwiza, E. I. (2020). African women at work during a pandemic: Case of Muundo Barakoa. In M. N. Kinyanjui, R. Thaker, and K. Toure (Eds.), *Covid stories from East Africa and beyond: Lived experiences and forward-looking reflections* (pp. 183-191). Bamenda: Langaa.

was a mix of concern, to stay safe, and humour, to keep stress levels down. We referred to the coronavirus as "the virus" and tried to go about our lives as normally as possible.

A week later, on March 11, 2020, the World Health Organization (WHO) declared covid19 to be a pandemic. What really brought things home for us was when, two days later, the Minister of Health of Kenya announced that someone in Nairobi had contracted the coronavirus disease (covid19). This was the first case to be reported in Kenya since the beginning of the outbreak in China in December 2019.

It was hard to process that, in the space of a week, we had gone from travel restrictions to worrying about a global pandemic and being anxious about a live case right on our doorstep in Nairobi. Two days later, in his address to the nation, His Excellency President Uhuru Kenyatta confirmed two more cases of the coronavirus in Kenya and declared measures to be taken by the public, schools and universities, the government, and private companies.

That announcement brought things home to us even more clearly. Several of our teammates and their family members had come to Kenya in the 14 days before March 15, 2020, and they now needed to self-quarantine for 14 days from the date of their return to Kenya. All meetings were being handled virtually to comply with the physical distancing regulations of the WHO and the country. Hand sanitizers were everywhere. And one of us was pregnant and had to take special care.

In all of this, however, we were the lucky ones. We kept our jobs, we could work from home, and we had written confirmation that our health insurance company would cover for infection from covid19. The company was not applying the epidemic or pandemic exclusion for treatment associated with the novel coronavirus. We were assured that we had coverage for treatment for coronavirus and coronavirus symptoms just as for any other condition.

Working from home, we engaged via Zoom or Microsoft Teams, and life took on a somewhat normal rhythm. Our day-to-day concerns were about how to get unlimited data options to ensure we could work from home seamlessly, cell phones for all those who hadn't received a work-issued phone, and wireless internet solutions for those who didn't have a reliable connection at home. Our offices were being cleaned properly and equipment and surfaces sanitized. And nearly all of us could avoid public transport and ride-hailing services. We worried about our welfare but focused on productivity and staying safe.

Then one day, it occurred us that the recommended safety measures were not easy for most people around us to practice. Many people did not have access to running water to observe the very basic preventive measure of regularly washing hands with soap and water. Nor did they (yet) have access to alcohol-based hand sanitizers. Avoiding public transport is a kiss of death because that is almost the only way besides walking to get to work and to the market. Practicing physical distancing is a challenge given the crowded living conditions in many households and neighbourhoods. Maintaining good respiratory hygiene by wearing a mask was not affordable to many people. And to top it all, some people working as domestic staff, as cooks, cleaners, or gardeners, were asked to stay home or were released altogether from their services, because their employers worried about them contracting the virus and infecting their households.

From the moment government announced the first case of covid19 in Kenya, the fear of hearing the numbers grow every day arose in us. The dramatic situation of Italy obsessed us day and night. We thought, if this is the situation in developed countries in Europe and North America, how will Africa cope? It became routine for us to wake up, switch on the TV, watch the global news, and follow the press conferences of the Permanent Secretary and Minister of Health.

For one of us, a woman four months pregnant, every risk takes on another dimension. A single worry is multiplied by a hundred. The week after we were requested to work from home because of the covid19 guidelines, our pregnant colleague had to miss an appointment for a 3D scan at a medical imaging facility. The exciting prospect of seeing her baby in real time changed to anxiety. Plans were on hold. Times were uncertain. How would things evolve? Which hospital would be available for a delivery? This was her first child. Her plan was to bring her mother-in-law living in Rwanda to help. Would she be able to travel? How would the household manage without her? How would the grandmother feel if she could not be present to help welcome her grandbaby into the world?

Our colleague's situation made us think of other women out there, with their own struggles. Like Dutta, a housekeeper we know, who is a single mum. Before the pandemic, her three children were in boarding school. She could survive on her monthly salary, being at home alone with her grandmother. But with three more people at home, she struggled to meet the monthly expenses, even though her employer continued to pay her salary. The question on our minds was, how long will this pandemic last? That question was a call for us to think urgently and in a sustainable manner about how to support not only Dutta but also other women in similar situations.

We decided to do something. It started with one, then two, then three colourful masks. We were alternating between working one week in the office and the following week remotely from home, as required by our physical distancing rules. Our colleague Lucilla was looking after her now homeschooling child and working part-time at the office serving tea. One day, she showed two of us who were working from the office some masks she had sown. We found them very attractive. We told her we would buy all that she had and that if she could make more, we would take those too. She beamed with joy. The first people to get the masks were the security guards, the cleaners, and the drivers, for themselves and their children. They selected the colours and designs they preferred.

The demand was so high that we asked Dutta if she wanted to join Lucilla in making masks. Dutta started doing this from home, where she had to stay, to protect herself and her three children and grandmother. We sent Dutta photos and design criteria and models and told her how many masks we needed. She manufactured them to perfection.

Lucilla and Dutta were making masks with three layers, including a filter layer in the middle and beautiful cotton kitenge cloth with African motifs on the outward-facing side. The cut, folding, and finishing were so beautifully done, with great care. These women had an impressive sense of colour, pattern, and style. Such quality! Such creativity! They adeptly mixed and matched fabric remnants. Every day they came up with new designs. They had quickly pivoted to develop a new source of livelihood during the pandemic.

Marketing was via Facebook. We posted photos of masks and of us modelling them. We took orders from neighbours and co-workers. Then orders started flying in, including from abroad, with people asking where they could get these masks.

That is how Muundo Barakoa handmade designer masks, in the traditions of haute couture, was born. It is an example of a covid19 pandemic rapid response using local solutions to meet demands for protective equipment and gear.

We had reoriented our personal anxieties into an initiative for women and for African cities. We called the initiative Muundo Barakoa, which is Swahili for "design mask." We agreed on three main goals. First, identify in Nairobi promising ongoing local initiatives for the production of masks, gloves, and protective gear, what is commonly known as personal protective equipment (PPE). Second, leverage existing capacities for mass manufacturing and distribution of PPE and other manufactured products to assist in the protection of disadvantaged populations from covid19 infections. Third, link up and network with local and international stakeholders in select segments of PPE supply chains to enable local and regional responses to the demand for covid19 protective gear, with a particular focus on opportunities provided by the African Continental Free Trade Area (AfCTA).

Based on our local knowledge, we realized that Africa in general, and Kenya in particular, has local manufacturing capacity for textiles at three levels: (1) mass manufacturing in existing factories that could be retrofitted to make PPE for domestic and export markets; (2) smaller scale manufacturing drawing on existing design and tailoring capacity and linked with in-country distribution chains; and (3) informal business-to-client (B-C) manufacturing, responding to individual needs, of made-to-order masks, gowns, and gloves.

We learned that, for rapid and differentiated covid19 responses in Africa, it is imperative to adopt a variety of approaches that respond to local contexts and situations. We also learned that these local approaches help address the massive loss of jobs created by physical distancing. They help ensure livelihoods and incomes for daily-wage household workers, informal traders, and other "non-essential" employees who were furloughed, let go, or asked to stay home with no wages.

Muundo Barakoa was designed to match informal demand for PPE with supply chains to serve that demand. We drew on processes already in place and adapted them to do other things. We contacted seamstresses and tailors – who had made dresses for us in the past using local materials – and networked them with women who had lost their jobs and other seamstresses and tailors. This growing pool of people is producing PPE in line with WHO design standards for safety. We linked the initiative to women-led distribution channels for other goods, which became supply chains for Muundo Barakoa PPE products.

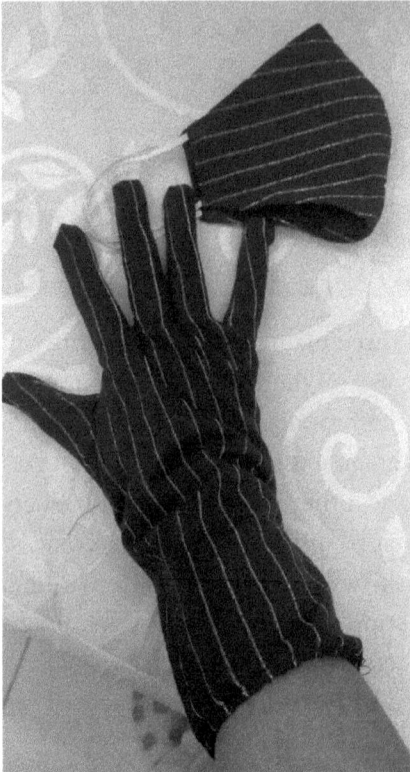

For such a complex project, one needs a coordination partner. We identified Pastoral Heritage Concern (PHC), an international non-profit organisation active in Kenya in capacity building and civic education for youth, women, persons living with disabilities, and albinos. PHC began coordinating production and distribution. They track where supplies are sourced, how the products are made, and to whom they are distributed. PHC is now a centrepiece of Muundo Barakoa. They help us get protective gear (masks and gloves) to people most affected by the pandemic in the informal sector of the economy and in Nairobi's informal settlements.

With a pool of one designer, 15 seamstresses and tailors, and 20 distributors, Muundo Barakoa had, within a couple months, distributed 10,000 masks to individuals with low income, underserved groups, and people leaving with disabilities. A similar initiative in Nairobi, run by renowned designer Ms. Deepa Dosaja, had distributed about 1,000 masks at about the same time.

This non-profit initiative is small compared to the need in Nairobi and indeed across eastern Africa and the entire continent. We are very conscious that it will not respond to all needs of those who suffer from structural discrimination, but we believe that even a small contribution at this time can save lives.

Muundo Barakoa has a long way to go, but we have a clear roadmap. We started working with a small group of women we knew in our daily lives, whose lives had been turned upside down. We involved colleagues, family, and friends in marketing very attractive locally-made masks and other products with African touches. We learned to scale local skills and capacity. We were astounded at and inspired by the adaptability and resiliency of our collaborators. This reinforced our determination to scale our collective efforts. Through multi-stakeholder partnerships, we are linking a small circle of workers in Nairobi to the broader chain of making PPE in Africa.

Covid19 started with one person infected in the city of Wuhan, a city and a name many of us had never heard of before the pandemic. Today, the virus has reached people of all walks of life, in communities and homes, and dramatically changed everyday life and economies. If we each do our part, we can make our way together through covid19. With all our hearts, we believe in the power of humanity, individual and collective creativity, and solidarity. We believe that what has been created in Muundo Barakoa will have lasting value after the covid19 crisis. This approach has demonstrated how to build an inclusive and sustainable social enterprise. Yes, together we can!

To learn more, please reach contact us at
MuundoBarakoa @ gmail.com

Ms. Aguere Yilma Bultcha *is Executive Assistant to the President and Chief Executive of the Trade and Development Bank (TDB). As a focal person to the Presidency, Ms. Bultcha is a hub for communication with senior government officials of the TDB member states. She is multilingual, including in French. She obtained her first degree in international relations and global studies, from New Generation University College in Addis Ababa. She also obtained an honours degree in international politics* *from the University of South Africa. She is finalizing her master's thesis in leadership and management.*

She has worked with Alliance Ethio Française *as a French teacher and, as Executive Associate/Office Manager, with Total Oil Company and the United Nations Development Programme. She served as team leader for the United Nations System-Wide Special Initiative on Africa. She also worked with the United States Agency for International Development in foreign disaster assistance. For the African Union Commission, she was the focal person and a jury member for the Kwame Nkrumah Scientific Awards, as well as focal person for the Global Monitoring for Environment and Security programme.*

Ms. Bultcha lends a helping hand to those often forgotten, making a difference for at least one person each day. Survivor of a car accident as a child that could have left her paralysed, sports (some daring ones) are among her hobbies, along with reading and cooking. She is a dedicated family person, who loves to travel, meet new people, and visit new places.

Dr. Frannie Léautier *is a finance and development professional, with long-standing global experience leading and transforming organisations in the private, public, and not-for-profit spheres. She held various leadership roles at the Trade and Development Bank (TDB) Group, including Vice Chair of the Board, first Independent Director on the TDB Board, and Special Advisor to the President, before becoming TDB's first Chief Operating Officer and then taking leadership of TDB's Asset Management business as its Executive Director. She was Senior Vice President at the African Development Bank and Vice President for nearly seven years at the World Bank Group. She recently joined SouthBridge Group as a Senior Partner.*

Dr. Léautier is known for her skills in operational management, transformational leadership, resource mobilisation, working with complex multi-constituency governance structures, and engaging with the highest levels of government. Her work has contributed to attracting innovative financing to Africa. She founded two companies and holds advisory and governance roles on several boards. She previously served on the board of the Nelson Mandela Institute for Science and Technology. She has authored several books and articles and lectured at Sciences Po, MIT, Harvard, and Tokyo University. She earned a master's in Transportation, a PhD in Infrastructure Systems, a doctorate in Humane Letters, and a doctorate in Law.

Ms. Eléonore Immaculée Nyamwiza *is Programme Coordinator in the Asset Management Department at the Eastern and Southern Africa Trade and Development*

Bank (TDB), stationed in its Regional Office in Nairobi. Her role involves engagement with service providers and Joint Venture Partners around fund management and administration issues, developing and managing the budgets of the department, and ensuring effective agenda-setting and smooth follow-up on strategic and governance-related meetings of the department.

Before joining the TDB Group in 2012, Ms. Nyamwiza was Human Resource officer at Oxfam Great Britain stationed in Haiti. She played a key role in the emergency recruitment of humanitarian personnel in response to the January 2010 earthquake. Working in Haiti helped her learn to manage in a crisis. This proved helpful in response to covid19; she took a lead in developing the Business Continuity Plan for the Asset Management Department at TDB. Prior to joining Oxfam, Ms. Nyamwiza was Administrative and Protocol Officer at the Embassy of the Republic of Kenya in Burundi, where she honed her diplomatic skills. She earned a master's in Project Management from the University of Salford in the United Kingdom and a Bachelor of Law from Lake Tanganyika University of Burundi. Ms. Nyamwiza is multilingual.

Engaging
systems

chapter 21

Rethinking Small-Scale Farming in Light of Covid[1]

Christopher Mubeteneh Tankou

With the outbreak of the covid19 pandemic, Cameroon has been brought to a lockdown. This has a lot of implications for the supply of food. A big concern regarding the restrictions enacted to control the spread of the virus is the flow of agricultural products from farms to consumers. The more these restrictions persist, the more the risk of food shortages. Shortages could materialize at any level of the food, feed, or livestock chain, with devastating consequences to both producers and consumers.

Impacts of the covid context on small-scale farming systems and society at large

The necessary containment measures put in place to limit the spread of coronavirus are profoundly impacting our food systems and exacerbating existing and longstanding economic inequalities and social injustices. The main suppliers of food are small-scale farmers. Their farm products are highly perishable. Many of the products cannot be stored due to the lack of appropriate equipment and products. Under such conditions, farmers could be forced to dish out their efforts at giveaway prices. Trade-offs could become particularly acute if farm production is severely constrained.

The pandemic has challenged many routines, and as a result many people will rediscover the value of small family farms and their healthy produce. The closure of and restrictions on informal and open-air markets are cutting off both sales outlets for farmers and provisioning channels for communities. Small-scale farmers face dilemmas. Those who happen to sell may do so at much reduced prices and end up spending their meagre income at drinking establishments and other leisure and entertainment

---

[1] Copyright © 2020 Christopher Mubeteneh Tankou
Tankou, C. M. (2020). Rethinking small-scale farming in light of covid. In M. N. Kinyanjui, R. Thaker, and K. Toure (Eds.), *Covid stories from East Africa and beyond: Lived experiences and forward-looking reflections* (pp. 195-199). Bamenda: Langaa.

centres that are enjoying the freedom to function following their recent official exemption from social and physical distancing measures. Some farmers, as resilient as they can be, are becoming very discouraged. Due to political and economic ideologies that threw the baby (farmers' produce) out with the bath water (restriction of sale to consumers due to the pandemic), the Western Highlands agroecological zone of Cameroon could go from being a regional breadbasket to a basket case. This would result in some farmers abandoning their businesses.

The farming system in the Western Highlands agroecological zone of Cameroon has changed over time. Before the devastating drop in the price of the major cash crops (coffee and cocoa) on the international market in the early nineties, the main cash crop of this zone was coffee. This crop usually occupied plots around the homestead and other land areas close to the home to assure efficient production. The proximity to the farms ensured accurate pest and nutrient management and, importantly, the ease of periodic harvest given that the maturity time of coffee berries is indeterminate. The health of one's coffee farm was highly related to the assurance and insurance of being able to borrow from others. This often went as far as families sponsoring children in institutions of learning on credit knowing that, after the harvest and sale of the coffee beans, the debt would be settled with no problem. The abrupt price drop in the early nineties was dramatic. Coffee prices were at record lows, even below costs of production, and coffee producers therefore faced a tightening cost-price squeeze. These challenges called for new strategies for farmers, the centrepiece of which was the substitution of coffee with more profitable crops.

This revolution can be understood through the mobility concept, which I have explored in my work[2]. The mobility of farmers during the coffee cash crop era was limited owing to the proximity of the coffee farms to the homestead. However, food crop farms (managed predominantly by the female segment of the household) were at some reasonable distance from the homestead and accounted for rural-rural mobility (from home to farm and vice-versa). The sale of coffee products did not require much movement because cooperatives were located in farmers' neighbourhoods,

[2] Tankou, C. M. (2013). *The interactions of human mobility and farming systems and impacts on biodiversity and soil quality in the Western Highlands of Cameroon.* Doctoral thesis, Leiden University (181 pages), http://hdl.handle.net/1887/22848

to facilitate engagement with them close to their homes and sites of production.

The more profitable substitutes for coffee in the area are cool-season crops like potatoes and cabbages. Most farmlands in the zone are situated between lowlands at about 1300 metres above sea level and highlands at altitudes between 1600 and more than 2000 metres above sea level. Coffee was commonly grown around the homestead situated mostly in the lowlands, but the cool-season substitutes require the highlands with the appropriate low temperatures for growth and development. The quest for limited farmlands in the higher altitudes provoked significant rural-rural mobility. Farmers were obliged to move from their lowland homesteads to grow cash crops at higher altitudes. The shift from coffee to cool-season cash crops resurrected devastated farmers due to the flexibility of these crops compared to coffee. These crops can be grown many times in a year; hence income is generated periodically as opposed to annually from coffee. These crops can also be consumed by farmer families as opposed to coffee which can only be sold. Many small-scale farmers transport their farm produce to urban markets where they can maximize profits. This results in significant rural-urban mobility.

The consequences of covid19 and the concomitant responses by governments and lawmakers are likely to harm people in segments of society that lack adequate resources and means to leap back after such catastrophic incidents. Small-scale farmers across Africa fit in this category. Covid19 has had significant negative effects on their lives.

Transport restrictions and quarantine measures have impeded farmers' access to input and output markets, curbing productive capacities and denying points of sale. Shortages of farm labour could disrupt the production and processing of food, notably for small-scale labour-intensive production systems. Food supply chains are disrupted; blockages to transport routes are particularly obstructive for fresh food supply chains and may also result in increased levels of food loss and waste.

Small-scale farmers are trapped to some extent, and many cannot profit from their farms. Consumers are equally trapped to the degree that they cannot access food to maintain their health. What a dilemma! The consequences include economic losses, which could limit the resiliency of small-scale farmers to continue their farming activities, and the deprivation of healthy foods, which could lead to malnutrition, starvation and even death among consumers, especially in cities. This would be in line with what Thomas Robert Malthus theorized in 1798 regarding how "positive checks" such as premature death from disease, starvation, or war limit population according to the availability of resources.

The covid19 crisis has dictated a paradigm shift in teaching, learning and evaluation. Educational institutions have realised the necessity of distance learning. Neglected before, it has become a cornerstone to continuity of education during the pandemic. In the same manner, the pandemic is revealing the importance of local food production systems. At this turning point, we must revisit our farming systems and integrate more home gardening.

Home gardening as an important part of African farming systems

Because almost everyone is quarantined, home gardening should become a hobby to counter the challenge of access to healthy foods. Home gardening is an old farming system that has provided and protected many households. Some years back, mixed farming – including both crop and animal rearing – was common. Such farming permits the family to procure a balanced diet, in a circular economy environment, where waste from one productive process serves another process. For example, in the Swine Quarters, as described by Francis Nyamnjoh[3], pigs in pigsties devour most forms of household refuse. This creates an agricultural biodiversity system less dependent on off-farm inputs (such as inorganic fertilizers and pesticides) and more economically and environmentally viable and sustainable. The decomposition of plant and animal wastes in the system results in fertile soil development. This ecological good permits the household to grow food with no dependence on costly inorganic fertilizers. Other outputs and benefits derived from home gardening, in addition to food, include clean air, raw materials used in other productive processes, and medicines.

Many households today still have large enough yards to accommodate a few seedbeds for fresh produce and space to raise small animal species such as rabbits and guinea pigs in addition to poultry. These gardens can grow most of the crops found in the markets: lettuce and other greens,

---

[3] *The Travail of Dieudonné* (2008), a novel by Francis B. Nyamnjoh (Nairobi: East African Educational Publishers, 172 pages), https://books.google.com/books?isbn=9966255575

peppers, tomatoes, plantains, bananas, maize, beans, herbs, etc. Most of these crops grow in a few months' time, and some allow harvests for about the same number of months it took to grow them. Home gardening has numerous advantages. These include containing the spread of covid by limiting the amount of time spent outside the house, saving time and resources previously invested in transport, and reducing monthly food expenses. In addition, gardeners have the opportunity to grow food organically. They monitor quality and can be confident that food is grown well. Gardening also puts people in contact with nature and is nurturing, thus reducing stress. Youths take on gardening responsibilities, benefit from intergenerational learning, and pick up skills that will serve them for their entire lives.

Another worthwhile option to consider in the face of this pandemic is the delivery of baskets of farm produce to customers' homes. Basket sales will surely grow during quarantine and help increase the profits of small-scale farmers. For consumers, they can reduce the need to leave home to shop.

People including decision makers at all levels should develop food practices and policies that support local agroecological food systems. Respect for those who produce food for communities, and in so doing care for the environment, should be at the forefront. Farmers should be able to procure up-to-date equipment such that farming consists of less drudgery and more dignity. Emphasis should also be placed on agricultural biodiversity, which is usually preferred by the local population and is a promising option for greater resilience in the face of the current economic and supply chain shocks.

A more just and sustainable food system must be based on the right of people to healthy and culturally appropriate food and their right to define their food and agriculture systems. The covid19 pandemic has caused us to pause to take a look at our systems and rethink them for the future

Christopher Mubeteneh Tankou *is Associate Professor in the Faculty of Agronomy and Agricultural Sciences (Department of Crop Science) at the University of Dschang in Cameroon. He is also Coordinator of the university's Centre for Distance Education.*

chapter 22

Evolving Story of Covid19 in Douala and Surrounding Towns[1]

Rose Chia Fonchingong

Covid19 left the confines of the medical world to become a social and political problem. Right from its entry and spread in Cameroon, there has been a deviation from the norms as far as prevention and case testing, tracing, and treatment are concerned. This short narrative explains my views on the approach to responding to covid19 in Cameroon.

How it began in Cameroon

When the SARS-CoV2 was spreading like wildfire in China and Europe, it was a regular news item on all local television channels. Social media was full of pictures of people dying in the corridors of hospitals in European countries. We read how in these hospitals, younger persons in respiratory distress were given preference over older persons for the limited number of ventilators. This frightened the medical corps because the required *plateaux techniques* or technological platforms for intensive care are not available in Cameroon. Not long after that, towards the end of February, we learned via social media about the first reported case of covid19 next door in Nigeria – and how the driver who picked the infected man up from the airport had disappeared into thin air. In as much as we laughed at the Nigerian situation, we knew that we should be expecting it at home.

On March 6, 2020, covid19 was announced to have arrived in Cameroon. The communiqué of the Minister of Public Health explained that a French national over 60 years of age was admitted to the Central Hospital of Yaoundé and that he was under good care. It also informed us that someone who was in contact with this person had been confirmed positive. Shortly after this announcement, what followed was very

---

[1] Copyright © 2020 Rose Chia Fonchingong

Fonchingong, R. C. (2020). Evolving story of covid19 in Douala and surrounding towns. In M. N. Kinyanjui, R. Thaker, and K. Toure (Eds.), *Covid stories from East Africa and beyond: Lived experiences and forward-looking reflections* (pp. 201-210). Bamenda: Langaa.

interesting: what I call the massive invasion of Cameroon by covid19 through the television.

The invasion of the novel coronavirus in Cameroon was visual. Those watching Cameroon Radio Television (CRTV) or other broadcasting houses in the country could see it, or at least hear about it. During the national televised news, we watched the Governor of the Littoral Region in Douala at the airport receive travellers who landed on Cameroonian soil on an Air France plane from Paris, France. We were told they were Cameroonians fleeing coronavirus who believed that SARS-CoV-2 could not survive the Cameroonian heat. To make matters worse, they were welcomed by the Governor as if they brought back trophies after performing some heroic acts for the nation. He even went as far as taking over private hotels and converting them into quarantine homes. Unfortunately, some hotel owners had lost trust in government and insisted that these prodigal sons and daughters of the soil pay for the rooms before occupation. After being refused accommodation in the designated hotels, these travellers went right back to the Governor's residence for him to intervene. We were not surprised to later learn that the Governor and his wife also caught the virus.

Cameroonians are tired of listening to government propaganda on issues with no action, so it was no surprise when hotel owners refused to lodge persons meant for quarantine. As would be expected, those with homes or relatives in town went home and others travelled to their hometowns.

The attitude of Cameroonians towards the presence of covid19

When coronavirus was still limited to Europe and China, many medical doctors came out to decry the fact that we did not have the minimum standards to manage covid19 cases. The Ministry of Public Health went ahead and reassured the masses that the Central Hospital of Yaoundé and Laquintinie Hospital in Douala were prepared to receive covid patients. One week after the arrival of our famous travellers from France, five of them tested positive for the virus.

Why did these Cameroonians, who know the situation in Cameroon, decide to leave state-of-the-art healthcare in France to return home for mediocrity? The truth is that they were not rushing to come and be treated in our hospitals. They, like the rest of us, thought this disease did not start in Africa so was not an African disease. We expected the disease to die down as it started. After all, China reported that they succeeded in controlling its spread across the country. It was believed to be a disease of the rich.

French physicians had started using hydroxychloroquine and other medications. This drug has been used for a long time to treat malaria, and my compatriots knew it would be available in Cameroon. Many believed the virus could not survive in Cameroon due to high temperatures. To add to this, it is generally believed that "flu" cannot kill people living in the tropics. These are some of the reasons why bushfallers, as Cameroonians who live in Europe and America are fondly called in the local slang, and other common Cameroonians did not take the disease seriously. To date, many still believe it is a disease of the rich.

Government action regarding the Air France passengers who brought in most of the early cases of covid19 also shows that government did not believe that Cameroonians would be infected; otherwise the passengers would have been quarantined under surveillance.

Response to covid

Back to my story on how this disease left the confines of the medical world to become a social and political issue. The response to any disease should be multisectoral and participatory, but the response in Cameroon became more or less political and partisan, with very little community involvement.

Early in February, the Minister of Public Health visited the Douala and Yaoundé international airports to ensure things were in place to screen passengers upon arrival. After all, we prepared for Ebola and SARS CoV1 in the same way, and no cases were identified. This was some sort of a window-dressing strategy to make people believe that we were prepared to fight SARS-CoV2. The entry of covid19 into Cameroon was neither through sea nor land. It came in by air – through the very points of entry that had been prepared.

It was believed that everyone who has covid19 is already symptomatic and needs to be in the hospital. The Central Hospital of Yaoundé and Laquintinie Hospital in Douala were selected for covid patients without ensuring their accommodation capacities. By the end of April, neither hospital had room to admit people who tested positive for covid and had symptoms of the disease. The prepared isolation sites, with only 20 beds each, were quickly overwhelmed.

I am tempted to say that, even though covid19 was going to eventually infect Cameroonians, its spread could have been contained had the government used a better approach.

Due to lack of well-prepared isolation sites, many people who brought in the virus disappeared into their family homes and villages. Even some symptomatic passengers refused to be confined because they were relatives of uniformed officers. It is even alleged that a uniformed officer took his wife out of one of the hotels that was accommodating travellers who either tested positive or had been in contact with an infected person. This couple subsequently infected the doctor who attended to them.

Covid19-related sigma and denial

One of the problems surrounding infection by the SARS-CoV2 virus is the associated stigma. Soon after confirming the first cases in Cameroon and till date, denial has been growing and presently has become a major contributor to the spread of the virus.

I chatted with a lady who was tested in one of the health facilities in Douala. Though asymptomatic, she was asked to isolate herself at home. Two days later, I saw this lady in the open market buying from some innocent vendor. She was not wearing a mask and was talking at very close range to the lady from whom she was buying tomatoes. I could not help but accost her to find out whether she deliberately wanted to infect everyone before being satisfied. The answer she gave really surprised me. She started by saying she was not infected. She then said she was on the Archbishop's treatment, which she believed worked wonders.

When I asked some people, who tested positive, why they were refusing to share their status with others, I received responses like: "I do not want to be discriminated at. I do not want to die alone. Even if I die, I'll want my parents to see and take care of my corpse." The simple truth is that covid19 has become synonymous with death. Even after continuous education, using all possible channels to share information with the masses, there has been very little behaviour change among Cameroonians.

To crown the fears, many persons who are admitted to the hospital with respiratory distress do end up dying. In Douala, the Deido Grand Moulin cemetery has become notorious for night burials. These night burials carried out by specially clothed people, with family members hanging around outside the fence of the cemetery, are a major contributor to the spread of rumours and fear. The inhabitants of the Grand Moulin quarters in Deido will tell you that the number of covid19-related deaths at the Laquintinie Hospital are higher than the reported deaths just by counting the daily burials by the special squad.

At times I share the fear and am also in denial. We were not prepared by the government to know that, unlike for other diseases, when you die of covid, your body is buried immediately by a special squad. No special burial ground has been prepared to bury the victims, so much so that we do not know where corpses are disposed. Most public cemeteries are full, and the squad quickly buries corpses with no respect for human dignity, sometimes in graves already occupied by another corpse. All of this is strongly against our customs and cultural practices.

More public education and sensitization should have taken place to explain why the bodies of those who expire from covid need to be buried immediately and under special conditions. The consequence of the lack of education and communication is that many family members of deceased persons have been arrested at burial grounds exhuming their loved ones who were buried unceremoniously by the squad. Another consequence is that people seek out traditional practitioners or informal healers if they suspect they might have covid, or, from a fear of stigmatisation, they disappear into thin air if they go for testing and the results come back positive.

Medical response

The confirmatory tests can be carried out in very few laboratories in Cameroon. At the outset, only one laboratory, based in Yaoundé, could carry out the tests. Subsequently, testing was decentralised to the regions. In the Southwest Region, testing only started toward the end of May, and tests are not available in sufficient numbers. Interestingly, many collected samples are stockpiled in laboratories, thus contributing to the spread of covid, because only persons with positive test results can receive any form of treatment. Fortunately, the rapid test kits, although not very sensitive, have been used to identify positive cases.

Before Cameroon saw its first covid19 patient, doctors could be seen on television discussing how prepared the Ministry of Public Health and its hospitals were to handle cases. It then clearly emerged that Cameroon had fewer than 20 ventilators and that these apparatuses were only found in a few private and public hospitals in Douala and Yaoundé. As medical personnel learned more about the disease, its progression, and how to treat it, they learned more about the appropriateness, or not, of ventilators, depending on the condition of the patient, and how to monitor patients on them.

It also came out that the country had few anaesthesiologists, doctors, and nurses. The rising mortality rate in Cameroon constantly highlights this shortage. Presently, the designated hospitals including and in addition to the Central Hospital of Yaoundé and Aquitaine Hospital in Douala are overwhelmed. There is no protective gear for the nurses and doctors. The infrastructure, mainly old colonial buildings without respect of building norms, is inadequate to manage these patients. Some wards have been converted to covid wards.

I heard the testimony of a patient who said that, in a six-bed ward in which he was admitted, five persons died over his four-day stay. He called for his employer to intervene and take him to a private clinic so he could survive. He said that even if coronavirus did not kill him, just the trauma of seeing people dying would have killed him.

The Minister of Public Health claims that treatment is free, but the only thing that is free is the test, hydroxychloroquine, and azithromycin. Patients must pay for every other service including ventilators, which were in use until hospitals were provided with oxygen masks sometime in May. In those days, given the scarcity of the ventilators, patients in respiratory distress who needed resuscitation but could not afford to pay for the use of a ventilator ended up dying. The very first Cameroonian coronavirus-infected medical doctor died for lack of an available ventilator. I met a 24-year-old young man with air hunger and severe chest pain. He told me that he was asked to make available 150,000 CFA francs (about $300) for a privately owned ventilator. This boy was not even in the ward because he had to go looking for money for his treatment. I do not want to imagine how many people he infected on that day and what happened to him.

The quality of care in the designated public health facilities leaves much to be desired, and that is why those who can afford it end up in private clinics. It is rather unfortunate that some of these private health facilities financially exploit patients. Cameroon has no national health insurance scheme, and about 80% of health financing is out-of-pocket and paid for by households. One private clinic was suspended and the doors sealed by the administration for issuing astronomical bills to a covid19 patient. This action, however, has not stopped persons with means from paying significant amounts for services.

As for those who cannot afford care in the private nor the public hospitals, they start taking all types of mixtures (lemon, ginger, garlic, honey, turmeric, pawpaw leaves, guava leaves, etc.). They cover themselves and inhale the steam. All sorts of treatments for covid19 are circulating on social media. Traditional practitioners and quacks are doing brisk business, producing all types of concoctions and selling them to hapless persons. They challenge health personnel, saying they are not capable of treating coronavirus patients. They forget that, when some of these persons end up in respiratory distress, they are rushed to the hospital and not to them.

Churches and many men of God have been organising prayers either online or one-on-one for patients who are religiously inclined. The most recent treatment is a plant-based production by the priest Archbishop Kleda. It has not yet been subject to a randomized study, although some patients claim it has helped relieve severe respiratory distress.[2] A colleague who tested positive for SARS-CoV2 and had breathing difficulties confessed to me that after taking the herbs for three days, his symptoms disappeared. Although the four Catholic hospitals in which this treatment is dispensed were not among those designated by the Ministry of Public Health, they have by default become covid treatment centres.

Since covid19 started spreading in Cameroon, hospital attendance has dropped, because many Cameroonians believe that hospitals are spreading the virus. The most affected sites are the so-called covid treatment centres, where doctors have been known to have contacted the virus and died.

---

[2] Cameroon's Ministry of Scientific Research Innovation, in collaboration with the Ministry of Public Health, is working with the Archbishop to carry out research on the efficiency of his treatment produced from medicinal plants.

Prevention of the spread of SARS-CoV2

The Cameroonian government has played the role of coordination very well, with the Prime Minister (Head of Government) and his cabinet coming out to regulate and give directions on how the population should prevent the spread of the virus through a 7-point strategy and subsequent 13 directives. This was welcome. It reassured the public that the government is taking things in hand to limit the spread of the virus as much as possible.

Unfortunately, the government failed to get people involved. Participation can go a long way in promoting measures and finding solutions when it comes to physical distancing, travel between regions, the closure of business places, and the use of protective gear in the general population.

Billboards line streets in the major towns, educating us on how to prevent covid19. Good handwashing practices are demonstrated on television, as is the use of hand sanitizer. There are videos on social media about how to use the mask. These are good initiatives if properly carried out by the population.

To ensure community engagement and see changes in behaviour, we need to involve the persons being protected. In this case, instructions were dished out by the government, and the next day we saw the mayors of the different constituencies going into action. One of the newly elected mayors of a constituency, in a bid to show his party his industriousness, positioned tanks of water at the entrances to his council area. He then convened the police and council workers. Instead of educating people on handwashing, people were forced to come out of their cars and dip their hands in the water, to show respect of the handwashing order, before continuing their journey. Interestingly, those water cans are still there, and nobody stops to wash their hands when the forces of law and order are not there.

Another example of a failed prevention strategy is the pseudo-lockdown in Cameroon. In mid-April, a Presidential decision came out limiting movements between towns and limiting the number of passengers to be carried in commercial vehicles. It also contained a decision on bars and restaurants, which were to open only during the day and close at 6 pm. This decision led us to wonder aloud whether our decision makers thought that the coronavirus could only be spread at night. We also realised that public buses were permitted to carry infected persons from one town to another, provided that the buses were not crowded.

People respected most of these decisions, because during this period the number of covid-related deaths increased, and there was real fear because well known people died of covid. Fear was also instilled by rumours. Two weeks after the beginning of the lockdown, the Prime Minister lifted it: bars and drinking spots would function like before, and public transport could continue with the usual overloading.

Of course, with the relaxation of the lockdown, there has been a steady climb in the number of infected persons. Many Cameroonians related the relaxation of the lockdown measures to the end of the coronavirus crisis. Some even went as far as saying that covid does not exist and that the government wanted to use the lockdown to kill Cameroonians. Some felt that because public transport companies and many businesses are government-owned, the lockdown caused the government to lose too much income. Cameroonians love drinking alcohol, in particular beer brewed by La Brasseries du Cameroon. According to social media, this company pushed the government to relax the lockdown. After all, when Cameroonians drink, they forget to criticize the government.

The government even used covid to impose its supremacy. Test kits and basic materials to fight covid are scarce, but the government rejected a donation from a group of people who support an opposing political party. Such responses increase the prevalence of conspiracy theories. Some even claim that Cameroon wants the number of infected persons to increase in order to receive money from international organizations. To seemingly confirm this, the President of the Republic, who stayed quiet throughout the onset of the spread of the virus, only came out one month after the first case was announced to collect financial support from the French ambassador to Cameroon. Soon after, we also read about a loan from the IMF.

People in all regions of Cameroon have contracted coronavirus. The very sick, for fear of dying abandoned and having no one to bury them in the big city of Yaoundé or Douala, prefer to go and die with their families. Hence, when they suspect that they have been infected, they leave town and head for their villages. That is how the virus has spread all over the country. When contacts of people who tested positive suspect that they might be infected, they prefer to go to any hospital other than where the victim was diagnosed. During the consultation, they hide their symptoms from unsuspecting ill-protected healthcare providers and thereby also infect them. Presently almost 200 healthcare providers have been infected. In the early days, at least three medical doctors and two nurses died.

This short narration relates what I observed once coronavirus entered Cameroon. No one was prepared, be it the population, the health system, or the government. The response became a political game with the ruling party exerting its powers at every opportunity. Cameroonians expected that the spread of the infections would be contained, because those who brought in the virus were known. However, due to a lack of organization and preparedness, these people went into towns and villages and infected uninformed community members. Covid has exposed the poor situation of the health system in Cameroon from the top of the pyramid right down to the periphery. No doubt, members of government and persons with means had never been treated in our hospitals, because they seek treatment abroad. This time, they were caught "pants down" and were admitted into dirty wards without running water. For the first time, their money is entering hospital coffers. It is high time for the government to implement all the strategies that are so well recorded in the strategic plan and to meet the health financing goal set out in the Abuja Declaration of allocating 15% of the national budget to health.

If one has to evaluate the impact of sensitisation and all other prevention measures put in place so far, it is evident that population behaviour change has not occurred. The virus is now spreading like wildfire, and recently the Prime Minister released yet another decision asking all drinking and recreation spots and places to close at midnight. There has not been community involvement or engagement in decision making. To curb the pandemic in Cameroon, we need to start discussing with community members. We do not need force but communication with all stakeholders. There is a health system in place. It is time we start using it.

Rose Chia Fonchingong is a *medical doctor and author of* Stifled by Justice: Detained for Six Years Without Judgement, *published by Langaa in 2016. She lives in Bua in the Southwest Region of Cameroon.*

chapter 23

Covid19 and Violent Extremism in Somalia[1]

Tabitha W. Mwangi

What leaders really do is prepare
organizations for change and help them
cope as they struggle through it.[2]

The covid19 crisis has unleashed unprecedented changes across the world in 2020. As governments work to curb the spread of the coronavirus, terrorist organizations have taken advantage of the diversion of governments' resources and attention from state security to human security, through provision of social services such as healthcare, to conduct attacks, recruit young people,[3] and spread their ideologies.

In Somalia, the federal government faces a complex challenge in dealing with the pandemic because al Shabaab (an al Qaeda affiliate) controls some territory. Consequently, the government is unable to collect data on the number of covid19 cases or serve communities living in the areas controlled by the group. The militant group has sought to remain relevant to the general Somali population by posing as a solution provider, yet there is a legitimate government responsible for responding to the pandemic situation. Leaders have a duty to help the nation and its people cope with challenges and changes, such as those brought on by the pandemic. The government of Somalia must demonstrate effective leadership by working to unite people, investing in social service provision systems, and promoting youth programs, lest young people fall prey to extremism during these challenging times.

[1] Copyright © 2020 Tabitha W. Mwangi
Mwangi, T. W. (2020). Covid19 and violent extremism in Somalia. In M. N. Kinyanjui, R. Thaker, and K. Toure (Eds.), *Covid stories from East Africa and beyond: Lived experiences and forward-looking reflections* (pp. 211-215). Bamenda: Langaa.
[2] "What leaders really do," by John P. Kotter, in *Harvard Business Review*, December 2001, https://enterprisersproject.com/sites/default/files/What Leaders Really Do.pdf
[3] "Youth, violent extremist recruitment, and covid-19 in Kenya," by Rukaya Mohamed, Ardian Shajkovci, Allison McDowell-Smith, and Mohamed Ahmed, 22 June 2020, www.hstoday.us/subject-matter-areas/counterterrorism/youth-violent-extremist-recruitment-and-covid-19-in-kenya

Al Shabaab's changing rhetoric about covid19

At first, al Shabaab released an audio message, in April 2020, stating that covid19 was a punishment from Allah to non-Muslims, which should be celebrated.[4] However, as cases of covid19 started being reported in Somalia, al Shabaab leadership pulled another tactic out of its hat, referring to reports by international health experts about the dangers of covid19. In June, in another radio statement, it was announced that the al Shabaab coronavirus prevention and treatment committee had set up a covid19 centre "about 380 km south of the capital Mogadishu" to treat those affected by the virus and that vehicles were available "to transport suspected coronavirus patients."[5]

Al Shabaab's changing standpoint on the covid19 crisis was a political move to gain popular support. The assertion that the virus was a punishment to non-Muslims was made at a time when the virus had not yet hit the African continent. It was a call to rally people to support al Shabaab's political ideology by using Islam, which is the dominant religion in Somalia, to widen their pool of supporters as much as possible. This is not a new tactic. The group claims to adhere to strict interpretations of Islam but in action defies the very core of Islamic teachings. Al Shabaab actions are full of contradictions. For instance, the group collaborates with commercial sex workers in Nairobi to get access to intelligence from law enforcement officers[6] on the one hand and on the other severely punishes Somalis engaged in adultery. Furthermore, there have been claims of pornographic materials and prophylactics found in al Shabaab camps by security agencies.[7]

---

[4] "Al-Shabaab call Muslims to rejoice in 'punishment' of covid-19 infected non-Muslims, as virus survey highlights Somali religious divisions," https://news.barnabasfund.org/Al-Shabaab-call-Muslims-to-rejoice-in--punishment--of-Covid-19-infected-non-Muslims--as-virus-survey-highlights-Somali-religious-divisions--/index.html

[5] "Somalia's al-Shabab 'sets up covid-19 treatment center'," updated 14 June 2020, www.arabnews.com/node/1689521/world

[6] "Worth many sins: Al-Shabaab's shifting relationship with Kenyan women," by Katharine Petrich and Phoebe Donnelly, published 2019 in *Small Wars and Insurgencies*, Volume 30, Issue 6-7 on Gender, Insurgency and Terrorism, pages 1169-1192, https://doi.org/10.1080/09592318.2019.1649814

[7] "Security agencies find porn, condoms and booze in al-Shabaab sex camp," by Hilary Kimuyu, 20 September 2017, https://nairobinews.nation.co.ke/news/kdf-find-porn-condoms-booze-al-shabaab-sex-camp-photos

The June 2020 message about the covid19 treatment centre south of the capital city was meant to show the community that al Shabaab cared about the wellbeing of people and would, in a show of solidarity, provide healthcare services. This technique has to do with identifying, acting on, and communicating about "mutuality of concern."[8] Mutuality of concern is the convergence of goals or aspirations of a group with those of an individual or group that faces the same situation. The logic goes like this: If al Shabaab could make itself useful to people in treating coronavirus, perhaps it could draw more people into its fold.

What the focus of the Government should be

During a crisis such as the covid19 pandemic, leaders must work to unite their followers by doing all that they can to help them understand and cope with the changes taking place. Consequently, corruption allegations regarding covid19 donations being sold in Mogadishu damage the public perception of the government.[9] In a country where al Shabaab rose from the Islamic Courts Union,[10] a group of Sharia law courts that was seen as a platform for justice, the government has a duty to effectively counter corruption to maintain legitimacy, especially because the 2020 elections have been pushed to 2021.[11] [12]

What should the government do? First, the government must maintain public support by promoting peace, security, and development by investing

---

[8] "Mutuality of concern: A key ingredient for team success," by AJ Powell, in *The Warfighter Journal*, www.warfighterjournal.com/2015/10/27/mutuality-of-concern-a-key-ingredient-for-team-success

[9] "Somalia: Former president alleges loss of covid-19 donations to black market in Mogadishu," 15 may 2020, www.garoweonline.com/en/news/somalia/somalia-former-president-alleges-loss-of-covid-19-donations-to-black-market-in-mogadishu

[10] The Islamic Courts Union "provided security and managed crime after the fall of Siad Barre's authoritarian regime," which was in place from 1969 to 1991. See Islamic Courts Union section of Stanford University's "Mapping Militant Organizations," last updated February 2019, https://cisac.fsi.stanford.edu/mappingmilitants/profiles/islamic-courts-union

[11] "Somali elections won't take place on schedule," by Harun Maruf, 28 June 2020, www.voanews.com/africa/somali-elections-wont-take-place-schedule

[12] Democratisation on hold in Somalia as first-past-the-post election is postponed," by Associate Professor of International Relations Fatuma Ahmed Ali and PhD candidate Doreen Muyonga, both of the United States International University-Africa, 20 July 2020, https://theconversation.com/democratisation-on-hold-in-somalia-as-first-past-the-post-election-is-postponed-142665

in systems to ensure access to healthcare, water, education, food, etc. because access to human security is essential for sustainable peace and development. This will require continued efforts through collaboration between the Somali National Army and other partners such as the African Union Mission to Somalia (AMISOM) to take over al Shabaab-controlled areas. This will put the government in a position to have credible information on the covid19 situation in Somalia.

Second, the virus has resulted in the closure of businesses and massive unemployment, so the government should provide tax breaks and basic needs for the most vulnerable families. In addition, the government should come up with youth-friendly programs to equip young people with skills to make them more likely to get employed and provide a stimulus package for small businesses.

Third, a lot of young people are idle, thus spending more time online, which exposes them to content from extremist groups such as al Shabaab. Therefore, the government should collaborate with the international communication, technology companies, and cybersecurity experts to detect, identify, and remove extremist content.

Fourth, women and girls are at increased risk of gender-based violence, including domestic violence, and need protection because they are spending more time at home due to the closure of schools and businesses. Women and girls living in camps for internally displaced persons and/or "from minority clans and marginalized communities face heightened risks of SGBV [sexual and gender-based violence], including abduction, forced marriage and rape," thus special support is needed.[13] This will require a rethinking of the proposed Sexual Intercourse Related Crimes Bill, given its problematic proposals that include leeway for child marriage and lack of clarity on how to protect victims and witnesses.[14]

Finally, the government must ensure that human rights for all are protected and be transparent about the management of resources. This entails arresting and prosecuting corrupt officials diverting resources from

---

[13] "Somalia country preparedness and response plan (CPRP): UN and partners' support towards the immediate humanitarian and socio-economic consequences of covid-19," April 2020,
https://reliefweb.int/sites/reliefweb.int/files/resources/Somalia%20COVID-19%20Country%20Preparedness%20and%20Response%20Plan.pdf
[14] "Somalia: Draft law a 'major setback' for victims of sexual violence," 11 August 2020,
https://news.un.org/en/story/2020/08/1070022

the covid19 kitty to their personal accounts or engaged in the sale of donated items, which undoubtedly is an uphill task because even more developed countries in the region are struggling with corruption. Even so, it can be done with enough political will.

Security in the greater of Horn of Africa region depends on security in Somalia

As long as there exist ungoverned and unregulated physical and virtual spaces in the governance of Somalia, there will always exist internal challenges in dealing with crises such as the covid19 pandemic and violent extremism. These challenges pose a threat to greater peace, security, and development in the greater Horn of Africa region. As such, neighbouring countries, regional organizations, and the international community have a duty to support the government of Somalia in ensuring both state and human security as a way of fighting violent extremism.

Tabitha W. Mwangi, *with a background in counterterrorism, homeland security, and international relations, currently heads the Security Program at the Center for International and Security Affairs in Kenya, coordinating research, policy formulation, learning forums, and trainings. Ms. Mwangi has been involved in projects to counter violent extremism, through engagement with government agencies and nongovernmental organizations. Her research interests span national and international security, counterterrorism, violent extremist groups, cybersecurity, and cyberterrorism. Her current research focuses on the role of the private sector in humanitarian assistance for internally displaced persons in North East Nigeria.*

Le confinement dû à la covid19 nous rend-t-il plus humain ?[1]

Nelkem Jeannette Londadjim

Le confinement dû à la maladie covid19 nous rend-t-il plus humain ? Cette question, je ne peux m'empêcher de me la poser. Comme beaucoup l'ont sans doute aussi vécu, tout s'est arrêté brusquement ! On disait que c'est en Chine que la maladie sévit. Mais la Chine n'est pas tout près, même si beaucoup de chinois « se sont faits proches » non pas à la manière du Samaritain[2] mais plutôt comme des hommes d'affaires pour ne pas dire des « nouveaux prédateurs » de nos richesses africaines. Un ami les a surnommés « nos nouveaux colonisateurs… ». Ceci pour dire comment certains Africains voient aujourd'hui les Chinois.

Tant que le coronavirus était en Chine, ce n'était pas encore notre problème. Voilà que tout d'un coup, il est arrivé aussi chez nous en Europe et puis en Afrique. On ne l'attendait pas si tôt ! Et pourtant… c'est aussi cela, la mondialisation ! Un grand sage de notre époque l'a dit : « Tout est lié[3] » ! Si tout est lié, ce qui arrive à l'humanité dans un bout de la planète m'atteint aussi à l'autre bout de la planète. De fait, en un rien de temps, les villes puis les pays sont devenus déserts et silencieux, un peu comme figés par cet « ennemi invisible » qui, de première vue, ne choisit pas ses cibles par la couleur de leur peau, leur race, ou leur statut social. Tous les humains sur la planète avaient à faire face à un combat, à une lutte commune : se protéger du virus d'où la décision rapide de confinement. Pour se protéger ? Peut-être…

---

[1] © 2020 Nelkem Jeannette Londadjim
Londadjim, N. J. (2020). Le confinement dû à la covid19 nous rend-t-il plus humain ? Dans M. N. Kinyanjui, R. Thaker, et K. Toure (Dir.), *Covid stories from East Africa and beyond: Lived experiences and forward-looking reflections* (p. 217-220). Bamenda : Langaa.
[2] Voir dans la Bible le récit de Saint Luc (chapitre 10, versets 25-37) sur le bon Samaritain.
[3] Pape François dans *Laudato si* (2015), www.vatican.va/content/francesco/fr/encyclicals/documents/papa-francesco_20150524_enciclica-laudato-si.html

Ce temps suspendu, pourrait-on dire, est rempli de petites histoires heureuses ou malheureuses, paraboles de vie qui, mises bout à bout, finissent par raconter une histoire qui a du sens. Comme le disait quelqu'un :

> Si les usines, les magasins et bureaux ont fermé leurs portes, je peux dire que les cœurs se sont ouverts. Qui n'a pas partagé à son voisin, à ses proches, des expressions comme celles-ci :« Prenez soin de vous », « Faites attention à vous, mais aussi aux autres ».

On entend et on lit cette dernière expression partout. C'est à croire qu'une nouvelle culture est née : la culture du soin, de l'attention, et du souci de l'autre. Comme ça fait du bien d'être témoin de cela ! J'ai l'impression que l'épreuve nous humanise et que ce qui devient premier, c'est protéger l'humain, se rendre utile aux autres… aider, partager.

Une femme africaine migrante à Paris, logée avec ses deux enfants dans un hôtel social en attendant, comme d'autres d'ailleurs, ses papiers de séjour, m'a expliqué que :

> Le confinement est un mal nécessaire. D'une part, c'est pour protéger nos vies, d'autre part, c'est un mal parce qu'il y a plusieurs effets négatifs. Par exemple, les familles comme nous, logées temporairement à l'hôtel, n'ont pas de moyens pour l'épanouissement de nos enfants. Nous sommes souvent plongées dans l'angoisse. Je dirais que c'est un calvaire pour nous les parents qui vivons à l'hôtel ! Cela permet de passer plus de temps avec nos enfants, et c'est bien. Mais d'un autre côté, il est difficile de tenir deux ou trois enfants hyperactifs dans un espace de cinq mètres carrés. Il n'y a pas d'espace, pas d'activités qui permettent aux enfants de dépenser leur trop d'énergie, ce qui les aiderait, le soir venu, de vite s'endormir. Du coup, cela fait de longues journées où les enfants ont du mal à s'endormir. Les enfants demandent à la maman, qui est seule à s'en occuper, d'être aussi constamment mobilisée, sans pouvoir elle-même souffler ou se poser un peu pour un moment de calme nécessaire à l'équilibre psychique de l'adulte.

Le confinement a été un temps pour aller à l'essentiel : être à l'écoute, se faire proche des personnes les plus vulnérables, prendre soin de ceux qu'on aime et de ceux qui sont seuls. Dans nos grandes villes, si le virus tue, durant le confinement, la solitude a sans doute fait beaucoup de ravages. Dans les épreuves, il y a des priorités auxquelles on cherche toujours à répondre surtout quand ça touche des personnes en précarité. Pour moi, avec le Secours Catholique[4], ça a été de maintenir des liens, coûte que coûte, avec les familles migrantes, ou non, logées dans les hôtels sociaux. Grâce au téléphone portable, cet outil, à la fois merveilleux et parfois diabolique (puisqu'on s'en sert aussi pour faire le mal), nous avons pu maintenir des liens de solidarité, organiser de l'aide, et secourir ceux qui étaient atteints et ne pouvaient s'en sortir seuls.

Je passais donc des heures au téléphone pour écouter des mamans frustrées ou même déprimées, prête à se jeter par la fenêtre me disaient l'une d'elles, pour abandonner son petit garçon qu'elle ne supportait plus de voir comme ça. Son garçon a une maladie qui le retarde dans sa croissance et il a un retard dans le langage. Il a des séances d'orthophonistes qui l'aident bien mais avec le confinement, ses séances s'étaient arrêtées. Peu à peu, en parlant au téléphone, en sollicitant des recettes de cuisine, en l'invitant à raconter sa vie, le goût de la vie a repris le dessus. Oui, avoir besoin de l'autre, de ses talents, lui a redonné le goût de vivre, d'avoir à nouveau des projets pour elle-même, pour son gamin. Finalement, grâce au téléphone, il y a eu un essai de séance à distance pour son fils.

Le confinement a ouvert nos yeux non pas sur le monde, mais sur « des mondes » que l'on côtoie sans voir. S'intéresser aux plus vulnérables en les rejoignant sur le champ de leurs décombres que nous ne voulions pas voir, invoquant souvent le manque de temps, a révélé nos sentiments ou indifférences vis-à-vis des gens qui vivent des situations différentes des nôtres. Les barrières qui séparent les riches des pauvres ne sont pas seulement extérieures à nous, elles sont aussi intérieures à nous : qui ne s'est jamais défendu d'être ouvert et accueillant ? Et pourtant, dans le concret des situations, on éprouve des résistances, parce que la différence et l'inconnu font toujours peur.

Durant ce confinement pour se protéger, je ne peux m'empêcher de m'émerveiller aussi devant l'engagement de tant de gens, en particulier des jeunes. Je pense à tous ceux qui sont allés à la rencontre des « sans domicile » dans les rues devenues désertes, pour leur offrir des soins, des vivres. Ou encore à ceux qui se sont portés volontaires, grâce aux remontées téléphoniques, pour offrir une formation pédagogique aux enfants venant de la rue, hébergés dans des hôtels avec leurs mamans, ou pour porter des

---

[4] Secours Catholique est une organisation non gouvernementale Catholique qui lutte contre la pauvreté et pour un monde juste et fraternel.

sacs de repas aux personnes âgées isolées, ou pour que sais-je encore ! En peu de temps, l'intelligence collective a fonctionné et la mutualisation des forces a fait des miracles pour le bien des personnes.

Bref, beaucoup de gens ont offert leur disponibilité pour aller à la rencontre des plus vulnérables, pour les servir, et ainsi les empêcher de sombrer dans la solitude ou dans des « misères humaines » multiples. Que deviendront toutes ces rencontres, ces attentions, ces liens tissés au fil des jours au téléphone, relayés parfois par des rencontres physiques ? Je ne sais pas trop, mais j'en suis certaine, ces liens tissés laisseront le « goût de l'autre ».

Oui, si les barrières de protection sont visibles, les personnes qui étaient invisibles avant la crise sont devenues visibles. C'est comme si la société découvrait pour la première fois le travail des personnes peu considérées. J'ai eu l'impression qu'on sortait d'un long sommeil, pour découvrir la vie simple, la vie qui est là, et qu'il faut défendre et protéger coûte que coûte. La crise sanitaire de la covid19 fera date. Elle aura marqué nos recherches de cohérence et d'unité dans nos relations humaines. Désormais, ce ne sont plus les promeneurs d'animaux qui font connaissance parce que leurs animaux les y ont entraînés, mais les gens se parlent parce qu'ils se découvrent voisins ou habitent le même quartier. Tout s'est arrêté ? C'est vrai ! Mais nous nous sommes aussi arrêtés. Cela nous a permis de « voir clair » pour reprendre une expression ivoirienne, et québécoise, pour que notre attention se porte sur l'autre, pour en prendre soin. Humain, nous nous nourrissons de la vie, les uns des autres, et ce sont ces liens maladroitement tissés, ou bien soignés, qui sont chemins d'Humanité !

Nelkem Jeannette Londadjim, *Sœur de Saint-Joseph et militante des Droits de l'homme, vit actuellement en France. Elle est membre de Justice et Paix France et travaille comme bénévole au Secours Catholique Caritas France avec les familles « sans papiers » hébergées dans les hôtels sociaux en les accompagnant dans le développement de leur « pouvoir d'agir », y compris pendant cette période de covid19. Avant cela, en Algérie, elle s'est efforcée de faciliter les relations entre les Algériens autochtones et les populations réfugiées et migrantes du pays. Elle a été en 2017 activiste en résidence à l'Université Avila à Kansas City aux États-Unis. Elle a également été active au sein de l'organisation non gouvernementale qui porte les préoccupations des Sœurs de Saint-Joseph au sein de divers organes et agences des Nations Unies pour discussion et action.*

Does Confinement Due to Covid19 Make Us More Human?[1]

Translated from French *

Nelkem Jeannette Londadjim

Does confinement due to the covid19 pandemic make us more human? I can't help but ask myself this question. Like so many others around the world, I experienced how everything stopped so abruptly! We heard that the disease was rampant in China. But China is not close by, even if many Chinese have approached Africa, not in the manner of the Samaritan[2] but as businessmen, not to say "new predators" interested in our riches. A friend nicknamed them "our new colonizers." This is to say how some Africans perceive some Chinese today.

As long as the coronavirus was in China, it wasn't our problem. All of a sudden, it came to us in Europe and then went to Africa. We didn't expect it so soon! And yet... that's what globalization is! A great sage of our time said it: "Everything is linked![3]" If everything is linked, what happens to humanity at one end of the planet also reaches me at the other end of the planet. In fact, in no time at all, cities and then countries became deserted and silent, as if frozen by this "invisible enemy" that, at first sight, does not choose its targets by the colour of their skin, their race, or their social status. All humans on the planet had to face a fight, a common struggle: to protect each other from the virus, hence the rapid decisions regarding confinement. To protect ourselves? Perhaps...

This suspended time, one might say, is filled with little happy or unhappy stories, parables of life, which, put together, end up telling a story that makes sense. I have heard people around me say the following:

[1] Copyright © 2020 Nelkem Jeannette Londadjim
Londadjim, N. J. (2020). Does confinement due to covid19 make us more human? In M. N. Kinyanjui, R. Thaker, and K. Toure (Eds.), *Covid stories from East Africa and beyond: Lived experiences and forward-looking reflections* (pp. 221-225). Bamenda: Langaa.
[2] See in the Bible the account of Saint Luke (chapter 10, verses 25-37) about the Good Samaritan.
[3] Pope Francis in *Laudato si* (2015), www.vatican.va/content/francesco/en/encyclicals/documents/papa-francesco_20150524_enciclica-laudato-si.html

> If factories, stores, and offices have closed, I can say that hearts have opened. Who hasn't shared with their neighbour, their relatives, expressions like these: "Take care of yourself," "Take care of yourself and others."

This last expression can be heard and read everywhere. It is as if a new culture was born: the culture of care, attention, and concern for others. How good it feels to witness this! I have the impression that the ordeal humanizes us, and that what comes first is to protect human being, to make ourselves useful to each other... to help each other, to share.

An African migrant woman in Paris, housed with her two children in a social hotel while waiting, like others, for her residency papers, explained to me that:

> Confinement is a necessary evil. On the one hand, it is to protect our lives. On the other, it is an evil because of the negative effects. For example, families like us, temporarily housed in hotels, have no means for the development of our children. We are often plunged into anxiety. It's an ordeal for us parents who live in a hotel! It does allow us to spend more time with our children, which is good. On the other hand, it is difficult to have two or three hyperactive children in five square metres for extended periods of time, day after day. There's no space, no activities that allow the children to expend their excess energy, which would help them fall asleep quickly in the evening. As a result, it makes for long days where the children have difficulty falling asleep. The children ask the mother, who is the only one to take care of them, to be constantly mobilised, without even being able herself to breathe or settle down for a calm moment of rest and reflection, necessary to the psychological balance and wellbeing of the adult.

Confinement has been a time to get to the essentials: listening, being close to people who are in precarious situations, taking care of those we love and those who are alone. In our big cities, if the virus kills, during confinement loneliness has undoubtedly taken a big toll on so many people. In times of hardship, humans try to respond to certain priorities. For me, with *Secours Catholique*[4], it was about maintaining connections, whatever the cost, with migrant families, whether or not housed in social hotels. Thanks to the cell phone, this tool which is both wonderful and sometimes diabolical (because we also use it in harmful ways), we have been able to

---

[4] *Secours Catholique* or Caritas France is a Catholic nongovernmental organization that fights for a just and fraternal world.

maintain links of solidarity, organize aid, and assist those who could not cope on their own.

I spent hours on the phone listening to frustrated or even depressed mothers, ready to throw herself out the window, one of them told me, to abandon her little boy whom she couldn't stand to see him cooped up anymore. Her boy has a disease that delays his growth, and he has a language delay. He had sessions with speech therapists who helped him out, but with the confinement the sessions stopped. Little by little, by talking on the phone, by asking for recipes, by inviting the woman to tell his life story, her taste for life regained the upper hand. Yes, needing the other and her talents gave her back the taste for life, to have projects again for herself and her child. Via the phone, finally, there was a trial remote session for her son.

Confinement has opened our eyes not to the world, but to the "worlds" we encounter without immersing ourselves in them. Taking an interest in the most vulnerable, joining them on the field of their rubble which we did not want to see, often citing lack of time, reveals feelings, even indifference, towards people who live in situations different from our own. The barriers that separate the rich from the poor are not only external to us, they are also within us: Who has never defended themself about being open and welcoming? Yet, in real-life situations, resistance comes to the fore. Because, so often, we find difference and the unknown so frightening.

During this confinement for protection, I cannot help but marvel at the commitment of so many people, especially young people. I think of all those who have gone to meet the homeless, in the streets that have become deserted, to offer them care and food. I think of those who volunteered for distance learning sessions with children housed in hotels with their mothers, or carried lunches to isolated elderly people, or who knows what else! In a short time, collective intelligence flowed and functioned, and the pooling of energies worked miracles for the good of people.

In short, many people came forward to meet the most vulnerable among us, and to serve them, thus preventing them from sinking into loneliness and other miseries and maladies[5]. What will become of all these

---

[5] See article about physical and spiritual health being a social effort and enterprise: "Donne's convalescence," by Mary Ann Lund, from 2016 in *Renaissance Studies* Vol. 31, No. 4, http://dx.doi.org/10.1111/rest.12246

meet-ups (virtual and in person), all this attention? What will become of these bonds woven over the days over the telephone, sometimes complimented by physical encounters? I don't know, but I am certain that these bonds will leave a "taste for the other."

Yes, if our protective barriers are visible, people who were invisible before the crisis have become visible. It's as if society is discovering the work of people who were little regarded. I have this impression that we were coming out of a long sleep, to discover the simple life, life that is simply, and divinely, there and that we must defend and protect.

The covid19 health crisis will make history. It will mark our search for coherence and unity in our human relations. From now on, it is no longer just those who walk their pets who will get to know each other because their animals lead them to that, but people will talk with each other because they have discovered they are neighbours or live in the same neighbourhood. Everything has stopped? It has! We also stopped. This allowed us to "see clearly," to use an Ivorian, and Quebecois, expression, to focus our attention on others, to take care of each other. Humans, we feed on life, on each other, and it is these awkwardly woven or well cared for bonds that are the paths of Humanity!

Nelkem Jeannette Londadjim, *a sister of St. Joseph and defender of human rights, currently lives in France. She is a member of Justice and Peace France and works as a volunteer for Secours Catholique or Caritas France with "undocumented" families housed in social hotels. She accompanied them in the development of their "power to act," including during this period of the covid19 pandemic. Before that, in Algeria, she worked to facilitate relations between native Algerians and the country's refugee and migrant populations. In 2017, she was an activist in residence at Avila University in Kansas City, USA. She has also been active in the nongovernmental organization that brings the concerns of the Sisters of Saint Joseph to various United Nations bodies and agencies for discussion and action.*

* *Laia Guyard Suengas* *has lived in Kenya for six years and is originally from France. She has a passion for her animals and especially her horse, named Cricket. Growing up in Kenya has always been a fun experience, and she loves everything about it. During covid19, however, she had to go back to France for a couple of months, leaving*

all her animals and her home. But she managed to get through it and get back to Kenya. She's now reunited with everyone she loves and is pursuing her studies at the International School of Kenya.

Thanks to a Laia Guyard Suengas for reviewing this chapter in French and its translation into English. Thanks to Dramane Darave, author of the Afterword to this Langaa collection of *Covid Stories from East Africa and Beyond*, for the translation of this chapter from French.

Transforming
towards
a
better
world

Covid et Africains : dénis et réveil[1]

Nelkem Jeannette Londadjim

J'entends beaucoup de gens dire autour de moi, « Y en a assez du coronavirus. On ne parle que de ça aux informations comme s'il n'y avait que ça comme problème dans le monde ! » Ces personnes ont sûrement raison en réagissant de cette manière. Quand on est connecté 24 heures sur 24, ça peut être de trop.

Mais des nouvelles venues de mon pays m'ont un peu consternée. Ignorance ou abus de pouvoir, je n'en sais trop ! Certains (ceux qui ont le pouvoir politique, économique), revenus des pays où beaucoup de personnes étaient infectées par le coronavirus, ont refusé de se soumettre aux consignes de quarantaine pour protéger les autres. Méchanceté ou abus de pouvoir ? Dieu seul sait ! Toujours est-il que ce sont les pauvres et les innocents qui en pâtissent le plus. Des amis me demandent souvent, « As-tu des nouvelles du Tchad ? Comment vivent-ils la covid là-bas ? »

Je réponds, « Je ne sais pas, j'ai peu de nouvelles. Il semble qu'il n'y a pas beaucoup de cas. Quelques personnes revenues de l'étranger, mais ce n'est pas grave ». Et voici qu'une vidéo[2] extraite des informations de Tchad Infos m'invite à la réflexion, à essayer de comprendre ce qui se passe dans la tête de certaines personnes de mon peuple.

La découverte d'une certaine mentalité à travers ces réactions

La situation est très compliquée, et les manières de se comporter sont différentes suivant les personnes et les lieux.

Quand j'appelle pour prendre des nouvelles des miens, j'apprends qu'ils sont allés rendre condoléances à un tel ou à une telle qui a perdu un proche.

---

[1] © 2020 Nelkem Jeannette Londadjim

Londadjim, N. J. (2020). Covid et Africains : dénis et réveil. Dans M. N. Kinyanjui, R. Thaker, et K. Toure (Dir.), *Covid stories from East Africa and beyond: Lived experiences and forward-looking reflections* (p. 229-232). Bamenda : Langaa.
[2] "VIDEO. Mathias, victime de stigmatisation après sa guérison du Coronavirus," by Nesta Yamgoto, 29 May 2020, https://tchadinfos.com/societes/video-mathias-victime-de-stigmatisation-apres-sa-guerison-du-coronavirus

Ou alors, ils sont allés visiter un tel ou une telle qui est malade. Je dis, « Mais enfin, vous n'avez pas peur de la maladie ? »

« Si, mais comment faire ? On ne peut pas l'abandonner dans son malheur, n'est-ce pas ? » Comment soutenir et aider sans se mettre en danger ?

On pourrait aussi évoquer d'autres personnes, qui par égoïsme ou réelle crainte, rejettent des personnes sans ressources, sans moyens. Bonne ou mauvaise occasion de se débarrasser des proches devenus trop encombrants ou trop lourds sur un budget familial déjà trop maigre pour prendre en charge tout le monde de manière convenable.

A côté de celles-là, il y a aussi des personnes qui refusent de respecter les interdictions de confinement, et d'autres qui disent que la maladie n'existe pas. Tenez, on m'a raconté une histoire extraordinaire : un sexagénaire revenu de l'étranger a été mis en quarantaine semble-t-il dans un hôtel réquisitionné par les pouvoirs publics à cet effet. Le sexagénaire a dit ne pouvoir rester à l'hôtel tout seul. Il a exigé que sa jeune compagne le rejoigne à son hôtel de confinement. Résultat de la course : il a testé positif pour la covid19, a développé la forme grave de la maladie et en est mort. Heureusement que sa compagne plus jeune, a survécu.

Parmi ceux qui ne croient pas en l'existence de la maladie, il y en a qui l'argumentent en cherchant des responsables. Certains disent que ce sont les Chinois, les Américains ou les Européens, ou bien des laboratoires ou des grandes sociétés, des ONG ou d'autres personnes mauvaises qui ont envoyé cette maladie pour tuer le maximum d'Africains « parce qu'ils sont trop nombreux. Et pour empêcher l'Afrique de se développer ». Cette « mentalité du complot » est très inquiétante, car elle empêche d'assumer nos responsabilités. Inutile de vous rappeler tout ce qui circule sur l'OMS, ou encore sur l'utilisation de l'hydroxychloroquine mis en place par certains médecins ou chercheurs.

La crise a réveillé nos vieux démons, complexes, et frustrations de peuples colonisés qui n'arrivent pas à s'en sortir malgré plusieurs années d'indépendance. Mais je suis à la fois heureuse et fière de constater « un réveil citoyen africain » à travers tout cela. Beaucoup dénoncent un modèle de développement imposé à nos pays africains, et j'ai été contente d'entendre l'autre jour à la radio des médecins africains revendiquer leur autonomie dans le choix des protocoles de soins contre la covid19. Les gens ne veulent plus de ces partenariats ou solidarités imposés où ce qui compte, c'est l'argent et le bien des autres au détriment de notre bien africain. Ils dénoncent ces échanges où nos capacités et nos richesses sont exploitées par d'autres, où la pauvreté gagne de plus en plus le terrain enfonçant nos pays dans des dettes qu'ils n'arrivent plus à rembourser.

En tout cas, il me semble que la crise a réveillé une prise de conscience qui était déjà là, mais qui donne de retrouver la foi en certains de leurs dirigeants qui osent affirmer ce dont l'Afrique est capable, et que le monde semble refuser de reconnaître ou du moins d'admettre. Beaucoup soutiennent le président malgache, en voyant que le remède qu'il propose à partir de l'artémesia est refusé. Il n'a pas eu peur de dire : « C'est parce que ce médicament est élaboré en Afrique. S'il venait d'Europe il serait accepté et utilisé ». Combien de chercheurs, d'intellectuels, d'inventeurs africains travaillent et produisent pour l'Europe ou l'Amérique, faisant avancer ces continents au détriment de leur continent ? C'est une question que l'on peut se poser !

Certes, beaucoup de personnes malades sont stigmatisées et même parfois rejetées par peur de contamination, mais je ne peux m'empêcher d'évoquer aussi les solidarités. On a vu naître sur les réseaux sociaux aussi une réelle solidarité mise en œuvre par des associations des jeunes dans les quartiers et les banlieues de Ndjamena. Il y a eu des dons reçus de l'étranger ; on a vu des masques donnés aux soignants qui étaient pourris, etc. Comme toujours, des personnes ont cherché à profiter de la situation pour leur propre intérêt, sans penser au bien commun, sans penser aux autres. Mais grâce aux réseaux sociaux, les gens ont osé dénoncer cela.

L'angoisse qui demeure et qui est celle partagée par beaucoup de gens en situation très précaire, c'est le manque de travail. Beaucoup de personnes travaillent au jour le jour, pour nourrir leurs familles. Elles font preuve de beaucoup de courage, de débrouillardise et de créativité pour cela. Mais avec le confinement et les règles à respecter, cela rend les choses plus difficiles voire les options inexistantes. Du coup, il n'y a tout simplement plus de travail, et c'est dramatique pour beaucoup de familles. Face à cela, prendre le risque ou respecter le couvre-feu mis en place, il n'y a pas de choix. Les gens prennent le risque tout simplement parce que la vie des proches en dépend. Il faut partir tôt ou rentrer tard, ce n'est pas pour braver une interdiction ou affirmer sa liberté comme j'entends dire ailleurs, mais pour continuer à vivre pour ne pas dire survivre.

Et c'est à l'heure où l'on parle de survie en Afrique, à l'heure où normalement quel que soit le coin de la planète où l'on se trouve, l'humanité ne devrait avoir qu'un seul ennemi à combattre : la covid19 ! C'est à l'heure-là qu'un autre choc plus terrible tombe sur nous : Un jeune homme de 46 ans meurt du fait de la violence policière et du racisme ! Que dire ? Que pensez ? Et avant cela une femme de 26 ans a été tuée la nuit dans son appartement par la police. Le rôle d'une police n'est-il pas de protéger des vies ? N'est-il pas d'éviter la violence quelle qu'elle soit ? Ces manifestations que nous vivons montrent le visage d'une société fracturée, où toute une partie de la population s'est sentie exclue. Ce qui fait une nation, c'est le sentiment d'appartenir à la même histoire. Ces révoltes sont le signe qu'une partie de la population américaine ne se sent appartenir à la même histoire que le reste du pays. Lorsqu'il y a trop de frustrations, trop d'humiliations subies par une population, il ne reste que la révolte. Qu'est-ce qui nous délivrera de la haine de l'autre ?

Que sera l'avenir à la sortie de cette crise pandémique ? Je n'en sais rien. Mais j'ose espérer que ces réveils qui pointent, ici ou là, nous conduiront à réellement jouer notre partition dans le concert des nations ! J'ose espérer que cette crise nous aura fait redécouvrir que « l'homme n'est pas l'ennemi de l'homme », mais qu'il est juste le frère ou la sœur sans qui je ne serai jamais homme ! Frère Georges Floyd, repose en Paix et en Pouvoir ! Sœur Breonna Taylor, repose en Paix et en Pouvoir.

Nelkem Jeannette Londadjim, *Sœur de Saint-Joseph et militante des Droits de l'homme, vit actuellement en France. Elle est membre de Justice et Paix France et travaille comme bénévole au Secours Catholique Caritas France avec les familles « sans papiers » hébergées dans les hôtels sociaux en les accompagnant dans le développement de leur « pouvoir d'agir », y compris pendant cette période de covid19. Avant cela, en Algérie, elle s'est efforcée de faciliter les relations entre les Algériens autochtones et les populations réfugiées et migrantes du pays. Elle a été en 2017 activiste en résidence à l'Université Avila à Kansas City aux États-Unis. Elle a également été active au sein de l'organisation non gouvernementale qui porte les préoccupations des Sœurs de Saint-Joseph au sein de divers organes et agences des Nations Unies pour discussion et action.*

Covid and Africans: Denial and Awakening[1]

Translated from French *

Nelkem Jeannette Londadjim

I hear a lot of people around me saying, "I've had enough of coronavirus. It's all they talk about in the news – as if it's the only problem in the world!" It's true, when you're connected 24 hours a day, it can be too much.

I was a little dismayed by some news from my country. Ignorance or abuse of power, I don't know which! Some people (with political and economic power) came back from countries where many people were infected with the coronavirus and refused to comply with quarantine instructions to protect others. Disregard for others or abuse of power? God only knows! Regardless, it is the poor and the innocent who suffer the most. Friends often ask me, "Have you heard from Chad? How are people experiencing covid there?"

I answer, "I don't know, I haven't heard much news. It doesn't seem like there are many cases. A few people have returned from abroad, but it's not serious." And then came a video[2] from *TchadInfos* that took me aback and made me think, to try to understand what is going on in the minds of some of my people.

The discovery of a certain mentality

The situation is very complicated, and ways of behaving are different in different places and for different people. When I call to check on my family, I learn that they have gone to pay their condolences to someone who has lost a loved one. Or they have gone to visit someone who is sick. I ask, "Well, aren't you afraid of illness?"

---

[1] Copyright © 2020 Nelkem Jeannette Londadjim
Londadjim, N. J. (2020). Covid and Africans: Denial and awakening. In M. N. Kinyanjui, R. Thaker, and K. Toure (Eds.), *Covid stories from East Africa and beyond: Lived experiences and forward-looking reflections* (pp. 233-237). Bamenda: Langaa.
[2] "VIDEO. Mathias, victim of stigmatization after his recovery from coronavirus," by Nesta Yamgoto, 29 May 2020, https://tchadinfos.com/societes/video-mathias-victime-de-stigmatisation-apres-sa-guerison-du-coronavirus

"Yes, but what do it? We can't abandon people in their misfortune, can we?" How can we support and help, without putting ourselves and others in danger?

There are other people who, out of selfishness or fear, reject those without resources, without means. The pandemic situation is an opportunity to ignore loved ones who have become too cumbersome, who weigh too heavily on an already too meagre family budget.

In addition, there are also people who refuse to respect containment protocols and then those who say the disease does not exist. I was told an extraordinary story about a 60-year-old man who had returned from abroad. He was quarantined, apparently in a hotel requisitioned by the public authorities for that purpose. The sexagenarian said he could not stay in the hotel alone. He demanded that his young companion join him in confinement. He tested positive for covid19, developed the serious form of the disease, and died from it. Fortunately, his younger companion survived.

Among those who do not believe in the existence of the disease, some look for those responsible. Some say it is the Chinese, Americans, or Europeans, or laboratories, big corporations, or NGOs, or just bad people who sent this disease to kill as many Africans as possible "because there are too many of them" and "to prevent Africa from developing." This "conspiracy mentality" is very worrying because it prevents us from assuming our responsibilities. It is useless to remind you of all that is circulating about the World Health Organization or the use of hydroxychloroquine.

The crisis has awakened our old demons, complexes, and frustrations of colonized peoples who are unable to cope despite several years of independence.

I am also both happy and proud to see "an awakening of African communities" through all this. Some people have denounced a development model imposed on our African countries, and I was happy to hear the other day on the radio African doctors claiming their autonomy in the choice of care protocols for covid.

People no longer want imposed partnerships or solidarities where what counts is money and the good of others to the detriment of our African good. They denounce relations in which our capacities and our wealth are exploited by others and where socioeconomic poverty gains ground, pushing our countries into debts they can no longer repay.

It seems to me that the crisis has awakened an awareness that was already there. Are people regaining some faith in leaders who dare affirm what Africa is capable of? That which the world seems to deny or at least not admit? Many support the Malagasy president. Seeing that the remedy he proposes based on artemesia is rejected, he was not afraid to wonder, "It is because this drug is developed in Africa? If it came from Europe it would be accepted and used." How many African researchers, intellectuals, and inventors work and produce for Europe or America, advancing these continents to the detriment of their continent? This is a question that we can ask ourselves!

Many sick people are stigmatized and even rejected for fear of contamination. At the same time, we have seen the emergence of real solidarity through social networks developed by youth associations in the neighborhoods and suburbs of Ndjamena, Chad's capital city. Donations have been received from abroad; we have seen used masks given to guards, etc. As always, people try to take advantage of a situation for their own interest, without thinking about the common good, without thinking about others. But thanks to social networks, people dared to denounce this.

The anguish that remains and is shared by many people in precarious situations is the lack of work. Many people work on a daily basis to feed their families hand to mouth. They show a lot of courage, resourcefulness, and creativity in that. But confinement and other measures make things more difficult and diminish options for survival. The situation is dramatic for many families. Between staying home and taking risks, there is little choice. People go out and takes risks simply because the lives of their loved ones depend on it. You have to leave early or come back late, not to brave a ban but to assert your freedom to continue to live.

Black Lives Matter

While talking about humanity's common fight against covid19 and survival in Africa and beyond, another more terrible shock falls upon us. A young man of 46 dies, before the eyes of the world, as a result of police violence and racism! What can I say? What to think? And before that, a 26-

year-old woman was killed in her apartment at night by the police[3]. Isn't the role of the police to protect lives? Isn't it to prevent violence?

These demonstrations **we are experiencing** show the face of a fractured society, where whole groups of people have been excluded and others privileged. What makes a nation is the feeling of belonging to a shared history and access to common resources to develop. These protests are a sign that part of the American population does not feel it belongs and that many people, of multiple ages and races, recognize that the country cannot progress, that people cannot thrive, if divided. When there are too many frustrations, too many humiliations and abuses suffered, only revolt remains. What will deliver us from hatred and oppression?

THE GREAT FIRE: A Special Issue, Edited by TA-NEHISI COATES

VANITY FAIR

BREONNA TAYLOR

What will be the future after this pandemic crisis? I don't know. But I dare hope that these awakenings, here and there, pointing to a better tomorrow, will lead us to really play our part in the concert of nations! I dare hope that this crisis will have made us rediscover that humxn[4] beings are not the enemy of humxn beings. Another humxn being is my brother, my sister without whom I will never be humxn! Brother Georges Floyd, rest in Peace and Power! Sister Breonna Taylor, rest in Peace and Power.

Nelkem Jeannette Londadjim, a sister of St. Joseph and defender of human rights, currently lives in France. She is a member of Justice and Peace France and works as a volunteer for Secours Catholique or Caritas France with "undocumented" families

---

[3] An image of Breonna Taylor, painted after her murder, featured on the cover of a special September 2020 issue of *Vanity Fair*, with author and journalist Ta-Nehisi Coates as guest editor, www.vanityfair.com/culture/2020/08/september-2020-issue-the-great-fire

[4] "Why humxn is not misspelled," by Bunny Young, 15 May 2020, https://abetterplaceconsulting.com/why-humxn-is-not-misspelled

housed in social hotels. She accompanied them in the development of their "power to act," including during this period of the covid19 pandemic. Before that, in Algeria, she worked to facilitate relations between native Algerians and the country's refugee and migrant populations. In 2017, she was an activist in residence at Avila University in Kansas City, USA. She has also been active in the nongovernmental organization that brings the concerns of the Sisters of Saint Joseph to various United Nations bodies and agencies for discussion and action.

* **Laia Guyard Suengas** *has lived in Kenya for six years and is originally from France. She has a passion for her animals and especially her horse, named Cricket. Growing up in Kenya has always been a fun experience, and she loves everything about it. During covid19, however, she had to go back to France for a couple of months, leaving all her animals and her home. But she managed to get through it and get back to Kenya. She's now reunited with everyone she loves and is pursuing her studies at the International School of Kenya.*

Thanks to a Laia Guyard Suengas for reviewing this chapter in French and its translation into English. Thanks to Dramane Darave, author of the Afterword to this Langaa collection of *Covid Stories from East Africa and Beyond*, for the translation of this chapter from French.

chapter 26

Collective Voice on
Ubuntu, Social Justice,
Gardens and Market Mammas[1]

Kundai Mtasa
Margaret LoWilla
Alexandra A. Lukamba

The extinction of ubuntu in the age of covid19?
Kundai Mtasa

Ubuntu, loosely translated to "I am because we are," is a Nguni Bantu concept that encapsulates a connectedness that prevails between people and all of humanity. The concept is rooted deeply in African philosophy. It acknowledges that our humanity is shared and, essentially, that we are each other's keepers. Within South Africa, the ideology has been associated with some of the country's great leaders such as the late Nelson Mandela. *Madiba*, as Mandela was known and is affectionately called, practiced ubuntu in word and deed. In one of his speeches, he eloquently laid out the foundation of this philosophy:

> As the years progress one increasingly realises the importance of friendship and human solidarity. And if a ninety-year-old may offer some unsolicited advice on this occasion, it would be that you, irrespective of your age, should place human solidarity, the concern for the other, at the centre of the values by which you live. – *Nelson Rolihlahla Mandela, 12 July 2008*[2]

---

[1] Copyright © 2020 Kundai Mtasa, Margaret LoWilla, and Alexandra A. Lukamba
Mtasa, K., LoWilla, M., and Lukamba, A. A. (2020). Ubuntu, social justice, gardens and market mammas. In M. N. Kinyanjui, R. Thaker, and K. Toure (Eds.), *Covid stories from East Africa and beyond: Lived experiences and forward-looking reflections* (pp. 239-247). Bamenda: Langaa.
[2] "Address at 6th Annual Nelson Mandela Lecture," by Nelson Mandela, 12 July 2008, Kliptown Soweto, South Africa, www.sahistory.org.za/archive/address-6th-annual-nelson-mandela-lecture-nelson-mandela-12-july-2008-kliptown-soweto

Twelve years later, the world finds itself at a pivotal moment of history as covid19 continues to reshape the practices and norms of life as we know it. The spirit of ubuntu, this ethos that is supposed to underlie the way Africans relate and treat one another – is it drowning?

The current climate of this pandemic has exacerbated the fragilities within society. If some people feel closer to each other in their neighbourhoods and in relationships of solidarity across space and time, life has been dismantled for many people across the continent.

I am thinking in particular about the increases in xenophobia directed toward African migrants living within the borders of South Africa. The hashtag #ZimbabweansMustFall was initiated as a campaign to fuel xenophobic propaganda against Zimbabwean foreign nationals within the country. Zimbabweans have been subjected to maltreatment in South Africa during covid19.

> Our Zim bros & sisters (parents & youths) forced into Mussina[3] illegally because sitting at home even to avoid COVID-19 isn't an option. Caught on camera by SA Army. This is why they now say #ZimbabweansMustFall but they don't understand the dire situation. One day they will.
> *(25 July 2020, with a link to a 2-minute video)*

> I am a South African but I will never support xenophobic attack on our fellow brothers [or…] supporters of this evil hashtag #ZimbabweansMustFall
> *(22 June 2020)*

> #ZimbabweansMustFall #SACitizensMustCome1st #SAHomeAffairsCorruption
> these people they want to destroy our country straight away
> *(21 July 2020)*

> #ZimbabweansMustFall
> Zimbabweans lives matter in Zimbabwe not here.
> *(3 August 2020)*

It seems that being African or being human is no longer enough safeguard for relations of mutual respect among Africans on the African

---

[3] Musina "is the northernmost town in the Limpopo province of South Africa. It is located near the confluence of the Limpopo River with the Sand River and the border to Zimbabwe." (Wikipedia)

continent. As hate crimes against fellow Zimbabwean foreign nationals continue to rise, ubuntu is being suffocated. "I can't breathe," says my sister. "I can't breathe," says my brother. The human experience of my Zimbabwean brothers and sisters in South Africa has been shaped by hostility and animosity, and the situation is getting worse with covid. Where has ubuntu gone?

Zimbabweans and other African foreign nationals have found it difficult to navigate the pandemic within South Africa. Measures put in place to protect South African citizens have left non-citizens further behind and desperately seeking any form of safe haven within the storm. For many years, the South African power structure has played South Africans off against fellow Africans from other African countries, encouraging fear and demonization. South Africans have put the blame on Zimbabweans and other foreigners for different societal problems including unemployment, increase in crime, and human and drug trafficking. Zimbabweans have suffered and continue to be persecuted. Within the context of covid19, they are largely disregarded in the fight against the pandemic.

This marginalisation brings about grave questions around whether the spirit of ubuntu still lives. Covid19 itself shows that as humans, we are all interconnected and equal. The virus has affected the rich and the poor, Blacks and Whites, people living in rural areas and in urban areas. In this sense, it is evident that we are all somewhat collectively responsible for each other's wellbeing. However, if we are not going to heed to this philosophy of ubuntu when it matters the most, does it still exist? If we can so openly and freely display hate for another African brother or sister, are beliefs about our common humanity senseless? Will the aftermath of covid19 bring about an extinction of ubuntu?

Kundai Mtasa *earned two degrees from the University of Pretoria: an undergraduate degree in Politics and International Studies and an honours degree in Development Studies. She is pursuing a master's in Leadership and Development at King's College London and is currently an Associate Fellow at the African Leadership Centre and a research intern with the African Centre for the Constructive Resolution of Disputes. Previously she worked with UNICEF and the World Wildlife Fund, and she has conducted research on human trafficking in South Africa.*

Harnessing collective voice for social justice
Margaret LoWilla

The covid19 pandemic caught the whole world unprepared. Health systems have been stretched, economies fractured, and leadership tested. Like other pandemics have done, the coronavirus is exposing and accentuating pre-existing socioeconomic inequalities. The question of social justice is being brought to the fore in various contexts worldwide, and despite the very real threat of the virus, people are coming together to stand up and speak out against injustices in their communities.

One such social ill is gender-based violence. With many women and girls trapped at home with abusers because of lockdowns and curfews, cases of gender-based violence have increased considerably. In addition, the growing presence of security forces to enforce government directives on curbing the virus contributes to state violence against civilians. Several countries across the continent have reported increased cases of sexual violence, including Liberia, Kenya, and Ethiopia.

In South Sudan, women took to the streets to demand justice for an eight-year-old girl who was gang-raped by three men in her home. Adorning masks and observing physical distance, the women marched through the streets of the capital city of Juba carrying placards that read:

Covid Walk against Rape

End Rape Culture in South Sudan

Justice Delayed is Justice Denied

Unfortunately, the case of the girl in Juba is not unique. A few days before the world learned what happened to her, there were 19 reported cases of women and girls who had been gang-raped during continued clashes in the mid-size city of Yei.[4] Even prior to that was the accusation

---

[4] Yei is a commercial centre about 170 kilometres (110 miles) southwest of Juba, toward the borders with Uganda and the Democratic Republic of Congo.

that government forces had committed various sexual offences against civilians in the town of Rubeke.[5]

The signing of the 2018 peace agreement in South Sudan brought a wave of hope for many South Sudanese women and girls. The post-conflict context signified an opportunity to transform inequitable and unjust systems. The formation of the government in February 2020 felt like a step in the right direction. However, the implementation of the peace agreement has stalled due to the urgency of the covid19 crisis.

At the time of writing, the Transitional Government of National Unity had not made much headway. In fact, intercommunal clashes persist in parts of the country, where women continue to be victimized by sexual violence. Aluel Atem from South Sudan, a facilitator of conflict transformation processes, writes in AfricanFeminism, an online dialogue platform:

> In the middle of a pandemic, a worrisome Peace Agreement, escalating intra and inter-communal violence, we have to brave reports of another girl, another woman raped, murdered or domestically abused. It feels like I have been in a constant state of emergency that just keeps getting critical.[6]

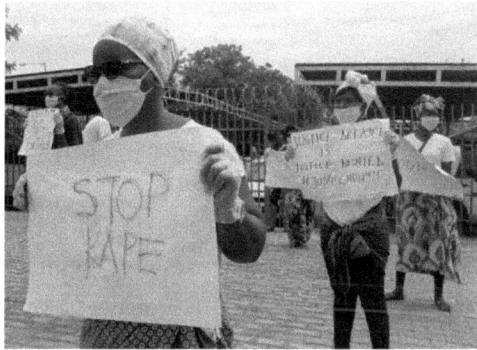

Furthermore, the impunity of perpetrators is enabled by a criminal justice system that lacks capacity and the legal instruments to protect the rights of women and girls. Cases of sexual violence are often referred to customary courts because the rule of law is largely non-existent in South Sudan. The patriarchal order embedded in colonial customs and traditional beliefs has long obstructed the realisation of women's rights. Due to the covid19 pandemic, efforts towards the establishment of justice

---

[5] Rubeke, between the larger towns of Wotogo and Asole, is southwest of Yei. The capital city of Juba, commercial centre of Yei, and town of Rubeke are all three in Yei County of the South Sudanese state of Central Equatoria.

[6] "Rape survivors defy shame culture to speak out on everyday violations in South Sudan," by Aluel Atem, 23 June 2020, https://africanfeminism.com/rape-survivors-defy-shame-culture-to-speak-of-south-sudan-every-day-violations The photo, by Ponl Victoria/Oxfam, associated with the article is included here.

systems, as provided for in the peace agreement, have taken a backseat, delaying access to justice for South Sudanese women and girls.

These obstacles, however, have not stopped women from demonstrating their desires and support for justice. Soon after the protest in Juba, a social media campaign with the hashtag #SouthSudaneseSurvivor (reminiscent of the #MeToo movement) was launched. South Sudanese women and girls from all over the world who had experienced sexual violence shared their stories in an effort to end the culture of silence within the community and provide a platform for survivors to be both seen and heard.

The hashtag creates a space for solidarity and sisterhood to flourish among South Sudanese rape survivors. It has also been used to name perpetrators and share mental health and other useful resources and tips on coping with the trauma. The tweets have included the following, from 17 and 23 June 2020 respectively:

> In solidarity with these young #southsudanese women (#SouthSudaneseSurvivor) exposing the rape/sexual abuse culture in our community. It about time somebody speaks on this, you all are very brave and I applaud you. Something need to change it's disgusting.

> We shall keep at it until change happens. The road won't be easy but our daughters should not experience the same! #EndRapeCulture #SouthSudaneseSurvivor

Covid19 has forced us to confront the harsh realities in our communities. Though we have been obliged to abandon our socialization habits, we are finding new ways to build a sense of community with each other. Though isolating for the sake of our health, we must continue to stand in solidarity to fight social ills. No one is alone.

Margaret LoWilla *holds a bachelor's in Economics and Business Studies from the Australian Catholic University, where she worked with Josephite Community Aid in Australia, engaging with Sudanese refugee children to aid their transition into a new educational system. She is completing a master's in Governance, Peace and Security at Africa Nazarene University in Nairobi, Kenya. Margaret has worked with local civil society organizations in South Sudan on women's rights, women's political participation, and advocacy against child and forced marriages. As assistant project coordinator of*

Leadership Crucible in Juba, South Sudan, she focused on the mobilization of young women for peace rallies and community dialogues and conducted trainings on good governance and the importance of democratic participation. Her research interests include women and the state in Africa, and the dynamics of conflict in the Horn of Africa. She is currently researching South Sudanese women's participation in peace processes after independence.

Findings solutions in our gardens in Kinshasa
Alexandra A. Lukamba

The arrival of covid19 in Africa starting in March 2020 created a sense of panic and questioning about the capacity of the continent to manage such a scary pandemic. The government of the Democratic Republic of Congo began to take measures to limit the spread of the virus. This created headache, heartache, pocketbook ache, fear, and panic in the lives of people in the country. The first major actions of the government were to close schools and churches and encourage companies to send their employees home.

These measures caused many to lose their jobs or to experience a significant decrease in their monthly income. Covid19 brought a sense of instability and uncertainty regarding the future.

The other side of the coin is that people sought solutions in these days of despair. As a young Congolese woman, I have been particularly interested in how women in the country's capital city of Kinshasa have been innovative. I was impressed with the seamstresses and market mammas. While many people were traumatized by what they heard in the media and by the numbers being circulated, these women seized the moment and emerged as a solution to the problem.

The seamstresses used what they had in hand – their talent and colourful fabrics – to contribute to the covid19 prevention campaign. The movement started with one, two, three women and then many more. In the face of adversity, they showed their talents and ensured revenue for their households. Today, people around the city wear masks in different colours and fabrics, showcasing the craftswomanship nimbleness, and innovativeness of Congolese seamstresses.

As for the market mamas, they advertised natural products – usually used to treat flus, colds, and even malaria – to help protect against getting covid19. At the entrance to markets are women selling ginger, lemon, bulukutu,[7] and Kongo-bololo,[8] plants known to have therapeutic virtues that strengthen the immune system. These women have gathered additional plants to sell in different markets in Kinshasa. They are not simply selling them but are also taking the time to educate their clients on their use. These plants have been part of the culture for centuries. My dad, who was born in the 1960s, told me that when he was around the age of seven, his mother initiated a family tradition to drink a glass of Kongo-bololo once a month to prevent any sickness.

The seamstresses and market women of Kinshasa have taught me several lessons. I will mention just three. First, these women adapted quickly during a crisis and had the reflex to look close to home for solutions. Second, in adapting quickly and strategically, they continued to make a living in the middle of a pandemic. Third, by working together they were able to learn from each other and also teach and set examples for others. While many people were waiting on a vaccine or on masks coming from other countries, these women showed that sometimes the solution is just in our gardens. These women are examples of true leaders.

Alexandra A. Lukamba is pursuing a dual master's in International Development and in Leadership and Development at Sciences Po Paris and King's College London. Before that she studied international relations, global affairs, and Spanish at Eckerd College in Florida, USA, where she was a member of the political science honour society.

---

[7] The leaves of the aromatic bulukutu (Lippia multiflora) plant, which grows as a shrub up to three metres tall, are used to prepare teas. The plant is a perineal with more or less woody stems. See Tropical Plants Database at
http://tropical.theferns.info/viewtropical.php?id=Lippia+multiflora
A 2016 comment on the web site says: "branches of lippia are traditionally placed in a bag containing cowpea to protect it against storage pests."
The bulukutu "leaves are dried in the sun, and then infused in hot water. The tea is consumed hot, with or without milk or sugar. Bulukutu is particularly researched for its medicinal properties: in traditional medicine it is used by itself or in combination with other medicinal herbs to treat illnesses such as lower back pain, anorexia, coughs, fevers or to alleviate muscular pain, joint- and stomachaches, to strengthen the kidneys and to cure hepatitis." It can be cultivated and also grows wild in the forest.
www.fondazioneslowfood.com/en/ark-of-taste-slow-food/bulukutu
[8] "DRC uses traditional medicine in virus fight," by Claudia Nsono, 23 April 2020,
www.africanews.com/2020/04/23/drc-uses-traditional-medicine-in-virus-fight

She worked with the social start-up, Wintegreat, which focuses on the reintegration of refugees in society through support for their professional projects. Alexandra interned with the NGO Committee on the Status of Women, New York. Since 2014 she has been involved with Sœur, Lève-toi, *a nongovernmental organization in Kinshasa, in the Democratic Republic of Congo (DRC), working on building young women's leadership skills through mentoring sessions with women in the workforce. Alexandra's research interests include development and the practice of leadership in government decision making. In the DRC, she is examining mutuality in the transfer of information to the public, and the government's response to the Ebola and covid19 outbreaks.*

chapter 27

A Tale of a Mother and a Son[1]

Haimanot Kebede Bayeh

No warning, no preparation. The world went into lockdown. I was on a new journey – to fulltime work from home and homeschooling. This of course was not unique to me. Many families around the world were confronted and challenged with new ways of doing life: the new normal.

I had relocated to Nairobi for work almost two years before the coronavirus outbreak. I moved with my son and with Muluye[2], who has helped me in raising him.

My six-year-old boy, let's call him Boaz, is energetic. He loves being around people. He is outgoing and knows his teachers and other classroom teachers and all his classmates' parents. Pre-covid, I was always greeted at his school, starting from the main entrance. "Mama Boaz" they call me. Many parents have let me know how sociable Boaz is.

He has also played a key role in introducing me to my neighbors back home in Ethiopia and here in Nairobi. The new normal of staying home and not meeting with others for the foreseeable future is going to be a challenge to my son and to a mother who has to make it work, for herself and for him.

Even though I have a certificate to teach English to adults, I never saw myself teaching children. I avoided teaching Sunday school at church for this reason. But in the covid context, there was no way out but to adapt as quickly as possible and run with it.

The first two weeks of virtual learning were a challenge. I had to juggle between my very busy work schedule (filled with meetings) and ensure Boaz got through his day's work. There were days he missed sessions, and we had to catch up over the weekend. Weekends, just like weekdays, we were pent up at home, so we could spare some weekend time for schoolwork.

---

[1] Copyright © 2020 Haimanot Kebede Bayeh
Bayeh. H. K. (2020). A tale of a mother and a son. In M. N. Kinyanjui, R. Thaker, and K. Toure (Eds.), *Covid stories from East Africa and beyond: Lived experiences and forward-looking reflections* (pp. 249-251). Bamenda: Langaa.
[2] Not her real name.

To my surprise, Boaz quickly adapted to the new way of learning from home. With very little supervision, he was able to follow through with schoolwork each day. He adapted, even to the new normal of not being around people. He kept himself busy with different activities outside of his schoolwork.

The days came and went just like that – the peace of mind a working mother needs. Credit also goes to Muluye, who behind the scenes has supported both Boaz and me in managing day-to-day life. I gain some quiet moments for myself when Boaz and Muluye spend time together. Considering the manner in which covid19 suddenly took over our lives, it would have been challenging to handle full-time work and full-time homeschooling plus household chores had it not been for Muluye.

I had to confront my own expectations of my son. Because he is an only child, I cannot compare his process of learning or of discovering himself with that of other children.

I think my expectations for him outsized his age. In taking more note of his schoolwork and observing the manner in which the teachers related to the children in my son's class, I was able to realign my expectations to his age. I have a better sense of what he is able to do. Covid's blessing in disguise.

In this journey of being at home, it was months before I realized that being at home with Boaz all day every day did not necessarily mean we were spending time with each other. That is a false belief.

I am a full-time working mother, and a lot of my off-the-computer hours were taken up by friends and family who also needed support during this season of uncertainty and lockdown.

I found myself on the phone late into the evenings and on the weekends. These conversations revolved around covid19 and its effects in different countries. Friends conversed, hoping to find out how serious the issue was. For some of us (and particularly me), these discussions were the only news source. Did I even have time to listen to the news?

These conversations helped me make it through, but they came at the expense of time with my son. I am grateful I realized this early enough to realign my priorities: take time, make conscious decisions, and put plans in place to ensure Boaz gets the attention and time he needs with his mother.

I acknowledge my son's resilience in the face of all these changes. He managed to cope with the new normal with very little support. I kind of wonder how he did it.

I must also mention my lovely neighbors with whom I built friendships during this period. It started out with a Saturday coffee, initiated by my neighbor. "Come with your cup of coffee and your chair. We'll physically distance, each at the entrance to their apartment."

Before we knew it, we were also able to celebrate Ethiopian New Year together. For New Year's at home, each member of the family has a bundled set of sticks. We stand outside in a circle and set fire to the bundles. These are our fireworks.

For Ethiopian New Year in 2020 in Nairobi, we sat on the balcony of our apartment with a cool breeze blowing and shared a meal with neighbors. Everything came together, simply and spontaneously. The convivial conversation and joyous laughter were like festive fireworks.

As the months go by and the dust sort of settles with the understanding that covid19 is here to stay, the fear component of the pandemic has been swept away, but not entirely. We have discovered resilience and skills we didn't know we had. We continue to be grateful, to take one day at a time, and to keep prioritizing what is important.

Haimanot Kebede Bayeh works as a Programme Policy Officer in the non-profit sector in the Horn of Africa. She has a master's in Global Management from the University of Salford Business School in the United Kingdom. For her thesis, she studied the tourism sector in Ethiopia. She completed her secondary studies in India. Outside of work, Haimanot enjoys spending time with her son.

chapter 28

Covid19: The Humbling and Humbled Virus [1] [2]

Francis B. Nyamnjoh

I have heard it repeated, *ad nauseum*: Covid19 is the ultimate symbol of globalisation as a homogenising process devoid of all trappings of hierarchies and inequalities. Every TV channel, radio station, press release, blog and Facebook post, and WhatsApp forward that have fed my anxious and eager palate have sought to reassure with sobering words.

Reassurances well captured by Zou Yue, CGTN anchor, in a viral WhatsApp video clip [3] thus: "Covid-19 respects no national borders, no social bounds, no political systems and no cultural values. It hits us just as hard. It levels the world." A sentiment echoed in March 2020 by Mike Ryan, executive director of the World Health Organization (WHO) Health Emergencies Programme: "Viruses know no borders and they don't care about your ethnicity, the color of your skin or how much money you have in the bank [4]."

Really? Yes, and No.

To what extent is covid19 no respecter of national borders? It may have been first identified in Wuhan, China, but covid19 has rapidly proven, through its invisible nimbleness of feet and wings, that it is *not only* a Chinese or a Wuhan virus. Its giant compressor ambition is no respecter of walls, real or imaginary. It has spread at lightning speed, metamorphosing almost at the blink of an eye into a truly global crisis that requires nothing short of a well-coordinated global response.

---

[1] Copyright © 2020 Francis B. Nyamnjoh
Nyamnjoh, F. B. (2020). Covid19: The humbling and humbled virus. In M. N. Kinyanjui, R. Thaker, and K. Toure (Eds.), *Covid stories from East Africa and beyond: Lived experiences and forward-looking reflections* (pp. 253-260). Bamenda: Langaa.
[2] A shorter and earlier version of this paper was published in *Corona Times*, www.coronatimes.net/covid-19-humbling-humbled-virus
[3] "What works against the virus?" 19 March 2020, https://news.cgtn.com/news/2020-03-19/What-works-against-the-virus--OZBF7I0PiU/index.html
[4] "WHO official warns against calling it 'Chinese virus,' says 'there is no blame in this'," by Morgan Gstalter, 19 March 2020, https://thehill.com/homenews/administration/488479-who-official-warns-against-calling-it-chinese-virus-says-there-is-no

In this regard, it is regrettable that whilst it has spread rapidly and sparing no corner of the globe, effective public health responses have remained rather local and national. This poses the "danger that Covid-19 will do long-term damage to migrant rights, as states continue to adopt inward-looking policies" partly to contain the movement of "people seeking better economic opportunities" as well as to keep out "those fleeing political persecution"[5]. In terms of compression of time and space, neoliberalism in its various guises and disguises runs the risk of losing out to the virus, bringing about a new global order, if current rates of transmission are not contained with imagination, creativity, and innovation.

As bubbly in generosity as it seems, covid19, just like neoliberalism, thrives on hierarchies and their interconnections, globally and locally. It follows, celebrates, and is encouraged by the same orifices of cosmopolitan fertility, melting pots, and triumphs.

Outside of Wuhan, even as it has hit major cities of Europe and the Americas more than anywhere else, it has not exactly ignored (nor can it afford to, given its global ambitions of dominance) the underdeveloped and the underprivileged North and South, East and West, urban and rural.

It is true – thanks largely to its invisibility and insensitivity to various technologies of containment and regimes of detection, detention, and deportation – that coronavirus is more aggressive at border crossings than capital, privileged forms of labour, the frequent flyer elite, consumerism, or any world religion has ever been.

Like a cockroach in the perforated luggage of an undocumented and underprivileged wayfarer at a heavily policed border crossing, covid19 has a debilitating ability to neutralise borders (physical, social, cultural, bodily, and ideological) that others hold in awe with norming ease and deadening silence. Notwithstanding its invisibility, its mode of travel and privileged crucibles of self-activation remain human.

Curiously, without much ado and almost with the press of a button, the virus has humbled strongmen of politics, and their penchant for hubris and for power without responsibility. It may have much in common with fake news in the digital age of post-truths. But it is far more real and potent than

---

[5] "Letter from Africa: Spare a thought for stranded migrants," 17 May 2020, www.bbc.com/news/world-africa-52645702

any digitally driven fake news virus. The vectors and vehicles that transmit covid19 are humans hungry for sociality, intimacy, and *ubuntu*.

Those who propagate it unknowingly do not need manipulation to desire and seek to be desired through relationships of interconnection with fellow humans. Being human in tune with the humanity of others does not require engineering or inducement to do what should come naturally to humans as social beings.

Unlike fake news viruses, covid19 does not need the hidden hand of tech giants, hackers, or spyware manufacturers to activate its potency as an efficacious malicious agent. Like Dracula, all it requires is our schooled taste and hunger for human warmth and connectivity as social beings to lure us, one and all, to its vampirish inferno of appetites.

Paradoxically, defeating the virus requires a different type of connectivity – one that is not necessarily physical, but certainly social and emotional. Humans must harness a virtual form of solidarity to enable coming together while staying apart. For, as is aptly and repeatedly stressed, coronavirus does not spread itself, people spread it. To discipline, punish, and curb its excesses in turn demands of us discipline enough to suspend our immediacy in the senses of touch, taste, and smell, by embracing technologies of presence in absence and absence in presence. This, of course, is not to deny the serious threat covid19 poses to the livelihoods of all those who depend exclusively on in-person presence in particular places and spaces to be effective in the services they deliver and/or seek.

It is true that covid19 is humbling leaderships, economies, and predictabilities globally. But that is the story at a general level. At a structural and layered level, the story is much more complex and nuanced. The more closely one looks, the clearer the pictures of power, privilege, and hierarchies become, at sub-national, national, regional, and global levels.

Globally, coronavirus has gained a reputation as a pandemic that kills without negotiation, mercy, or remorse, making of everyone a potential victim. Stories of death and dying are truly horrendous. As Father Mario Carminati from a small town in northern Italy, an area hard hit by the virus, put it: "Authorities didn't know where to put the coffins.[6]"

---

[6] "Italy small town priest deals with death on industrial scale," by Flavio Lo Scalzo, 28 March 2020, www.reuters.com/article/us-health-coronavirus-italy-coffins-idUSKBN21F0M6

However, while every social category is affected, not everyone is affected to the same degree. Everywhere, elderly people are dying disproportionately to the young. Could this turn out to be Africa's saving grace as a youthful continent, where three quarters of the population is aged below 35?

There are also gender differences in how the virus affects humans. Writing for BBC Future, a science site, Martha Henriques observed: "In the US, for example, twice as many men have been dying from the virus as women. Similarly, 69% of all coronavirus deaths across Western Europe have been male. Similar patterns have been seen in China and elsewhere.[7]" On the other hand, with the confinement measures, women are "losing jobs at higher rates" and "were making less money to begin with.[8]"

There is discrimination along racial lines as well. In Europe and North America, racialized people are dying in inverse proportions to their white counterparts. In Chicago, for example, Blacks "account for half of all coronavirus cases in the city and more than 70% of deaths, despite making up 30%" of the city's population[9]. At face value, this reflects the inaccessibility of affordable and quality healthcare as well as systemic exclusion from other societal services and benefits. It also reflects their lowly positions on the hierarchy of socioeconomic and political visibility that neoliberalism and legacies of the institution of slavery have enshrined and perpetuate even in camouflage. Hence, former President Barrack Obama's comment: "A disease like this just spotlights the underlying inequalities and extra burdens that black communities have historically had to deal with in this country.[10]"

Ethically, how does one negotiate and navigate the delicate balancing act of representing these disproportionalities, scientifically, journalistically, politically, and otherwise, without implying that the lives of those most adversely affected matter less?

---

[7] "Why covid-19 is different for men and women," by Martha Henriques, 13 April 2020, www.bbc.com/future/article/20200409-why-covid-19-is-different-for-men-and-women
[8] "Why covid-19 is different for men and women," by Martha Henriques, 13 April 2020, www.bbc.com/future/article/20200409-why-covid-19-is-different-for-men-and-women
[9] "Coronavirus wreaks havoc in African American neighbourhoods," 7 April 2020, www.bbc.com/news/world-us-canada-52194018
[10] "Coronavirus: Obama criticises Trump administration's virus response," 17 May 2020, www.bbc.com/news/world-us-canada-52694872

While the economic effects globally are devastating for most all and sundry as the virus drives productivity into hibernation, some people are losing their businesses and jobs faster than others. In many an African country where citizens have mostly failed over the years to jolt the reigning dictatorships out of their slumber of inaction and complacency, covid19 has succeeded in attracting, at the level of hollow rhetoric at least, the attention of government to the urgency of the moment. Even if only to regret, or appear to regret, the deplorable public health systems they have ignored or underfunded with impunity for decades – preferring, as they often have, to head elsewhere for more prestigious healthcare for themselves and their immediate families.

If aggressive and massive testing is necessary to contain the ravages of covid19, how do African countries of preponderantly modest means and underfunded public health services afford the testing and personal protective equipment needed by medical and public health practitioners to do justice to such an expectation? And what will be the long-term impacts that "the huge focus" on the virus has had on "other health issues being neglected"[11]?

The potentially devastating economic effects, especially on the poor of the continent, are frightening to contemplate. The reports of ordinary folks driven to disarmingly horrendous levels of desperation are widespread and surging. In Kenya for example, Peninah Bahati Kitsao, a Mombasa-based widow, was reportedly "cooking stones for her eight children to make them believe she was preparing food for them," hoping "they would fall asleep while they waited for their meal."[12] While her story caught the attention of many Kenyans who apparently rallied to her aid, it is not impossible to imagine thousands or even millions of fellow Kenyans and Africans in similar positions not being as lucky, as they run the risk of dying as much from hunger as from covid19.

Hopefully, the current show of concern does not simply result in handing over the African populace to be used as guinea pigs and experimented upon to guarantee salvation for the lives of others higher up the reigning hierarchies of humanity.

---

[11] "Coronavirus in Africa: Contained or unrecorded?" 20 May 2020, www.bbc.com/news/world-africa-52702838
[12] "Coronavirus: Kenyans moved by widow cooking stones for children," 30 April 2020, www.bbc.com/news/world-africa-52494404

There are legitimate concerns about a lingering "colonial mentality" in Europe, an attitude that has drawn widespread condemnation as well as suspicion and the circulation of rumour and conspiracy theories among Africans towards trials for "a vaccine that works worldwide – and not just for richer nations."[13]

A related concern around Covid-Organics, a "herbal cure" proposed by the Malagasy Institute of Applied Research (IMRA) and promoted by President Andry Rajoelina of Madagascar as a "herbal tea [that] gives results in seven days,"[14] poses the additional problem of the unresolved tensions between the competing and often conflictual healthcare traditions on the continent – one generally termed "plant-based," "traditional", "African" or "endogenous" and the other roughly equated with being "medical," "scientific," "orthodox," "Western" and "colonial" in origin.

According to President Rajoelina, people would not be so sceptical if a European country had discovered the remedy. As he told France 24's Marc Perelman and RFI's Christophe Boisbouvier in an interview: "What if this remedy had been discovered by a European country, instead of Madagascar? Would people doubt it so much? I don't think so.[15]"

The President is categorical that what is truly in question about Covid-Organics as a "preventive and curative remedy" is the assumption that nothing good can originate from Africa: "What is the problem with Covid-Organics, really? Could it be that this product comes from Africa? Could it be that it's not OK for a country like Madagascar, which is the 63rd poorest country in the world... to have come up with (this formula) that can help save the world?"[16]

---

[13] "Coronavirus: Why Africans should take part in vaccine trials," by Anne Mawathe, 18 May 2020, www.bbc.com/news/world-africa-52678741

[14] "Coronavirus: Caution urged over Madagascar's 'herbal cure'," 22 April 2020, www.bbc.com/news/world-africa-52374250

[15] "Exclusive: Madagascar's president defends controversial homegrown covid-19 cure," 12 May 2020, www.france24.com/en/africa/20200512-exclusive-madagascar-s-president-defends-controversial-homegrown-covid-19-cure

[16] "Exclusive: Madagascar's president defends controversial homegrown covid-19 cure," 12 May 2020, www.france24.com/en/africa/20200512-exclusive-madagascar-s-president-defends-controversial-homegrown-covid-19-cure

Reported resurgence in prejudice, stereotyping, discrimination, and physical and social distancing from Africans in China[17] is worrying, and another test of whether African governments truly care beyond declarations of intent.

The IMF and World Bank are predicting downturns and recessions for economies globally and especially on the African continent[18]. According to some estimates, because of covid19, extreme poverty in the world may rise to embrace about 50 million people in 2020, undoing all the progress made in poverty reduction since the launch of the Sustainable Development Goals (SDGs) in 2015[19]. Calls for intelligent, rigorous, and robust responses by African governments are greeted with the proverbial beggars' bowl, outstretched, unscrupulously and unashamedly, and not without dubious intentions in some cases, West and East, notwithstanding that these regions are facing their own worst economic nightmares. With the covid19 death toll at more than 500,000 worldwide, and with many of the traditional countries Africa usually relies on for aid reported as having the most deaths, it is easy to see that reprioritisation of resources would likely affect Africa[20].

In addition, the African Union has hurriedly put in place a committee to seek urgent assistance from developed economies towards addressing

---

[17] "Victimisation of Africans in China threatens Afro-Sino relations," by Mills Soko and Mzukisi Qobo, 14 April 2020, www.dailymaverick.co.za/article/2020-04-14-victimisation-of-africans-in-china-threatens-afro-sino-relations

[18] "Coronavirus: 'World faces worst recession since Great Depression'," by Szu Ping Chan, 14 April 2020, www.bbc.com/news/business-52273988, and "Sub-Saharan Africa faces R1.4-trillion output loss and food crisis due to covid-19, says World Bank," by Bekezela Phakathi, 13 April 2020, www.businesslive.co.za/bd/national/2020-04-13-sub-saharan-africa-faces-r14-trillion-output-loss-and-food-crisis-due-to-covid-19-says-world-bank

[19] "Turning back the poverty clock: How will covid-19 impact the world's poorest people?" by Homi Kharas and Kristofer Hamel, 6 May 2020, www.brookings.edu/blog/future-development/2020/05/06/turning-back-the-poverty-clock-how-will-covid-19-impact-the-worlds-poorest-people/?preview_id=804150

[20] According to the BBC article, "Which countries are reporting the most deaths?" of 29 June 2020, "More than 501,000 people have died after contracting coronavirus, according to a tally by Johns Hopkins University in the US. Here are 10 countries reporting the highest number of deaths: United States: 125,803; Brazil: 57,622; United Kingdom: 43,634; Italy: 34,738; France: 29,781; Spain: 28,343; Mexico: 26,648; India: 16,475; Iran: 10,508; Belgium: 9,732," www.bbc.com/news/live/world-53216079

the crisis[21]. If the rest of the world has in the past and under relatively normal times not been that generous or effusive in their *ubuntu* towards Africa, there is little to suggest that, plagued by their own problems under the coronavirus tsunami, they are suddenly going to become evangelists of selfless philanthropy.

Beg, borrow, or repatriate misappropriated funds, one thing is certain: Fighting covid19 requires not rhetoric and vacillation but appropriate action, creativity, and innovative modes of solidarity.

Francis B. Nyamnjoh is *Professor of Anthropology at the University of Cape Town in South Africa. He has taught at universities in Cameroon and Botswana, and worked with the Council for the Development of Social Science Research in Africa (CODESRIA) in Senegal.*

---

[21] "Trevor Manuel in bid to find international support for Africa," by Linda Ensor, 13 April 2020, www.businesslive.co.za/bd/economy/2020-04-13-trevor-manuel-in-bid-to-find-international-support-for-africa

chapter 29

Rediscovering Neptune: Towards Care[1]

María José Moreno-Ruiz

Let's travel – and reflect – together…

1.   Through history there are times when we build worldviews, societies, and artefacts that seem to work and to remain relatively stable, or that simply lean slightly as does the Tower of Pisa. We tell ourselves we should not react with "hysteria" because perhaps the situation is not so serious or, with some luck, will not fall in the end or in any case may fall on others. It may collapse and fall on those coming after the next election, on the next generations, or on strange people who live far away and of whom we have a notion by reading the fifth page of the newspaper, but whose faces we do not know.

2.   Before this improbable black swan event, the coronavirus pandemic, many people in different domains had warned of imminent danger. Living with the dread of downfall, people at the edges – essential workers and unemployed persons –, academics, organizers and measured visionaries tried, mostly unsuccessfully, to be heard. They translated their thinking, experiences and voices into articles, reports and actions. Specialists, each of us from our perspective, warned of potentially catastrophic threats: systemic discrimination by gender, race, class, nationality, religion, or sexuality; obscene inequalities, within and among countries, that degrade human lives and in their worst expressions have reinvented slavery; the emergence of authoritarianism, the rise of "strong men" (giving a bad reputation to strength through that expression), the loss of credibility of democratic institutions and systems, and the manufacture of public consent, all reflecting and underpinning patriarchal mentalities servile to hierarchical constructions and relationships; dismantling of

[1] Copyright © 2020 María José Moreno-Ruiz

Moreno-Ruiz, M. J. (2020). Rediscovering Neptune: Towards care. In M. N. Kinyanjui, R. Thaker, and K. Toure (Eds.), *Covid stories from East Africa and beyond: Lived experiences and forward-looking reflections* (pp. 261-268). Bamenda: Langaa.

welfare states, thus breeding precariousness, fear and often short-sighted identity movements that deny others; massive migrations as a result of entrenched and forgotten conflicts, lack of economic opportunities, or ecological disasters following extractivism and predatory relationships with the planet; international economic architectures erected on solid bridges between power and law – constituted, for example, by those of us who would participate in Davos – and global criminal networks – led by powerful people but who, in principle, would not participate in such summits. We could of course keep adding.

3.   People from around the world, in different specialities, have shouted loudly and clearly that it is important – urgent – to act and that the consequences of inaction will be dire. It is important to act in relation to each issue, but perhaps we need to look for overarching theories or approaches which enable us to gain a better panoramic view of the present in order to better delineate the future we want and definitively discard the futures we cannot afford. Like a group of blind people in which each one approaches a different part of an elephant and interprets what they touch, each of us would be right when we talk about the existence of an ear, a trunk, or a foot, or when another discerns the beats of a heart. However, despite having identified these parts of the animal, if we do not connect our knowledge we do not realize that it is an elephant. If we take a long time arguing about its sections, the pachyderm can die in front of us.

4.   We were in those deliberations when suddenly the pandemic arrives and shakes us up, big and small, in the North and the South, putting us in front of a collective mirror. While many of us stay at home, the news runs on our screens, offering us different chapters of who we collectively are. From our trenches we can observe facts that answer great questions. What is the state of our families? In which houses and in which neighbourhoods do we live? What is the quality of healthcare services? Are they "selective" or do they include care for those who are ill and do not have money to pay for their healthcare? Can we leave our elderly in retirement homes with peace of mind, knowing they will be well cared for? What is the quality of our political classes, at international, national, and local levels? Can we assume that they will make decisions pursuing the public good now and in the future? What are our social welfare systems like when we need them most? Who do they protect and who they exclude? What is life like in places where the majority of people have to procure resources daily to buy their food, and suddenly they are decreed to stay home? How does news become news and how is it communicated? What capacity for empathy have we developed in our societies for our next-door neighbours? For our neighbours all over the planet? The Gross Domestic Product tries to count goods and services, but unfortunately, we have developed few indices that annually explore our progress and setbacks in the above areas.

5.   In the mirror the pandemic provides, we have important sources of inspiration and hope for our species in the here and now. Millions of people have altruistically sympathized with practical actions and behaviours to alleviate suffering and need. Exemplary leaders have made a difference with their responses towards the common good, recognizing mutuality and interdependence. Health workers and people in essential services have demonstrated values associated with heroism. We have witnessed an international women's and feminist movement more dynamic, strong, and interconnected than ever and which has shown the capacity to analyse, propose, take up space, and lead narratives. The mirror tells us that we are also that.

6.   However, this cannot hide other aspects of the landscape that the pandemic has allowed us to see. Indicators in many areas show alarming trends. How have we built our families so that in a situation of lockdown in "our homes," gender-based and patriarchal violence has multiplied? Who are these police, military or even private "security forces" serving considering that in so many countries, in the name of enforcing new lockdown rules, they have abused, beaten, and murdered, people? Such chastisement is not wielded on just anyone but usually on those in situations of vulnerability where running over them is "cheap" and without consequences. How have we articulated our production and distribution systems so that the smallest parenthesis at the workplace leads millions of people directly to hunger? What values guide us if Amazon, one of the companies considered as a symbol of success, one of the few companies in fact that has exponentially enhanced its proceeds "thanks" to the pandemic, reminds of the exclusion of certain workers when it comes to the protection of wages in case of illness?[2] Why is the world more prepared to wage wars than to prevent pandemics? What explains the immeasurable gaps between the incomes of soccer players and scientists? Why is part of the elite international political class more involved in creating fake news against opponents, to massage their egos or shielding their interests, than in protecting the people affected by the pandemic?

7.   To rectify the reflection that the pandemic returns to us of our families, communities, countries, and the international arena that we share, we can and must act in each of the aforementioned areas. However, given the urgency, and in honour of the somewhat arrogant name we give to our species, Sapiens, we must identify the common elements that will make an important difference in all the areas of concern. After the discovery of Uranus, it was observed that its orbit and that of other planets did not behave as predicted by the laws of gravitation, and scientists set to find the cause of this unexpected phenomenon. The result of that search was the discovery of Neptune, a planet that explained that those "abnormal" orbits were in fact to be expected. Today, the feminist ethic of care could be the invisible planet that could help us anticipate deformations of trajectories and build better futures.

8.   The present historical moment of neoliberal globalization has accompanied its great transformations with a particular ideology and set of values, a radical transformation in the narrative, with profound implications for care. Politics, economies, and societies have been transfigured through the implementation of privatization and austerity, the reduction of the state, the deregulation of capital markets, the elimination of price controls, and the emergence of new narratives. The commitment to constant growth "whatever it takes" and the metamorphosis of inequality into a "natural" functional of "development" have been presented for decades as "fatalistic" options, that is, without possible alternatives. The world, or each village, was simply the sum of winners and losers, of the strong and the weak, with the weak being those who are sick, poor in money or assets, unemployed, or victims of ecological catastrophes and conflicts,

---

[2] "Revealed: Amazon told workers paid sick leave law doesn't cover warehouses," by Sam Levin, 7 May 2020, www.theguardian.com/technology/2020/may/07/amazon-warehouse-workers-coronavirus-time-off-california

and who are at best a temporary "burden" and in the worst cases "parasites" for national institutions or the international aid systems that "generously" deal with them – sometimes anyway. Human vulnerability is turned into shame. The fact that part of each person's life includes vulnerability, that every person is born dependent and remains so for years, that all people experience vulnerability and need for care, and that we are interdependent disappeared from any neoliberal equation, be it in the organization of families, countries or international architectures. In this light, the responses to the coronavirus pandemic, and to crisis more generally, would not prioritize boundless economic growth and the status quo over the wellbeing of the population, the health of the planet or over the lives of their most vulnerable.

9. It is no coincidence that in this context, care work in most societies across the planet is in practice feminized, invisible, and considered and rewarded as a subordinate occupation. People employed in domestic work – caring for children or the elderly, sick people, people living with disabilities, or simply those needing care during a period – tend to be poorly paid, when they are paid, lack robust protection systems, and have a precarious social status. These are not socially shiny or glamourous occupations. Caregivers are not the ones who take out their business card at social gatherings and get admiring glances accompanied by the classic "very interesting" exchange of phone numbers and lunch invitations. These jobs are simply considered by the majority, and therefore by the value system that unites us, jobs that do not require specific skills and that are performed by people who have not found something better to do with their lives. It is not by chance, therefore, that in our social and economic hierarchies, such thankless work is carried out mainly by women, migrants and, in general, people of "low social extraction" according to the neoliberal patriarchal perspective. People at the "top" of our social and economic hierarchies can buy care work at prices more than convenient for them, thus occupying almost invisible people who are minimally heard or seen in social debates. Some of these people are now among millions who experience this pandemic and live their vulnerability without safety nets or social protection. They are left to doing their best in their neighbourhoods to cope and to support each other, and there they have given many of us the greatest examples and hopes.

10. The pandemic has blatantly exposed the precarious balances, fragile narratives, and dubious values that govern our common life, whether across town or across the planet. The magnitude of the numbers and the exceptional nature of the situation have given visibility to people and organizations that make up the "weak links" of the chains that unite us. We see (or at least hear about) the millions of patients who do not have access to the quality, public and free healthcare they need. We see millions of nurses and other healthcare system personnel on precarious contracts trying to plug, with superhuman effort and often at the cost of their own health, the cracks in the system. We see the millions of domestic workers and men and women working in informal economies around the world being put out in the street overnight, facing not just the challenge of the virus to their lungs but also the threat of hunger. We see the fragility of our international cooperation network in which many civil society organizations, providing care across territories and frontiers large and small, are also in danger of death, or at least in urgent need of a ventilator after the coronavirus tour de force.

11. The neoliberal system continues to rely on a patriarchal perspective that organizes in a binary and hierarchical way, dividing between men and women, strong and weak, mind and emotion, autonomy and relationship, productive work and care work, compatriots and foreigners, we and the others, the people and organizations that have to be cared for / saved and those that can be dropped. The cost of the degradation of care – care that is provided and the idea of care itself – in our societies, narratives, and value systems is staggering. The survival of the fittest in the neoliberal system never achieves "herd" immunity because the competition is perpetual, and hierarchies always have one step above and one step below. The neoliberal vessel is sinking, and if we do not change boats, narratives, and values, we risk the lives of many people and of humanity itself.

12. Feminism, one of humanity's great revolutionary movements, has shown the important links between patriarchal authority in the home and patriarchal authoritarianism in our societies, economies, and policies and between the degradation of care in families and

communities and the construction of political and socioeconomic systems that consider some lives disposable. The feminist ethics of care proposes a new paradigm that is urgent today. Care according to this ethic is not a burden but a constant that responds to the vulnerability, mutuality, and interdependencies that shape and build us personally and collectively. Men and women would not come respectively from Mars and Venus, but both would have the capacity and the emotional and intellectual education to give, receive, experience, and consider care not as a minor task but as an embodied response to our commitment to social justice and mutuality. The collective admission of vulnerability and human interdependence, and the need for care, in practice, would profoundly transform the architecture of our institutions and transboundary dynamics towards the democratization of the hierarchical and patriarchal constructions that today govern us.

13.   Communication about this pandemic has highlighted trends showing that women-led countries have had a more effective response to the coronavirus threat than the rest. It has also become apparent that countries ruled by "strong men" – who do not bother to hide but rather flaunt their strong patriarchal and racist inspirations, with Trump or Bolsonaro at the helm – have failed miserably, with the leaders once again consummating their disdain for life, science, and truth and exhibiting their fantastic ability to craft alternative facts and seed mayhem and discord. From feminist perspectives, the different outcomes obtained by women leaders and the patriarchal leaders mentioned above should not encourage us to reinforce binary theories of men and women being intrinsically different and consequently some being worse than others or vice versa. Evidence points to the fact that societies better protected from the pandemic of binarism and patriarchy in their narratives and social organization, which includes those in which women candidates have options to be elected by public vote, show an advantage in their ability to respond effectively to crises, trying not to leave anyone behind.

14.   A student asked the anthropologist Margaret Mead about the first sign of civilization in a culture. Mead replied that the time was around 15,000 years ago with the discovery of a broken femur that had subsequently been healed. A broken femur does not heal without the care of other people and without a community that makes it possible. What the renowned scientist highlighted as the beginning of civilization was not tools nor language but the ability to care for others in a community. **This pandemic gives us the opportunity to prevent anthropologists of the future from identifying the moment in which civilization collapsed.**

Dr. María José Moreno-Ruiz *works as Global Director for Gender Justice at Oxfam International. Before that she worked with the African Development Bank Group based mainly in Ivory Coast. She has also worked with the German Corporation for international cooperation in Latin America and the Maghreb, the Latin American School of Social Sciences, and the United Nations Development Programme. She studied sociology and gender. She moved from Tunis to Nairobi in late 2019 and happily settled in an apartment just before the covid-related curfew was instituted by the Government of Kenya. Even under lockdown, she enjoys continuous glimpses of the country.*

Afterword

Dramane Darave

The year 2020 was marked by the beginning of the covid19 pandemic, which changed the lives and habits of the world's populations, including on the African continent. If the pandemic caused fears, reminded us of the fragility of human life, and plunged some families into mourning, it also provided an opportunity – because of the need to respect and adapt to the necessary measures to limit the spread of the disease – to experiment and discover new modes of working and of living together.

The idea behind producing this collection of stories and reflections was to provide a record of a moment in time. People in East Africa and beyond recount how they experienced the pandemic and what they were thinking at the time. Their lived experiences and contemplations provide insight into adapting to and supporting each other in crisis and also into shaping the future.

The process of producing the book began with the establishment of an editorial committee and then the sharing of a call for chapters through the Langaa Research and Publishing Common Initiative Group website and social media platforms. As chapter proposals were received, a virtual community of authors gradually took shape.

The editing phase consisted of the editorial team engaging in dialogue with the contributors to refine the chapters with comments, questions, and suggestions. During this editing phase, the virtual community of authors was further strengthened through conversations with human touches.

The finalization phase was devoted to the creation of a table of contents which organizes the contents of the book for greater accessibility. It also involved assembling the chapters, collecting photos and short biographies of the authors, and creating a cover design and promotional posters.

The experience related to the production of this book has been very enriching on both human and intellectual levels. The magic of the internet has allowed us to interact on a daily basis with authors from several African countries on how they experienced the covid19 pandemic and to actively participate in the creation of this oeuvre.

We hope *Covid Stories from East Africa and Beyond: Lived Experiences and Forward-Looking Reflections* will provide information, insight, and inspiration now and into the future – on responding rapidly, adapting to new realities, working with the most vulnerable, engaging systems, and transforming towards a better world, where care is at the heart of human and planetary relations.

Dramane Darave *is an Information and Communications Technology professional. He has extensive experience in knowledge translation and digital communications and has worked in the field of education and with international development organizations, the United Nations, the media, and publishing houses in Africa. He is passionate about helping people, communities, and organizations use technology in ways that enhance connectivity, creativity, and human relations.*

About the Authors, Editors, and Artist

-·- Authors -·-

Aguere Yilma Bultcha is Executive Assistant to the President and Chief Executive Office of the Trade and Development Bank (TDB). She is multilingual, with 21+ years of work experience in African and international organisations and companies. Co-Founder of Muundo Barakoa, she is finalizing her master's in Leadership and Management. She obtained her first degree from New Generation University College in Addis Ababa and a second from the University of South Africa.

Alexandra A. Lukamba is pursuing a dual master's in International Development and in Leadership and Development at Sciences Po Paris and King's College London. Since 2014 she has been involved with *Sœur, Lève-toi*, a nongovernmental organization in Kinshasa, in the Democratic Republic of Congo, working on building young women's leadership skills through mentoring sessions with women in the workforce.

Awuor Onguru is a 17-year-old female from Nairobi, Kenya. She has been writing poetry and short stories since she was 12 years old. Her work has appeared in *Menacing Hedge* and *Polyphony Lit*, among other publications, and has been recognised by Hollins University and the Alliance for Young Artists and Writers.

Catherine Mongella-Kalokola is a visionary with over 10 years of experience in the nongovernmental sector in East Africa. She works as a consultant with HC&A Solutions, a consultancy firm which helps build human capital and supports organizational development using Solution Focused Approach and Theory of Change.

Catherine Muyeka Mumma is a human rights lawyer and defender who has served on the Commission for the Implementation of the Constitution and the Kenya National Human Rights Commission. She is part of human rights teams that have championed the right to health in Kenya including

HIV/AIDS-related human rights and is keen to see the poor and vulnerable not getting further disenfranchised by this pandemic.

Chimwemwe A. Fabiano holds a bachelor's in Social and Political Philosophy from the University of Malawi. Chimwemwe has 12 years of work experience and is particularly interested in gender justice. Currently, Chimwemwe is a Fellow at the African Leadership Centre under the Peace and Security Fellowship for African Women.

Christopher Mubeteneh Tankou is a Systems Agronomist and an Associate Professor in the Department of Crop Science, Faculty of Agronomy and Agricultural Sciences, University of Dschang, Cameroon. He is currently the Coordinator of the university's Distance Education Program.

Diana Kinagu is a third-year student at the University of Nairobi undertaking a bachelor's degree in Anthropology. She is a keen researcher who wants to understand the human context of development.

Didi Wamukoya is a Kenyan lawyer and author. She currently works at African Wildlife Foundation. Didi is the author of two fiction novels, *Wamukoya Netia* and *Wakaba Will Marry*, and the author of the fiction blog "Wooden Glass" (*www.nairobiborn.com*).

Dramane Darave is an Information and Communications Technology professional with extensive experience in knowledge translation and digital communications. He has worked in the field of education and with international development organizations, the United Nations, the media, and publishing houses in Africa. He is passionate about helping people, communities, and organizations use technology in ways that enhance connectivity, creativity, and human relations.

Eléonore Immaculée Nyamwiza is Programme Coordinator in the Asset Management Department at the Trade and Development Bank, in its Regional Office in Nairobi. Co-Founder of Muundo Barakoa foundation, she earned a master's in Project Management from the University of Salford in the United Kingdom. She has also lived and worked in Haiti and in Burundi. Ms. Nyamwiza is multilingual.

Essa Njie, an African Leadership Centre Fellow, earned a master's in Security, Leadership and Society from King's College London and another in Human Rights and Democratisation from the University of Pretoria. He earned a bachelor's in Political Science from the University of The Gambia where he lectures. He has worked as a conflict monitor for the Economic Community of West African States (ECOWAS) in The Gambia.

Francis B. Nyamnjoh is professor of Social Anthropology at the University of Cape Town, South Africa. Recent publications include *Drinking from the Cosmic Gourd: How Amos Tutuola Can Change Our Minds* (2017), *The Rational Consumer: Bad for Business and Politics: Democracy at the Crossroads of Nature and Culture* (2018) and "Covid-19 and the Resilience of Systemic Suppression, Oppression and Repression" (2020).

Frannie Léautier, Senior Partner and Chief Executive Officer, SouthBridge Investments, is a well-known finance and development expert, experienced in transforming complex multi-constituency organizations. Thought leader, author, and member of Responsible Leaders Network, Dr. Léautier is Co-Founder and Chair of Muundo Barakoa.

Haimanot Kebede Bayeh works as a Programme Policy Officer in the non-profit sector in the Horn of Africa. She has a master's in Global Management from the University of Salford Business School in the United Kingdom. For her thesis, she studied the tourism sector in Ethiopia. She completed her secondary studies in India. Outside of work, Haimanot enjoys spending time with her son.

Ibrahim Mohammed Machina holds a master's in International Relations and Diplomacy from Nile University of Nigeria, Abuja and is pursuing another master's in Security, Leadership and Society at King's College London. Ibrahim has taught courses in International Law and Diplomacy and in Nigerian Government and Politics for undergraduate students of political science at Federal University, Gashua in Yobe State in Nigeria.

Ikran Abdullahi holds a master's in International Relations from the United States International University-Africa in Kenya. She has worked with Somalia's Ministry of Constitutional Affairs and on gender equality awareness and empowerment with women affected by gender-based violence. She is interested in the crossroads of human rights and peacebuilding and is researching relations between leadership and customary law approaches to addressing sexual and gender-based violence.

Joanne Ball-Burgess is a Bermudian, born and raised in Bermuda, of Afro-Caribbean descent. She has been living in Nairobi, Kenya for nine years. She is a dancer and educator as well as a writer. She wrote "An underworld education," published in *Take This Journey with Me: Bermuda Anthology of Memoir and Creative Non-Fiction*. She also wrote *The Lizard and the Rock: A Fable of Bermuda's Discovery* and *The Priceless Hogg Penny: A Tale of True Treasure*.

Kundai Mtasa earned two degrees from the University of Pretoria: an undergraduate degree in Politics and International Studies and an honours degree in Development Studies. She is pursuing a master's in Leadership and Development at King's College London and is currently an Associate Fellow at the African Leadership Centre and a research intern with the African Centre for the Constructive Resolution of Disputes. Previously she worked with UNICEF and the World Wildlife Fund, and she has conducted research on human trafficking.

Margaret LoWilla holds a bachelor's in Economics and Business Studies from the Australian Catholic University, where she worked with Josephite Community Aid in Australia, engaging with Sudanese refugee children to aid their transition into a new educational system. She is completing a master's in Governance, Peace and Security at Africa Nazarene University, in Nairobi, Kenya. Margaret has worked with local civil society organizations in South Sudan on women's rights, women's political participation, and advocacy against child and forced marriages.

María José Moreno-Ruiz lives in Nairobi and works as Global Director for Gender Justice at Oxfam International. Previously, she worked with the

African Development Bank Group based mainly in Cote d'Ivoire. She has also worked with the German Corporation for international cooperation in Latin America and the Maghreb, the Latin American School of Social Sciences, and the United Nations Development Programme. Dr. Moreno-Ruiz studied sociology and gender.

Marloes Hamelink is a cultural anthropologist and journalist. Her research themes include gender, social media, and religion. Currently she is doing research on the online lives and morality of Muslim women in Zanzibar. She lives in Dar es Salaam with her family and invests in youth education initiatives.

Mary Amuyunzu-Nyamongo earned a PhD in Social Anthropology from the University of Cambridge in the United Kingdom. She is the Founder Director of the African Institute for Health and Development. She has over 30 years of experience in social development with a focus on health, social safeguards, social protection, and poverty alleviation. With regard to covid19, her focus is on identifying and mitigating the social impacts in the immediate, medium, and long term.

Meseret Kassahun Desta has a PhD in Social Work from the Jane Addams College of Social Work, University of Illinois at Chicago. She has taught at the School of Social Work at Addis Ababa University. Her research interests include gender issues, child protection, urban governance, migration, and peace and security issues. She is the founder and a researcher at EMAH Social Development Consulting. As a consultant, she carries out formative studies and evaluations of social programs in Ethiopia and the Horn of Africa more broadly.

Mirka Eikelschulte came to Rwanda as Marketing Director in 2015, when her Dutch employer founded a food producing subsidiary in Kigali, Rwanda. Ever since, she and her husband have been living between Kigali and Rotterdam.

Nahya Khamis Nassor is an Environmental Health Officer and Assistant Researcher at the Zanzibar Health Research Institute. Previously, Nahya worked as an Environmental Health Officer at Pennyroyal Gibraltar Ltd,

Zanzibar. She graduated with honors from State University of Zanzibar with a degree in Environmental Health.

Neema Rubaba is a medical student at Hubert Kairuki Memorial University (HKMU) in Dar es Salaam, Tanzania. During the closure of her university due to covid19, she stays with her family in Kigoma. She is President of the Rotaract Club of HKMU.

Nelkem Jeannette Londadjim, from Chad, is a sister of St. Joseph, currently living in France and working with schoolchildren. Before that, in Algeria, she worked with migrants. In 2017, she was an activist in residence at Avila University in Kansas City, USA. She taught in a girls' high school in Cote d'Ivoire and helped found the "Young Peacemakers" organization in Senegal.

Nelkem Jeannette Londadjim, du Tchad, est une sœur de Saint-Joseph. Elle vit actuellement en France et travaille avec des écoliers. Avant cela, en Algérie, elle a travaillé avec des migrants. En 2017, elle était activiste en résidence à l'Université Avila à Kansas City, aux États-Unis. Elle a enseigné dans un lycée de filles en Côte d'Ivoire et a aidé à fonder l'association « Jeunes artisan·e·s de la paix » au Sénégal.

Nyambura "Nash" Kariuki is an illustrator, designer and self-taught animator living and loving in Nairobi, Kenya. She has always enjoyed and even found kinship in the zany worlds of various cartoon characters. She began seriously exploring the cartoon medium in 2015 and continues to self-teach to date. She has worked with various brands such as the Qai Qai doll, Joanna Kinuthia Cosmetics, Think Equal organization, and many others. She is currently freelancing as an illustrator and designer.

Nyawira Muraguri in her writing depicts life as she experiences it and passes on light-hearted messages of self-acceptance and compassion. She is a full-time investor interested in the innovative ways finance can address the failures of a capitalist society.

Nyawira Wahito holds a bachelor's in Sociology and Philosophy from the University of Nairobi and is pursuing a master's in Security, Leadership and Society at King's College London. Nyawira is a feminist young women's rights activist with over eight years' experience working, most recently via the Resource Center for Women and Girls in Kenya, with adolescent girls from disadvantaged and underserved backgrounds.

Rose Chia Fonchingong is a public health physician, with a passion for HIV/AIDS management. She has spent the last five years working as a technical advisor for an international NGO fighting HIV/AIDS in Cameroon. She is the author of *Stifled by Justice*, a true-life account published by Langaa Research and Publishing in 2016.

Sarah Nasimiyu Sikuku is a post-graduate student of Monitoring and Evaluation at Daystar University in Nairobi, Kenya. She is an economic and social justice advocate. She currently works at Clean Start, a social enterprise that works to restore the dignity and hope of women and their children impacted by the criminal justice system.

Susan Karungi is a governance specialist, social analytical writer, and passionate development practitioner working to positively transform and improve communities in Uganda. She is a mother who outside her work enjoys spending time loving and nurturing her two daughters.

Tabitha W. Mwangi is an Early Career Fellow at the African Leadership Centre. She is researching the role of the private sector in humanitarian assistance for persons displaced as a result of the insurgency in Nigeria. She studied for a master's in Government Counter-Terrorism and Homeland Security at the Interdisciplinary Center Herzliya in Israel and earned a bachelor's in International Relations from the United States International University-Africa in Kenya.

Toseef Din was born into a humble family in Nairobi. Dr. Din is an accomplished management professional with over 15 years of experience in finance, eight of which are in healthcare at M. P. Shah Hospital in Nairobi, Kenya. She attended primary and secondary school in Nairobi. At present, she holds the position of Chief Executive Officer at the Hospital. She has three sisters and is married with three children. She is a certified Kaizen (change for the better) practitioner and a member of the Institute of Certified Public Accountants of Kenya.

Ukaiko A. Bitrus-Ojiambo is a communications instructor at St. Paul's University. Her scholarly contributions and interests are in media cultural studies, autoethnography, and the role of language in communication. Ukaiko has experience in faculty development and quality assurance in higher education. Born in Nigeria, she has lived in Kenya for over three decades. Ukaiko is currently undertaking doctoral studies in human communication at Daystar University in Kenya.

-·- Co-editors-·-

Mary Njeri Kinyanjui is a researcher and writer on women's movements and the informal economy in Africa. She earned her PhD from the University of Cambridge, United Kingdom, and taught at the Institute for Development Studies, University of Nairobi, Kenya.

Roopal Thaker works with community-based organizations to shape public policy from the ground up. She currently works on adolescent health and life skills education programs in Kenya.

Kathryn Toure is a researcher and writer. She promotes the circulation of African worldviews and facilitates community inquiry to deepen understandings of her/history and culture.

-·- Artist-·-

Anna Rarity studied Fine Art in London, focusing on painting and printmaking, and occasionally dabbling in pottery. She taught Community Arts in schools for many years and most recently in Kenya. She still teaches some private lessons but enjoys finding more time for her own art. She recently moved to the coast of Kenya and, during covid, is soaking up the scents, colours, and heat of the coastal region.

Here are words of appreciation shared by a teacher in August 2020: "In the midst of many difficult situations there are bright spots of joy. Artist Anna Rarity, who recently moved to the coast, has volunteered to give art lessons to some of our students. It becomes a combined cycling, art, swim, and snack time. Art has not been taught in schools here, so it is a new venture for these kids but one they enjoy. With schools closed since March, outings are welcome and probably necessary."

A photograph of her "New Beginnings" painting (114h x 94w cm, which is 3 ft x 4 ft) features on the cover of this book, *Covid Stories from East Africa and Beyond*. She completed the painting in March 2020 as a response to covid19, taking a positive slant on the situation. "I looked at Covid as a way of awakening populations and governments to environmental and health issues, an awakening which will hopefully lead to a more balanced, symbiotic relationship with Mother Earth."

The experimental painting on canvas is about growth, birth, and cell division, based on drawings made of microscope images. It is a mixed media collage which includes iron oxide, gold leaf, and acrylic. Red is the first colour that humans perceive after black and white, a colour of strength and vitality. The iron oxide, often used as a red or rust colouring medium in ceramics, adds an earthy tone. The "New Beginnings" painting was part of the "Red" eclectic exhibition – a response to covid – at One Off Contemporary Art Gallery[1] in June and July 2020 in Nairobi.

END

---

[1] www.oneoffafrica.com/red.html

We at Langaa hope you enjoyed reading
Covid Stories from East Africa and Beyond:
Lived Experiences and Forward-Looking Reflections

We would very much appreciate it if could take a moment to send a brief commentary about the book to
info@langaa-rpcig.net for the web site of Langaa Research and Publishing. Please indicate if your comments are anonymous or if we may share them with your name. Your insights and contribution help valorise and promote African worldviews and African publishing.

You may peruse the catalogue of other Langaa books and the list of Langaa authors at www.langaa-rpcig.net

Follow Langaa on Facebook fb.me/langaarpcig and
Twitter @langaa_rpcig

Langaa Research & Publishing CIG
Mankon, Bamenda

Nous, à Langaa, nous espérons que vous avez apprécié ce livre intitulée
Covid Stories from East Africa and Beyond:
Lived Experiences and Forward-Looking Reflections

Nous vous serions très reconnaissants si vous pouviez prendre un moment pour envoyer à info@langaa-rpcig.net vos opinions et commentaires sur ce livre, pour qu'on puisse les partager sur le site web de Langaa. Merci de spécifier si votre commentaire est anonyme ou si nous pouvons le publier avec votre nom. Vos idées et votre contribution aident à valoriser et à promouvoir les perspectives africaines du monde ainsi que l'édition africaine.

Vous pouvez consulter la liste des auteurs de Langaa
et le catalogue des autres livres de Langaa sur
www.langaa-rpcig.net

Suivez Langaa sur Facebook fb.me/langaarpcig
et Twitter @langaa_rpcig

Langaa Research & Publishing CIG
Mankon, Bamenda

www.ingramcontent.com/pod-product-compliance
Lightning Source LLC
Chambersburg PA
CBHW060027030426
42334CB00019B/2219

* 9 7 8 9 9 5 6 5 5 1 5 4 5 *